Prosperity Comes in Cycles
Bikeways and the Virtuous Cycle

Rick Pruetz

Also by Rick Pruetz

Smart Climate Action Through Transfer of Development Rights

Ecocity Snapshots: Learning from Europe's Greenest Places

The TDR Handbook: Designing and Implementing Transfer of Development Rights Programs
(co-author with Arthur C. Nelson and Doug Woodruff)

Lasting Value: Open Space Planning and Preservation Successes

Beyond Takings and Givings: Saving Natural Areas, Farmland and Historic Landmarks with Transfer of Development Rights and Density Transfer Charges

Saved By Development: Preserving Environmental Areas, Farmland and Historic Landmarks with Transfer of Development Rights

Putting Transfer of Development Rights to Work in California

Copyright © 2021 Rick Pruetz

All rights reserved.

Arje Press
ISBN: 978-0-578-32863-8

DEDICATION

To Adrian, Jay, Erica, Gena, Jeromy, Josh, Kayla, Cate, Evie, and Sienna

CONTENTS

1 The Virtuous Cycle 8
    The Economic Benefits of Bicycling 8
    A) Reduced cost of transportation benefits local economies 12
    B) Reduced cost of transportation benefits economic resilience and mobility 13
    C) Reduced healthcare costs 13
    D) Increased property value due to proximity of bike infrastructure 15
    E) Improved transport efficiency benefits 16
    F) Reduced cost of roadway and parking improvements 17
    G) Economic benefits of reduced energy consumption and pollution 18
    H) Other economic benefits 18
2 Abington – Damascus - Whitetop, Virginia: Saved by the Creeper 19
3 Austin, Texas: Closing Gaps - Opening Opportunities 23
4 Atlanta, Georgia: The Beltline - Economic Development Engine 24
5 Blackstone River Greenway, Rhode Island: Birthplace of the American Industrial Revolution 30
6 Boise, Idaho: Gathering at the River 33
7 Charlotte, North Carolina: Bicycling and the Redevelopment Playbook 37
8 Chattanooga, Tennessee: The Trail to Revitalization 40
9 Chicago, Illinois: Building on a Green Legacy 43
10 Cockeysville, Maryland – York, Pennsylvania: Torrey C. Brown Trail – Heritage Rail Trail County Park: Cycling through History 46
11 Colorado: High on Bicycling 49
12 Covington – Mandeville - Slidell, Louisiana: Tammany Trace Builds Community 52
13 Dayton – Cincinnati, Ohio: Little Miami Scenic Trail Generates Big Results 56

14	Delaware and Lehigh Trail, Pennsylvania: A Trail of Two Revolutions	59
15	Des Moines, Iowa: It Pays to Make Connections	62
16	East Bay Bicycle Path, Rhode Island: A Car-Free Way to Get In and Out of Town	64
17	Erie Canal Trail, New York: Transformational Then and Now	67
18	Farmington Canal Heritage Trail, Connecticut: A Key Link in Two Long-Distance-Trail Chains	72
19	Great Allegheny Passage/C&O Canal Trails: Trails and Trail Towns Are Good for Each Other	76
20	Greenbrier River Trail, West Virginia: Boom Towns, Ghost Towns, and Bike Towns	81
21	Greenville, South Carolina: The Swamp Rabbit Inspires More Trail Reproduction	83
22	Gulf Coast, Alabama: Snow Birds Flock Here	87
23	Harmony - Lanesboro - Preston, Minnesota: Root River Trail Links Art and Crafts	90
24	Hattiesburg - Prentiss, Mississippi: Adding Spokes to Hub City	93
25	Indianapolis - Carmel, Indiana: Slowing Down Pays Off	97
26	La Crosse – Madison - Milwaukee, Wisconsin: The Route of the Badger	100
27	Lackawanna River Heritage Trail, Pennsylvania: From Electric City to Coal Country	104
28	Louisville, Kentucky: Getting Everyone in The Loop	107
29	Maine: Seeing the Light	110
30	Minneapolis, Minnesota: Learning from the Grand Rounds	113
31	Minuteman Commuter Bikeway: Declaring Independence from the Automobile	118
32	Montreal - Quebec, Quebec, Canada: *Route verte* - Green in Many Ways	121
33	New Hampshire: Bridging the Old and the New	124
34	New Jersey: Cultivating the Garden State	127
35	New Mexico: Gearing Up for Bicycles	130
36	Philadelphia: At Liberty to Bicycle	133
37	Pittsburgh, Pennsylvania: From Steel City to Cycle Town	137
38	Portland, Oregon: Bicycling and Portland's Green Dividend	141
39	Raleigh-Durham, North Carolina: New Roles for the Tobacco Legacy	145

40	Razorback Regional Greenway: On Track to Becoming a World-Class Bicycling Destination	148
41	South Haven - Kalamazoo, Michigan: Adding Trails to the Tourism Mix	151
42	Sacramento, California: The Great California Delta Trail Promises Great Results	154
43	San Francisco Bay Region, California: The Bay Trail Is Getting Around	157
44	Smyrna, Georgia – Alabama State Line: Silver Comet Trail Keeps Growing	162
45	St. Louis – Sedalia - Kansas City, Missouri: The Katy Trail Is Just the Beginning	166
46	Tallahassee – St. Marks, Florida: Capitalizing on Bicycling	170
47	Tucson, Arizona: Connecting the Dots	173
48	Utah: Seeing the Beauty of Bicycle Tourism	176
49	Vancouver, British Columbia: Copenhagenizing in Canada	179
50	Vermont: Bikes Help Green the Green Mountain State	183
51	Washington State: Going Long on Trails	185
52	Yellowstone-Grand Teton Loop Bicycle Pathway, Wyoming-Idaho-Montana: Thinking Big Out West	189
References		193
About the Author		228

CHAPTER 1

The Virtuous Cycle

Bicycle trails are good for business. They attract restaurants, brewpubs and retail shops catering to those who walk or pedal for fun, exercise, health, and to get from place to place. When trails connect centers of employment, recreation, education and culture, they also generate residential development aimed at people who increasingly prefer active transportation to fighting traffic. And when trails are extended and linked with one another, they expand tourism revenue from a growing breed of vacationers who want to get out of their cars and experience places at a more leisurely and enjoyable speed.

As bicycle trails succeed, they increase business activity, employment, income, property value, and tax revenues in a self-reinforcing upward spiral, motivating additional trail improvements, boosting trail use, growing more trail-adjacent businesses, expanding property investments, enlarging tax revenues, generating public support for further trail improvements, and creating, pardon the pun, a virtuous cycle.

The 51 profiles that follow this chapter primarily explore how communities are using bicycle trails and other cycling infrastructure to attract and grow commercial businesses. But this chapter serves as a reminder that bicycling also reduces healthcare expenses and costs associated with traffic congestion while increasing real estate values and generating other economic benefits.

The Economic Benefits of Bicycling

As detailed in the 51 profiles in this book, communities increasingly recognize bicycling trails as an important economic development tool because cycling infrastructure supports businesses that serve cyclists. In many cases, trail-oriented businesses generate millions of dollars annually in retail sales while growing employment, income and tax revenues (Fulsche 2012).

Statewide - The economic impact of bicycling is sometimes calculated on a statewide basis and occasionally achieves benefits measured in billions of dollars. The State of Washington is ranked as the most bicycle-friendly state in the nation with over 1,240 miles of off-road trails which partly explains the estimate that bicycling contributes over $3.1 billion per year to the state economy. Of this, $113,494,490 represents equipment purchases and the remaining $3 billion comes from trip related expenditures (Earth Economics 2015).

Bicycles annually inject $1.6 billion into the Colorado economy, including $511 million spent on lodging, food, beverages and transportation by bicycle tourists (BBC 2016).

A 2010 study concluded that bicycle recreation in Wisconsin approached a billion dollars of benefit, generating $924 million in economic impacts and supporting 13,191 full-time-equivalent jobs (Grabow, Hahn & Whited 2010).

Although statewide benefits are lower in other states and provinces, they still generate economic impacts greater than a third of a billion dollars. Bicycle tourism in the Canadian province of Quebec generated $700 million in spending in 2015, creating 6,800 jobs and generating $100 million in tax revenues for the Quebec government as well as $38 million for the Canadian government (Velo Quebec 2016).

A 2009 study calculated that trail bicycle riding in Minnesota generated $427 million in total spending, supporting 3,736 jobs with employee compensation of $87 million and state and local tax revenues of over $35 million (Venegas 2009).

Traveling cyclists spent almost $400 million in Oregon in 2012, supporting 4,630 jobs with a payroll of $102 million and tax receipts of almost $18 million (Dean Runyan Associates 2013).

A 2011 study estimated that recreational riders alone contributed $365 million to the Iowa economy (Lankford, J. *et al.* 2011).

Even states with lower estimated benefits still experience economic impacts in nine figures from cycling and cyclists. A 2012 report estimated that bicycling contributed over $300 million annually to the New Mexico economy in equipment purchases and travel related expenses (Atencio 2012). A 2014 study estimated that bicycles and bicycling add $224 million per year to the Michigan economy: $175 million in retail spending, $38 million on bicycle events and tourism plus $11 million on bike related manufacturing (BBC Research & Consulting 2014). Bicycle tourism in Utah annually produces a total economic impact of $121.9 million in spending, supporting 1,499 jobs with $46.73 million of employment income (Feer & Peers 2017).

Regional Benefit Estimates – Several studies document the benefits of multiple trails on regional economies. Trails in the seven-county Minneapolis metro area were estimated to experience almost 86 million person-days of walking, bicycling, running and inline skating in 2008, generating over $487 million in trail spending (Venegas 2009). In 2012, cyclists in the Portland metro area generated $89 million in spending, accounting for 700 jobs, $18.7

million in earnings and $4.1 million in state and local tax revenues (Dean Runyan Associates 2013). The 70 miles of trails that form the spine of the East Coast Greenway in the Raleigh-Durham region of North Carolina generate over $87 million in economic benefits annually and support 800 temporary and permanent jobs (East Coast Greenway Alliance 2017). Similarly, bicycling in Northwest Arkansas contributes $51 million per year to the regional economy including $27 million from the spending of out-of-state bicycle tourists at local businesses throughout the region. (BBC Research & Consulting 2018). The Little Miami Scenic Trail and four other trails in Ohio's Miami Valley are estimated to generate a total direct economic impact of up to $15.4 million a year for this region (Miami Valley Regional Planning Commission 2017). Similarly, the multiple trails radiating from downtown Des Moines, Iowa are estimated to generate an economic impact of $15 million and support almost 215 jobs (Fleming *et al.* 2013).

Individual Trail Benefits - As illustrated in the following chapters, studies have also quantified the economic benefit of several individual trails. Some of the most economically-productive trails are longer and anchored by one or more large cities. For example, the 61.2-mile Silver Comet Trail northwest of Atlanta, creates a total annual impact of almost $120 million within the State of Georgia while supporting roughly 1,300 jobs and producing $37 million in earnings plus $3.5 million in income tax, sales tax and business tax revenues (Alta 2013). In 2000, cyclists on Route verte, the 3,100-mile network stretching between and around Montreal and Quebec, spent $64.6 million, supporting 2,000 jobs and generating $15.1 million in tax revenues for the Quebec government as well as $11.9 million for the government of Canada (Velo Quebec 2003). Similarly, the 335-mile Great Allegheny Passage/Chesapeake and Ohio Canal Trail between Pittsburgh, Pennsylvania and Washington, DC was estimated to generate an impressive $40 million in direct spending and $7.5 million in wages during 2008 (The Progress Fund 2009).

Many other trails succeed at generating economic benefits in the eight-figure range. The 37-mile-long Spokane River Centennial State Park Trail contributes $30 million to the regional economy (Stark 2014). The 240-mile Katy Trail in Missouri annually attracts 400,000 visitors, generating a total impact of $18.5 million to local economies and supporting 367 jobs with a payroll of $5 million (Synergy/PRI/JPA 2012). The 44-mile trail formed by Maryland's Torrey C. Brown Rail Trail and Pennsylvania's Heritage Rail Trail County Park generates between $13.5 and $14.4 million per year to the local economies (Knoch 2017; Trail Facts 2005). In fiscal year 2015-16, the 25-mile Tallahassee – St. Marks Trail in Florida produced a total direct economic impact of $13,065,398, generating $890,913 in state sales tax and supporting 209 jobs (Florida Department of Environmental Protection 2016).

Shorter trails in or near major cities often generate economic benefits in the seven-figure range. The 14-mile Butler Trail in Austin, Texas singlehandedly attracts 2.6 million visitors annually and generates $8.8 million in economic impact, supporting 88 full-time equivalent jobs, $3.2 million in labor income and almost $200,000 in state and local tax revenue (Angelou Economics 2016). The 17-mile Swamp Rabbit Trail in Greenville, South Carolina annually contributes $6.7 million to local businesses (Maxwell 2014). In Charlotte, North Carolina, the six-mile Sugar Creek Greenway generates over $5.2 million per year in sales revenue, supporting 73 jobs with over $2 million in labor income (North Carolina Department of Transportation 2018).

Regardless of the size of the communities they link, some trails nevertheless generate remarkable economic benefits. The 31-mile Tammany Trace, connecting Covington and Slidell, Louisiana, annually contributes an estimated $7.3 million to local economies (Hammons 2015). The 77-mile Greenbrier River Rail Trail, anchored by Marlinton, West Virginia, population 1,000, annually generates $3.1 million of economic impact, which is a meaningful contribution for a region striving to transition from its lumber mill past (Magnini and Uysal 2015).

The 42-mile Harmony-Preston/Lanesboro-Houston Root River system in Minnesota was estimated to be responsible for trip spending of over $2.2 million even though the largest of the four villages linked by this network has a population of less than 1,300 people (Kelly 2010).

This report focuses primarily on the economic benefits that bicycle trails and networks create for trail-oriented businesses in terms of sales, employment, income and tax revenues as briefly sketched above. However, before proceeding directly to the profiles that form the bulk of this book, below are a few reminders that bicycling and cycle infrastructure also produce economic benefits in other ways including the following:

- Reduced cost of transportation benefits local economies;
- Reduced transportation cost benefits economic resilience and mobility;
- Reduced healthcare costs;
- Increased property value due to proximity of bike infrastructure;
- Improved transport efficiency benefits;
- Reduced cost of roadway and parking improvements;
- Economic benefits of reduced energy consumption and pollution;and Other economic benefits.

Because they drive less, the people of Portland have an estimated $1.1 billion "Portland Green Dividend" to spend on purchases from local businesses.

A   Reduced cost of transportation benefits local economies

The paragraphs above summarize the economic benefits of bicycle-oriented business. A slightly different benefit occurs when people have more money to spend on local goods and services because of the savings in transportation costs made possible by good walking, bicycling and public transport services. Expenditures on cars and fuel typically involve the outflow of money from local economies while reduced auto-dependency generally supports local economies. The less people drive, the less they spend on driving and the more money they have to spend on other things. According to a 2007 study, since Portlanders drive 20 percent less than average Americans, they have an extra $1.1 billion in their pockets, a so-called Portland Green Dividend. Furthermore, by reducing expenditures on cars and gas (which primarily leave the state), this $1.1 billion has a better chance of being spent in economic sectors with higher local multiplier effects including restaurants and brewpubs (Cortright 2007). Of course transit, walking and compact development as well as bicycling account for Portland's lower auto-dependency. But together, the green dividend concept suggests that Portland's economy is strong because of, rather than despite, its sustainability successes.

B   Reduced cost of transportation benefits economic resilience and mobility

Good bicycling infrastructure inherently promotes social justice by improving mobility options for families regardless of whether or not they own an automobile. The low-cost option of commuting by bicycling increases employment opportunities and improves the potential for improving household income. In addition, bike-friendly communities improve the ability of employers to attract and retain employees, particularly lower-wage workers without personal automobiles. Therefore, the ability to bike to work promotes upward economic mobility for lower-income households and improves the prosperity of the city as a whole.

Several studies confirm that walkable/bikeable cities promote economic resilience - the ability to overcome unanticipated financial reversals including reduced incomes or unexpected expenses (Litman 2020). Walkable cities also advance intergenerational upward economic mobility – the ability of children from lower income households to move up the economic ladder in adulthood. A 2018 study documented a strong relationship between walkable cities and economic mobility. In these cities, the lack of an automobile is less of a barrier to upward mobility. In fact, the ability to accomplish things without a car was found to be a key factor in upward mobility. In addition to decreased reliance on cars, people living in walkable cities have a greater sense of belonging to their communities, a feeling associated with documented changes in social class (Oishi, Koo and Buttrick 2018).

C   Reduced healthcare costs

Medical costs are lowered by the improved health and fitness created by bicycling, walking and other forms of active transportation. Modern life has taken a toll on the medical condition of many people in the United States and other developed countries. Manufacturing occupations and other active jobs of a generation ago have largely been replaced by desk jobs that entail sitting in a chair and staring at a screen. Auto-dependency has reduced people's inclination to walk just about anywhere. And now, ride-hailing companies offer door-to-door service, thereby eliminating even the effort of walking to your car. In 2018, less than a quarter of American adults met the guidelines from the Centers for Disease Control for aerobic and muscle strengthening activity (Centers for Disease Control 2019).

Sedentary lifestyles have created a medical emergency. Half of American adults do not get enough of the physical activity needed to help reduce and prevent chronic diseases. Not surprisingly, half of all U.S. adults have at least one chronic disease and a quarter have two or more. Adequate physical activity could prevent one tenth of premature deaths from breast cancer, colorectal cancer, diabetes and heart disease. In monetary terms, inadequate physical activity is associated with $177 billion in healthcare costs every year. Considering that one quarter of young adult Americans weights too much for military service, physical inactivity is also considered a risk to defense readiness (Centers for Disease Control 2020).

Walking and bicycling improve healthcare outcomes. A 2017 study involving 263,540 participants in the United Kingdom concluded that commuting on foot reduces the risk of cardio-vascular disease and that commuting by bicycle lowers the risk of mortality from all causes and cancer as well as cardio-vascular disease (Celis-Morales 2017). Similarly, a 2013 study found that walking lowers the risk of mortality from all causes by up to 20 percent and from cardiovascular disease by up to 30 percent (Sinnett et al 2013).

Several researchers have estimated the monetary value of improved health resulting from walking and cycling. A 2013 study from Australia monetizes the average health benefits of walking at $1.68 per kilometer and the improved healthcare outcome of bicycling at $1.12 per kilometer (Mulley et al 2013). Similarly, a 2008 New Zealand study monetized health benefits as $3 per mile of walking and $1.6 per mile of cycling (Litman 2013).

Another study calculated that shifting trips of five kilometers or less from cars to bicycles for 250 days generates 1,300 euros of heath care benefits annually to the rider and 30 euros per year of benefit to all city residents from improved air quality. The health benefit from improved air quality for bicyclists however varies depending on whether the cycling occurs on separated bike paths or on roads shared with motor vehicles (Rabl and de Nazelle 2012).

A study of 11 metropolitan areas in the Upper Midwest of the United States estimated that $8 billion per year in health benefits would result from air quality improvement and increased physical activity if car trips of eight kilometers or less were eliminated and half of all short trips were made by bicycle (Grabow et al, 2012). Similarly, bicycling in Northwestern Arkansas was estimated to generate $86 million in healthcare benefits (BBC Research & Consulting 2018).

The healthcare benefits of cycling are sometimes calculated on a statewide basis. In Michigan, bicycling was estimated to save $256 million in health care costs and $187 million in the cost of work absenteeism as part of a study that found a total annual economic impact of $667 million from cycling (BBC Research & Consulting 2014). In 2011, bicycling was estimated to annually produce $87 million in healthcare savings for the State of Iowa (Lankford, J. et al. 2011).

Some studies take the next step and monetize the healthcare benefits of pedestrian and bicycle infrastructure. A 2011 study analyzed the $138 million to $605 million that Portland had invested and planned to invest in bicycling infrastructure over a 40-year period. It concluded that this investment would save from $388 million to $594 million in healthcare costs alone. This outcome suggested that the disease-fighting results would single-handedly justify expenditures in robust cycling systems. In addition, the statistical value of the lives saved by physical activity on the Portland system was estimated to range from $7 billion to $12 billion, which represent staggering returns on investment (Gotschi 2011). In Austin, Texas, a single bicycle trail was estimated to annually produce $4.3 million of medical cost savings (Angelou Economics 2016).

D   Increased property value due to proximity of bike infrastructure

A growing portion of the population is demonstrating its preference for walkable/bikeable neighborhoods. In a 2017 survey, the National Association of Realtors found that over half of all Americans prefer to live where they can easily walk to community amenities and believe that walkability contributes to quality of life (National Association of Realtors 2017).

Walkability can be quantified by Walk Score, a publically-accessible index that rates locations on a scale of 0 to 100 based on pedestrian routes to everyday destinations like schools, parks, grocery stores, restaurants and retail. In 2012, Walk Score launched a similar program called Bike Score, which rates places from 0 to 100 for bike-friendliness based on bike lane infrastructure, hilliness, the percent of commuting done by bicycle and the destinations that can easily be reached by bicycle (Walk Score 2020).

In a 2009 study of 15 U.S. cities, home values typically increased from $500 to $3,000 for each Walk Score point (Cortright 2009). A more-recent study of 14 U.S. major metro areas concluded that every Walk Score point can increase the value of a home 0.9 percent, or $3,250 on average. Despite large variations between real estate markets, this study suggests that real estate prices demonstrate preferences for walkable neighborhoods (Bokhari 2016).

As with walkability, bike trails generally increase the value of nearby property. A 2008 study reviewed five hedonic studies that used actual property values and found that trails had consistently positive effects for nearby homes. For example, one study found that 14 percent ($13,056) of predicted prices could be attributed to the Monon Rail Trail, the popular 27-mile rail trail connecting Indianapolis with its northern suburbs. Another study estimated that single-family residential properties increased in value by $7.05 for each foot they are located closer to the Little Miami Scenic Trail in Ohio (Karadeniz 2008). Similarly, homes within a quarter mile of the Razorback Greenway in Northwest Arkansas were found to sell for $15,000 more on average than comparable homes two miles from the trail (BBC Research & Consulting 2018).

Some research calculates the impact of bicycle trails on the property value of entire regions. A 70-mile stretch of the East Coast Greenway was estimated to add $164 million to regional property value in the Raleigh-Durham Region of North Carolina (East Coast Greenway Alliance 2017). The Silver Comet Trail in Northwest Georgia produced a total value increase of $180 million and additional property tax revenues of over $2 million per year for the jurisdictions and school districts adjacent to the trail (Alta 2013). Similarly, Tucson's 131-mile Loop trail was found to add $300 million in tax base, thereby generating more than $3 million per year in extra property tax revenue for this metro area (Pima County 2013).

Property values increase with proximity to the Monon Rail Trail, the popular 27-mile rail trail connecting Indianapolis with its northern suburbs.

The redevelopment potential of trail networks is evident in larger cities. The Beltline trail system that will eventually encircle downtown Atlanta is projected to ultimately remediate 1,100 acres of brownfields, build 5,600 affordable housing units, generate $10 to $20 billion in economic development, create 30,000 permanent jobs and support 48,000 one-year construction jobs (Atlanta BeltLine 2018a).

E   Improved transport efficiency benefits

The public right of way theoretically belongs to the entire public. But personal cars occupy much more of this space than pedestrians and cyclists, causing roadways to be congested, inefficient and unpleasant, even for motorists. Pedestrians and cyclists require less than a quarter of the space consumed by a single occupant vehicle (SOV) traveling 30 kilometers per hour and less than five percent of the pavement needed for a SOV traveling at 60 kilometers per hour (Litman 2000). This difference is unfair to all pedestrians and cyclists but also raises a social justice issue for people who have no options other than walking and cycling.

Walkability and bikeability reduce auto dependency, consequently lowering traffic congestion and related costs of time delay and accidents. In 2007, congestion was estimated to cost the economy of the United Kingdom 20 billion pounds due to wasted time, pollution caused by inefficient motorized transportation and various health problems including respiratory diseases and stress-related illnesses. Expanding roadway capacity does not necessarily relieve congestion since increased traffic often overwhelms the new capacity. But switching from cars to bicycling has a quantifiable benefit. A 2007 study estimated that one person switching from car use to cycling for 624 kilometers per year annually reduces the cost of roadway congestion by 68.64 pounds in rural areas and 137.28 pounds in urban areas (SQW 2007).

Some studies quantify the monetary benefits from reduced congestion produced by individual bicycling trails. For example, the trail encircling Lady Bird Lake in Austin, Texas is estimated to annually produce $727,103 of traffic reduction benefits (Angelou Economics 2016).

F   Reduced cost of roadway and parking improvements

Due to vehicle weight, size and speed, the cost of constructing and maintaining infrastructure is much lower for pedestrians and cyclists than motor vehicles. One study estimated that changing from driving to cycling or walking saves five cents per urban mile and three cents per rural mile in terms of infrastructure construction and maintenance (Litman 2020).

The annualized cost of an urban parking space ranges between $500 and $3,000 depending on whether the space is located in a surface parking lot, a multi-level parking structure or some place in between. Because ten to 20 bicycles can be stored in a single parking space, switching from cars to bicycles reduces parking costs by 90 to 95 percent (Litman 2020). Since parking bicycles is typically cost-free, increasing the ability to bicycle rather than drive further promotes mobility for people who have no car or who simply would prefer to spend less on transportation and more on other things.

Some business owners resist eliminating on-street parking for bike lanes or bike corrals under the assumption that car drivers are better customers. However, surveys of customers at bars, convenience stores and restaurants in Portland, Oregon, found that although cyclists spend less per visit than motorists, they tend to visit more often and consequently spend almost 25 percent more per month than their car-driving counterparts (Clifton, Morrissey & Ritter 2012).

A study conducted in Davis, California found that cyclists there not only make more trips per month to downtown businesses but that they also spend more per trip and contribute more to local businesses than their car-bound counterparts (Davis 2014). Another study found that the same square meter of parking space in downtown Melbourne, Australia generates over three times more in retail sales per hour when used by bicycles rather than cars for various reasons, including higher turnover and the smaller area needed by cycles (Lee and March 2007).

G   Economic benefits of reduced energy consumption and pollution

Switching from motor vehicles to walking and bicycling saves an average of one to four cents per mile in energy costs (Litman 2020). In total, fuel consumption can be reduced by two to four percent for every one percent shift from motor vehicles to active transportation (Komanoff and Roloff 1993).

Motor vehicles generate local impacts, such as noise, particulates, and carbon monoxide, as well as regional and global impacts, including ozone, carbon dioxide, and methane. A review of several studies developed a reasonable conclusion that a driver switching from driving a motor vehicle to walking or cycling reduces these multiple impacts by ten cents per urban mile during peak traffic hours, five cents per mile in urban areas during non-peak hours and one cent per mile in rural areas (Litman 2020).

H   Other economic benefits

The construction of bicycle infrastructure creates more jobs per dollar of investment than the installation of roads for motor vehicles. A study of 58 projects in 11 U.S. cities, found that the construction of bicycling infrastructure creates 11.4 full-time-equivalent in-state jobs per $1 million while the construction of road-only projects creates 7.8 jobs per $1 million. The greater job-generation ratios occur because the construction of bicycling infrastructure is more labor intensive and generally requires less importation of materials from other states (Garrett-Peltier 2011).

Because pedestrians and cyclists consume less urban space than cars, cities that emphasize active transportation can be more compact, diverse and ultimately successful. Compact cities with well-designed, multi-use neighborhoods consume 75 percent less energy and other resources than cities that follow the wasteful, business-as-usual model popular in the late 20th century (International Resource Panel 2017).

CHAPTER 2

Abington – Damascus – Whitetop, Virginia: Saved by the Creeper

In addition to spa treatments, golf rounds and theater performances, the Martha Washington Inn will shuttle you and your bike to the far end of the Virginia Creeper Trail, allowing a 34-mile ride back to this historic hotel in Abington, Virginia. The 'Martha' and many other local businesses are wisely capitalizing on one of the country's most scenic rail trails and a well-deserved honoree in the Rail Trail Hall of Fame (Traillink 2018). Bike shops, brew pubs, restaurants and all forms of lodging have gravitated to the Virginia Creeper both in Abington and Damascus, the aptly-nick-named "Trail Town USA" at the trail's midpoint. Economic studies have documented that this apparent success story in the heart of the Blue Ridge Mountains is real.

The steam engines that originally used this rail line literally crept up the long, uphill slope from Damascus to Whitetop Station, now the southern trailhead. The grade in this section is definitely noticeable, which is why many visitors choose to shuttle rather than pedal to the top. No fewer than eight outfitters are more than happy to provide this sweat-free uphill lift. The downhill ride is both exhilarating and spectacular, passing waterfalls and crisscrossing mountain streams as the Creeper winds though mile after mile of the Jefferson National Forest. Most riders pause at Green Cove where the original rail station still welcomes visitors with a dose of history and, occasionally, some live local music. Further downhill, it is practically mandatory to stop at the Creeper Trail Café for something cold or hot depending on the weather (Stark 2013).

A great trail with spectacular scenery explain why the Virginia Creeper became a Rail Trail Hall of Famer.

Arriving in Damascus, riders can taste a locally-crafted concoction from the Damascus Brewery, linger in a cafe or stay the night at any of more than a dozen inns, cottages, or B&Bs. We chose the Damascus Old Mill Inn, which overlooks a waterfall and mill pond teaming with ducks, geese and fishermen. The 2000-plus-mile Appalachian Trail intersects the Virginia Creeper Trail in Damascus and uses the sidewalk on the main street here before climbing back into the hills on the other side of town. Every spring, Damascus hosts Trail Days, attended by roughly 20,000 cyclists, hikers and other nature lovers hoping to catch the rhododendrons and mountain laurels at peak bloom (Stark 2013). Wayne Miller, President of the Virginia Creeper Trail Club, gives the following opinion of the trail's importance. "Damascus is a little mill town that was saved by the trail. It was on its last legs. The old industries were shutting down. Now it supports eight bike shops that service the trail" (Stark 2013).

Heading north, the scenery changes from forests to farms as cyclists pedal the remaining 17 miles to Abington where they are greeted by a 1907 steam engine tailored to the Creeper's tight curves, steep grades and wooden trestles (Stark 2013). On bike-friendly Pecan Street, cyclists soon enter the Abington Historic District, listed in the National Register of Historic Places. Here, the previously-mentioned Martha Washington Inn, dating from 1832, was a residence and college before becoming an upscale hotel in 1935. An 1831 building across the street became a theater in 1933 called the Barter Theatre because people could attend plays by bartering fruit and vegetables from their farms and gardens during the depths of the Great Depression. The Barter now welcomes over 120,000 visitors a year with a year-round schedule (Barter Theatre 2013). Further up Main Street, the county still dispenses justice in a courthouse built in 1869 (National Park Service 2018).

By connecting destinations, like the Barter Theater, the Virginia Creeper prompts visitors to stay longer (and spend more).

In addition to history and bike trails, Abington offers visitors other reasons to hang around including a winery, brewery, art museum, craft stores and art galleries plus several outstanding restaurants like The Tavern, serving traditional German meals in a landmark building that originally housed a stagecoach inn. Kevin Worley, Abington's Director of Parks and Recreation, is working to get more people on the Creeper for economic as well as health reasons: "They come in to do the Creeper, then come in to do other things in town. The trail brings a lot of economic benefit to the town" (Stark 2013).

Formal economic studies support these personal observations. For his

2004 master's degree thesis, Joshua Gill conducted an extensive survey of Virginia Creeper users. The survey responses allowed him to estimate the percentage of users who travel here primarily to ride this rail trail. The survey also distinguished between day users and overnight users. For example, of the 39,367 primary-purpose, non-local trips, 33,642 were day trips and 5,725 were overnight trips. The overnight trips involved lodging revenue as well as higher per-trip expenditures on food, bike rentals and shuttles. Consequently, primary-purpose, non-local overnight users were estimated to spend roughly four times more than their day use counterparts. As a bottom line, Gill calculated the Creeper's total economic impact at $1.6 million per year when applying a multiplier to direct expenditures (Gill 2004).

A 2007 report estimated that 106,000 people used the Virginia Creeper in the study year. The authors calculated that the $1.6 million in total annual economic activity supported 27 jobs and $610,000 in labor earnings. That represents a sizable portion of the local economy considering that Abington had a population of 8,186 and Damascus was home to less than 800 people (Bowker, Bergstrom & Gill 2007).

In 2011, a team from the Virginia Tech Economic Development Studio surveyed local businesses as well as trail users. More than half of the commercial respondents reported that trail use generated over 61 percent of their income. The report concluded that Damascus owes its economic success to trail-based tourism, with many local entrepreneurs naming the Virginia Creeper as a motivation for opening a business here (Economic Development Studio 2011).

As shown by these studies, despite the disappearance of the steam locomotives essential to bygone industries, the Virginia Creeper is still an economic engine.

CHAPTER 3

Austin, Texas: Closing Gaps - Opening Opportunities

Austin thrives in the heart of Texas largely because of water. Logically, much of Austin's bicycle network follows creeks and surrounds Lady Bird Lake, an impoundment of the Colorado River that gives this city of 950,000 people a picture-perfect foreground for its downtown skyline. Although this network required some expensive gap-closing boardwalks and bridges, the city is doubling down on its investment, knowing that a well-designed bicycle system is good for business as well as mobility, health, recreation and the environment.

Austin is the only city in Texas to be recognized as a Gold Level Bicycle Friendly Community (League of American Bicyclists 2020). This ranking reflects Austin's bicycle plan which aims to create a network for all ages and abilities from 8 to 80 years of age. As of 2014, Austin already had a 210-mile bicycle network linking neighborhoods, schools, parks, greenspace and public institutions as well as employment and commercial centers (Austin 2014).

Part of this system is formed by 16 greenbelt trails that generally follow creeks flowing down to Lady Bird Lake (Austin 2020a). On the west side of downtown, the 6.8-mile Shoal Creek Greenbelt Trail connects five parks and passes Austin Community College, with 60,000 total enrollment, before merging with other trails at Shoal Beach on the north shore of Lady Bird Lake. Northeast of the Texas state capitol building, Waller Creek bisects the University of Texas campus, home to the Lyndon B. Johnson Presidential Library. Further downstream, the Waller Creek Greenbelt Trail, connects several parks and neighborhoods before ending at Waller Beach on Lady Bird Lake.

Austin's 85 hike-and-bike trails total 125 miles in length (Austin 2020a). Although most of these trails are short, the network has remarkable exceptions. At the northern end of the eight-mile Barton Creek Greenbelt

Trail, Zilker Park is home to a botanical garden, a nature preserve, a science center and a miniature railroad. Further south, the trail passes Barton Springs Pool, a three-acre, outdoor swimming pool fed entirely by natural spring water which annually attracts 800,000 visitors. Further up Barton Creek, mountain bikers can climb the trail into Barton Creek Wilderness Park, the largest of 15 nature preserves in Austin's 2,200-acre nature preserve system (Austin 2020b).

The crown jewel of Austin's trail system is the 14-mile Ann and Roy Butler Trail which now forms a complete loop around Lady Bird Lake thanks to the closing of a 1.3-mile gap in 2014 using a $28-million complex of boardwalks and bridges over the water (Austin 2020c). Traveling counter-clockwise from Festival Beach, cyclists can pedal the Butler Trail though a continuous park system lining the north shore of the lake. On one of four possible options, cyclists can ride the Pfluger Pedestrian and Bicycle Bridge to reach the south side of Lady Bird Lake at an entertainment complex that includes a performing arts center, a theater and an outdoor concert space.

The Butler Hike and Bike Trail offers views of the Austin skyline over Lady Bird Lake.

Continuing east on the Ann and Roy Butler Trail, riders can stop to rent boats, kayaks and paddle boards or simply take a break at a restaurant patio overlooking the lake. After navigating the boardwalk and bridges, the trail enters 400-acre Roy G. Guerrero Colorado River Metro Park featuring a wildlife sanctuary as well as volleyball courts, softball diamonds, fitness stations and Secret Beach, a sandy, shallow stretch of river where kids can splash in a natural wading pool.

The Butler Trail alone attracts 2.6 million visitors annually and generates $8.8 million in economic impact, supporting 88 full-time-equivalent jobs, $3.2 million in labor income and almost $200,000 in state and local tax revenue. A 2016 study found that monthly rental rates increase by $0.28 per square foot of office floor area for every quarter-mile of proximity to the trail. That study also estimated that the trail annually produces $495,182 of environmental benefits, $727,103 of traffic reduction benefits and $4.3 million of medical cost savings (Angelou Economics 2016).

Economic return is one reason why Austin's bicycle plan proposes 220 miles of on-street facilities and 150 miles of off-street urban trails. Implementation of this plan carries a price tag of $161 million. But Austin recognizes that this investment will benefit mobility, congestion management, health and the environment as well as the local economy (Austin 2014)

CHAPTER 4

Atlanta, Georgia: The Beltline: Economic Development Engine

Ladybird Grove & Mess Hall proclaims its address as Mile Marker 9.5 on the Atlanta Beltllline. That's one measure of the success of this city's ambitious project to redevelop and connect 45 neighborhoods encircling downtown using the conversion of 22 miles of abandoned rail corridors as the catalyst. Ladybird Grove owes much of its popularity to its quirky, summer camp vibe and huge selection of craft beer. But the main attraction here is a huge deck overlooking the Beltline where people can take a break from their walking, running, or biking and watch others passing by under their own non-motorized power.

Proximity to the Beltline is in high demand. "Beltline Living" is a common advertising slogan seen on the banners hanging from new apartment buildings under construction here. Taking its cue from Ladybird Grove, New Realm Brewing has opened a beer garden not far down the trail. Anchoring the Eastside Trail is Ponce City Market. Once a Sears & Roebuck regional distribution center built in the 1920s, this two million square-foot building has been repurposed as a multi-use complex with 259 apartment units, 550,000 square feet of office space and 330,000 square feet of retail including a Central Food Hall featuring famous chefs and international cuisine. Ponce City Market incorporates bike storage, showers, and bike-friendly elevators in order to take maximum advantage of its location on the Beltline (Urban Land Institute 2016).

In 1999, the Beltline concept was first proposed in a thesis written by Ryan Gravel, a Georgia Tech graduate student. Grassroots support for the idea was nurtured by Friends of the Beltline and a 2004 Trust for Public Land study demonstrating the feasibility of the project using a Tax Allocation District (TAD). By 2005, a plan and the TAD were approved and the first trail segment was open by 2008 (Atlanta BeltLine 2018b). As of 2016, the project had created seven parks and hundreds of affordable housing units as well as $3 billion in residential complexes, commercial buildings, affordable housing and other forms of private investment (Atlanta BeltLine 2018a).

Ladybird Grove and Mess Hall uses its Beltline mile marker as a business address.

The Beltline is all about connecting Atlanta. While the Atlanta region is famous for sprawl, the older parts of the city of Atlanta concentrate many recreational, cultural, residential and commercial destinations within easy bicycling distance via the Beltline. The Eastside Trail segment of the Beltline passes through 185-acre Piedmont Park. In 1887 and again in 1895, this park was the site of international expositions, two of many reasons why the park is now listed on the National Register of Historic Places. Some elements from this era still survive, including Lake Clara Meer, which once featured water slides and diving platforms. A 1912 Olmstead Brothers plan influenced the park's current look, which offers the Atlanta Botanical Garden, a swimming pool, a tennis academy, ball fields, playgrounds, dog parks, a community garden and a Saturday morning farmers' market (Piedmont Park Conservancy 2018).

Just south of Ponce City Market, a consortium has transformed an area previously plagued by flooding and neglect into the Historic Fourth Ward Park, a model of multi-functional green infrastructure. This 17-acre park includes a playground, splashpad, skatepark, sport areas, and passive green space. In addition, the two-acre lake here serves as a storm water detention basin as well as a stunning bit of landscape architecture (Atlanta BeltLine 2018a).

On a spur called the Freedom Park Trail, cyclists can pedal one mile west to the Martin Luther King Jr. National Historical Park. The Visitor Center here explores the life of Dr. King and the Civil Rights Movement. Surrounding the Center are Dr. King's birth home, grave and the Historic Ebenezer Baptist Church, where Dr. King was co-pastor from 1960 until his death in 1968 (National Park Service 2016).

So far, Atlanta's Beltline has generated $3 billion of private investment in residential complexes, commercial buildings and affordable housing.

Just east of the Beltline on Freedom Park Trail, cyclists encounter the 35-acre campus of the Carter Center, a non-governmental organization founded by former US President Jimmy Carter promoting conflict resolution, civil rights, democracy, disease prevention and mental health. The beautifully landscaped grounds here showcase a particularly-moving sculpture depicting a child leading a man stricken with river blindness, a disease that the Carter Center and its partners are in the process of eradicating throughout the world (The Carter Center 2018). Visitors to the Carter Presidential Library & Museum can take selfies in a life-size replica of the Oval Office and wander through a maze of exhibits on the life and times of Jimmy and Rosalynn Carter, with understandable emphasis on 1977 through 1981, the turbulent four years of the Carter Presidency (Jimmy Carter Library 2018).

Going further east, the Freedom Park Trail becomes the Stone Mountain Trail and a trail spur leads to Dinosaur Plaza, an outdoor space in front of the Fernbank National History Museum dominated by a family of *Lophorhothon atopus* dinosaurs recreated in bronze. The 75 acres surrounding the museum are home to Fernbank Forest, the largest old-growth Piedmont forest within the urban United States. In the heart of the city, hikers can wander two miles of paths beneath trees more than 16-stories tall. The WildWoods exhibit here features an elevated walkway where visitors can experience forest life from a treetop perspective (Fernbank 2018).

The destinations sketched above are connected by the Eastside Trail, one of four segments of the Beltline that are currently in use. On completion in 2030, the Beltline will connect 2,400 acres of parkland with a 22-mile streetcar loop and 33 miles of multiuse trails. Atlanta BeltLine estimates that the project will ultimately remediate 1,100 acres of brownfields, build 5,600 affordable housing units, generate $10 to $20 billion in economic development, create 30,000 permanent jobs and support 48,000 one-year construction jobs (Atlanta BeltLine 2018a). Considering the huge success of the Beltline segments finished so far, these estimates might actually be conservative.

CHAPTER 5

Blackstone River Greenway, Massachusetts and Rhode Island: Birthplace of the American Industrial Revolution

Slater Mill, built in 1793 on the Blackstone River in Pawtucket, Rhode Island, was the first water-powered textile mill in America. It is often credited with sparking this country's transition from an agrarian to an industrial nation. Today, cyclists and hikers on the Blackstone River Greenway absorb this history as they pass the 19th century mills that have often been restored and repurposed to meet modern needs. As a means of transportation, recreation, and tourism, the trail has essentially become part of a new economic era.

The northern portion of the greenway is home to the Blackstone River Canal and Heritage State Park in Massachusetts, which preserves many remnants from the time when the Blackstone Canal, completed in 1828, linked Providence, Rhode Island and Worcester, Massachusetts. The canal transformed Worchester into an inland port and spawned a rash of textile mills that took advantage of the river's 438-foot drop in elevation. However, the Providence & Worcester Railroad, which began service between these two cities in 1847, was more reliable and rendered the canal obsolete. Today, much of the former canal's towpath has been put to use as the route of the Blackstone River Greenway (Traillink 2021).

The trailhead in Woonsocket, Rhode Island, is located near the Museum of Work and Culture, showcasing 19th-century mill town life within a former textile mill. French-Canadians once immigrated to work in the mills of Woonsocket and their influence can be felt throughout the city. St. Ann Arts and Cultural Center was originally built as a church here for French-

Canadians in 1913 and its walls and ceilings still display North America's largest collection of fresco paintings (St. Ann 2021).

South of Woonsocket, cyclists pass several reminders of why the Blackstone Valley is called the birthplace of the American Industrial Revolution. Former mills have been restored and converted into residences including Highland Falls in Albion and Ashton Mills in Cumberland, where the River Lofts complex markets its apartments by touting the brick walls, exposed wood beams, and the industrial-sized windows overlooking the river. The 1867 mill and its surrounding village of mill-worker housing is listed in the National Register as the Ashton Historic District. Downstream, the Town of Cumberland is home to the Berkeley Mill Village, the Arnold Mills Historic District, and the Lonsdale Historic District, all listed in the National Register. Further south, the City of Central Falls earned the title of Chocolateville from a 1782 mill here that once ground cacao beans to satisfy the hot chocolate craze of the late 1700s (Mitchell 2021).

The 1867 Ashton Mill has been restored and repurposed as apartments featuring brick walls, exposed wood beams, and industrial-sized windows overlooking the Blackstone River

Further downstream, the City of Pawtucket welcomes visitors to a grouping of historic structures illustrating the pivotal role of the Blackstone Valley in America's Industrial Revolution. The star attraction here is Old Slater Mill, named for inventor Samuel Slater who designed this and several other mills as well as pioneering the Rhode Island System in which a mill employed entire families, including children, as workers and housed them in adjacent villages of company-owned housing (McBurney 2021).

In 1986, the United States Congress designated the entire valley from Worcester to Providence as the Blackstone River Valley National Heritage Corridor. Since then, federal, state, and local efforts have been removing dyes, chemicals, and other industrial wastes from the Blackstone River, which was once one of America's most polluted rivers. Today, ongoing work within the corridor supports community renewal and economic development with help from over 10,000 sites of scenic, historic, and ecological importance within the valley (Mass Humanities 2021).

The Blackstone River Greenway will eventually be a continuous, off-road trail for the entire 50 miles from Providence to Worcester. But today, the longest uninterrupted path links the 12 miles between Woonsocket and Cumberland. Even with its current gaps, the Blackstone River Greenway is attracting cyclists and their dollars. In 2014, the trail saw 2,314 daily users of which three quarters were bicyclists. The total economic benefit was estimated to be $5.44 million at that time (Leonard 2014). Creating a continuous, gap-free trail will increase both ridership and revenue.

Completion of the Blackstone River Greenway should also be motivated by the fact that the Blackstone forms part of the route for the East Coast Greenway, the mega-path that will one day connect 450 communities in 15 states from Florida to Maine. In addition to increasing options for alternative mobility and healthful recreation, closing the remaining gaps in this trail will ensure that Rhode Island receives its share of the bicycle tourists who will be unable to resist the challenge of a 3,000-mile bike trip..

CHAPTER 6

Boise, Idaho: Gathering at the River

In 1964, a planning consultant proposed that Boise create a continuous greenbelt of public land along the banks of the Boise River. By 1967, a grassroots campaign had been launched to clean up the previously-neglected waterway and benefactors had donated three parcels of land as the nucleus of the trail. Today, the greenbelt offers 25 miles of riverside pathways, connecting dozens of Boise's most important civic and recreational venues. In addition to providing a pleasant way to commute, exercise and enjoy nature, the city also recognizes the greenbelt as an important economic development asset.

The greenbelt evolved from earlier efforts to restore and manage the Boise River itself. In the first half of the 20th century, the river was an unnavigable maze of shallow, shifting channels dotted with debris-strewn islands. Floods periodically swept through the valley, prompting the Army Corps of Engineers to build the Lucky Peak Dam in 1955, which helped carve a single channel and control flow, particularly when the river was swollen by snowmelt and heavy rains (Boise State University 2014).

Prior to 1949, the city allowed dumps to be located on the banks of the river and used its waters for the disposal of raw sewage. But, after two failed attempts, the voters finally passed a bond to build the city's first sewage treatment plant and the Boise City County prohibited dumping except at approved landfills. The river changed from a contaminated eyesore to a treasured asset, prompting the Jaycees to hold its first "Keep Idaho Green" raft race in 1959. Since then, locals and visitors flock to the river for the tubing and rafting season. Boise's Parks & Recreation Department now manages the Boise Whitewater Park featuring a wave-shaping dam that adjusts to create ideal conditions for kayakers and surfers. Today, bicyclists on the greenbelt often see fly fisher-persons in chest-high waders angling in what is now considered one of the finest urban trout streams in the country.

(Boise Parks & Recreation Department. 2019; Boise State University 2014; Idaho Department of Fish and Game. 2019a).

The once-degraded Boise River is now popular for fishing, kayaking, river surfing and rafting.

At the center of the greenbelt, the Anne Frank Human Rights Memorial creates an outdoor classroom dedicated to respect for human dignity and diversity. Heading east on the north side of the Boise River, cyclists encounter Julia Davis Park, one of several riverside parks in Boise's 'Ribbon of Jewels' and home to Zoo Boise, the Boise Art Museum, the Idaho State Historical Museum, the Discovery Center of Idaho and the Idaho Black History Museum. Further east, the Morrison Knudsen Nature Center features an underwater viewing window for visitors to peek in on the river's aquatic life. Next is the natatorium with an elaborate enclosed slide known as the Hydrotube.

Past the golf course in Warm Springs Park, cyclists can continue to Marianne Williams Park and cross over to the south side of the river at Barber Park, where rafts can be rented and launched for a float down the river. After five miles, cyclists approach Boise State University, home to 22,000 students, the nationally-famous Broncos football team and the bright-blue artificial turf adorning the playing field within the 36,000-seat Albertsons Stadium. At one time, this campus turned its back to the river. But in 1977, a bike-pedestrian bridge to Julia Davis Park strengthened the university's connection with the greenbelt. In 1984, the riverfront formed the entrance to the Morrison Center, a 2,000-seat theater called Idaho's Premier Performing Arts Theater (Boise State University 2014).

In another mile, the greenbelt bisects Ann Morrison Park, the take-out point for raft and tube float trips, and Katheryn Albertson Park, with walking loops through urban wildlife habitat. Further west, the Riverside Hotel has taken maximum advantage of its location on the greenbelt, offering restaurants and live-music venues including the Sand Bar, situated directly on the trail and overlooking the river.

In another mile, the southern leg of the greenbelt enters Garden City, which approved extending the trail through the town in 1988. In the next jurisdiction, the City of Eagle, the greenbelt steers clear of Eagle Island State Park in an effort to reduce impacts on birds and other wildlife. This park is part of the Idaho Birding Trail encompassing 20 miles of the river in and around Boise that is home to waterfowl, water birds, shorebirds, song birds and raptors, including Bald Eagles (Idaho Department of Fish and Game. 2019b).

In addition to greenway extensions, Boise and its neighbors are supplementing existing bike lanes and bike friendly streets with corridors designed to improve safety using new intersection configurations and rider-activated warning signals. By 2021, the Ada County Highway District plans to complete an additional bicycle corridor to Camel's Back Park in Boise's North End (Berg 2018). These spurs link the greenway with neighborhood parks, playgrounds, and community facilities including Jack's Urban Meeting Place, or JUMP, equal parts experimental art studio, creative space, educational center and tractor museum (JUMP 2019).

Idaho recognizes trails like the Boise Greenbelt as vital to the state's tourism industry. Roughly ten percent of Idaho vacationers hike or bike during their visits. In 2012, biking and hiking tourists contributed $500 million to Idaho's economy. By 2035, the state plans to add 650 more miles of shared use paths, creating a branded 1,000-plus-mile system aimed at attracting more than 1.2 million new users annually and adding $135 million per year in new tourist revenue (Idaho 2014).

According to a 2013 trail-user survey, people use the Boise greenbelt to run errands and commute to work as well as exercise and enjoy outdoor recreation. Over 12 percent of the 1,000-plus respondents to a 2013 survey reported that they use the trail to go shopping and almost 20 percent said they take the greenbelt to restaurants. Roughly half of the people walking or biking on the greenbelt live within a mile of the trail and 40 percent live within a half mile. While most trail users live in Boise, the 2013 survey found that about eight percent are tourists, suggesting that the greenbelt is generating economic activity from beyond the larger Boise region (Vos 2014).

Ada County, home to Boise, is already recognized as bike friendly by the League of American Cyclists. The League also names Boise State University as a Bicycle Friendly University. By 2035, the state aims to increase this list to 20 bike friendly communities and make Idaho one of the top ten bike friendly states (Idaho 2014).

In addition to being a key draw for tourists, Idaho understands that trails are an important economic development tool, enabling employers to attract and retain highly-skilled and creative workers (Idaho 2014). Although it is only one ingredient, multi-use trails in general and the greenbelt in particular are at least partly responsible for Boise's phenomenal success as demonstrated in its appearance on numerous "best" lists including Best Places to Live, Best Places to Retire, Healthiest City, Best River Town in America and Best Cities for Raising a Family (Boise State University 2014).

CHAPTER 7

Charlotte, North Carolina: Bicycling and the Redevelopment Playbook

The City of Charlotte and Mecklenburg County plan to complete a Cross Charlotte Trail stretching 30 miles from the South Carolina border to the PNC Music Pavilion near the northern county line. They have a head start on that project with the already-existing Sugar Creek Greenway near downtown Charlotte and the Toby Creek Greenway that bisects the University of North Carolina – Charlotte. But even more attention is being paid these days to the economic development flocking to a corridor connecting downtown Charlotte with its South End neighborhood, a former industrial district that is currently a hotbed of revitalization generated by a new light rail line and the multiuse trail that runs alongside it.

When the LYNX Blue Line light rail began operating in 2007, the path paralleling the tracks was seen as a way of simply getting passengers to and from the stations in Charlotte's South End. However, a 2012 plan reimagined this corridor as a linear park with a trail that people could use for active transportation, recreation, exercise, people-watching and pedestrian/bike-friendly access to and from the bars, restaurants, stores and residential complexes that are sprouting up along this corridor. Between 2005 and 2017, 10,000 new housing units were built in this corridor. Public art abounds here as well as craft beer. The Sycamore Brewing Beer Garden abuts the trail, attracting crowds with food trucks and live music. As of 2017, 14 breweries, distilleries, taprooms and brewpubs were located on or near the rail trail. Futobuta, a ramen restaurant on the ground floor of an apartment building here, has no street access other than the trail, indicating confidence in the viability of trail-oriented development (Goodwin 2017).

Bike lanes connect the South End Rail Trail with Charlotte's Sugar Creek Greenway, which currently begins just east of downtown in Elizabeth Park. This is also the start of Charlotte's Trail of History as commemorated by a statue of Captain Jack who rode his horse to the Continental Congress in Philadelphia carrying the Mecklenburg Declaration of Independence in 1775. Further south, the trail passes restaurants that have strategically positioned outdoor patios for a good view of the walkers and cyclists on the path below. After a few more miles, cyclists enter Freedom Park, home to the Charlotte Nature Museum and an amphitheater featuring free summer jazz concerts.

Although there are two gaps in this six-mile trail, the Sugar Creek Greenway nevertheless produces notable economic benefits. Roughly 382,600 trips are made by cyclists and pedestrians annually, generating over $5.2 million in sales revenue and supporting 73 jobs with over $2 million in labor income as a result of these expenditures. This sales volume also annually creates $179,000 in state and local tax collections (North Carolina Department of Transportation 2018).

Restaurants and pubs line the trail in Charlotte's South End.

The Toby Creek Greenway adds another three-mile segment of completed multi-use trail to Charlotte's bicycle network. This path bisects the 1,000-acre campus of the University of North Carolina at Charlotte with an enrollment of roughly 30,000 students. The Toby Creek Greenway connects to the university's extensive pathway system which links residence halls with classrooms, athletic facilities and the student union as well as the woodlands and stream corridors that dominate the campus. North of UNCC, the Toby Creek Greenway intersects the Mallard Creek Greenway and the Clark's Creek Greenway which create a meandering linear park through several residential neighborhoods.

The success of the existing trail segments has motivated the City of Charlotte and Mecklenburg County to complete the 30-mile Cross Charlotte Trail linking the destinations already served by greenways with additional parks, commercial centers and other special places. For example, just north of downtown, the Cross Charlotte Trail will reach NoDa, (for north of Davidson Street), a vibrant arts district featuring outdoor murals, galleries, live music venues, offbeat eateries and, of course, craft beer breweries and pubs.

Murals abound in Charlotte's NoDa arts district.

When completed, over 140,000 residents and 130,000 jobs will be located within walking distance of the trail and its connecting greenways. City and county citizens are supporting the Cross Charlotte Trail, approving millions in transportation bonds that include funding for further trail development. With this commitment, greater Charlotte is likely to achieve its goals, which include making it possible for residents to travel safely without a car and putting Charlotte in the top 25 US cities for most multiuse trails (Charlotte 2018).

CHAPTER 8

Chattanooga, Tennessee: The Trail to Revitalization

Chattanooga's Walnut Street Bridge is a historic landmark and a symbol of this city's renaissance as well as a key link in the highly successful Riverwalk trail network here. Completed in 1891, this 2,376-foot-long bridge was closed to traffic in 1978 and slated for removal. But activists, preservationists and public officials started a community campaign that raised local funds and secured federal grant money for restoration, resulting in the reopening of the bridge for bicyclists and pedestrians in 1993. Today, it is listed on the National Register of Historic Places (National Geographic 2018).

The bridge restoration was just one part of the redevelopment of downtown Chattanooga. In the first half of the 20th century, Chattanooga had a growing population and a thriving manufacturing-based economy powered largely by the Tennessee Valley Authority's Chickamauga Dam. But over time, suburbanization and deindustrialization took their toll and, by 1990, Chattanooga had become a Rust Belt city with a semi-deserted downtown. The turn-around began when a public-private partnership produced Vision 2000 which led to the building of the Tennessee Aquarium and the evolution of the Riverwalk trail network as well as the reopening of the Walnut Street Bridge to bikes and pedestrians. A ball park, museum and a movie theater also located near the water and were soon joined by residences, hotels and restaurants. On the shore opposite downtown, the site of a former Coast Guard reserve station became Coolidge Park, motivating walkers and cyclists to use the Walnut Street Bridge to go north as well as south. According to a study by the Brookings Institution, implementation of the Vision 2000 plan led to higher median income, lower rates of poverty, population growth, and a 25-percent increase in tourism-related employment during the 1990s (Eichenthal and Windeknecht 2008).

From the south end of the Walnut Street Bridge, the Riverwalk leads to the Tennessee Aquarium, which became the largest freshwater aquarium in the world when it opened in 1992 (Eichenthal and Windeknecht 2008). The aquarium looks over Riverfront Park, home to the Riverbend Festival, an 8-day music event featuring nearly 100 artists. Docked nearby, the Southern Belle Riverboat annually takes over 100,000 passengers on cruises up and down the Tennessee River. Until recently, the trail ended at a new Marriott hotel with a patio restaurant perched on the Tennessee River. But now, Riverwalk has been extended several miles downstream and enhanced with parks, public art and upscale townhomes.

Heading east from the Walnut Street Bridge, cyclists and walkers cross a glass bridge and enter the Bluff View Art District. The Hunter Museum here features American artists like Thomas Cole, Winslow Homer, Mary Cassatt, Thomas Hart Benton and Andy Warhol in an architecturally stunning building. Those who would rather remain outside can enjoy the Bluff View sculpture garden which includes some pieces that cling to the steep slopes above the river. Further on, art studios and galleries are appropriately supported by trendy restaurants and wine bars.

Riverwalk links many of Chattanooga's cultural attractions, including the Hunter Museum.

East of the Arts District, the Riverwalk trail bisects the Chattanooga Rowing Center and meanders, often on elevated boardwalks, through wooded terrain and the Amnicola Marsh. At Riverpoint, historic markers briefly describe the Civil War battles of Chickamauga and Chattanooga that swept through this area in 1863. The South Chickamauga Creek Greenway splits off at Riverpoint and extends for 14 miles (with gaps) past the Tennessee Valley Railway Museum to Camp Jordan Park, a 275-acre park with a 10,000-seat amphitheater. The main stem of the Riverwalk continues to hug the south bank of the Tennessee River, linking with 11,000-student Chattanooga State Community College and ending at the Chickamauga Dam, built in the late 1930s by the Tennessee Valley Authority as a New Deal project.

The development of Riverwalk and the reopening of the Walnut Street Bridge is also credited with helping to revitalize the north bank of the Tennessee River. As mentioned above, Chattanooga created 13-acre Coolidge Park here in 1999 and over time added an interactive water feature, floating restaurant and restored 1894 carousel. At the east side of this park, the Chattanooga Theatre Center annually attracts over 50,000 playgoers (Chattanooga Theatre Center 2018).

West of Coolidge Park, Chattanooga remediated a former industrial site on the north bank of the Tennessee River that was leaching contaminants into groundwater. The resulting 23-acre Renaissance Park, completed in 2006, features a floodplain forest and a constructed wetland that manages and treats storm water. In addition, the park is home to public art, a 490-seat amphitheater, plus historical commemorations of the Trail of Tears and an encampment of liberated slaves. One study credits the park with stimulating the redevelopment of seven nearby properties and many other neighborhood investments. As proof, land within one quarter mile of the park experienced an 821-percent increase in value between 2005 and 2013 (Landscape Architecture Foundation 2018).

Another study by the Trust for Public Land recounts the transformation of the entire Chattanooga riverfront from a liability into a community asset that attracts tourists and residents. Between 1988 and 1996, businesses, full-time jobs, and property value in this area more than doubled. To highlight the significance of the trail system to this turnaround, the chairman of the Chattanooga City County stated: "There is a feeling not that we've arrived, but that we are on the right path – and 'path' is a good word for it, since our progress is closely linked to paths" (Trust for Public Land 1999, p13).

CHAPTER 9

Chicago, Illinois: Building on a Green Legacy

Illinois almost gives bicyclists too much choice. The Illinois Prairie Path, which preserves the natural ecology of a 61-mile-long corridor west of Chicago, was one of the country's first rail trails and an early inductee into the Rail-Trail Hall of Fame. The 56-mile Des Plaines River Trail, the 45-mile Fox River Trail, 33-mile DuPage River Trail and 17-mile Great Western Trail explore the forest preserves surrounding Chicago. Several trails now use the corridors originally carved by canals, including the 70-mile Illinois & Michigan Canal State Trail and the 104-mile Hennepin Canal Parkway, which is one of the planned gateways to the almost 4,000-mile Great American Rail-Trail across the US. Not surprisingly, this extensive network is producing economic as well as health, environmental and mobility benefits.

Chicago's 19-mile Lakefront Trail is wildly popular and a key ingredient in the Windy City's pursuit of sustainability and livability. In the heart of the city, this trail offers a planet-friendly way of reaching many of Chicago's biggest attractions including Soldier Field, Adler Planetarium, Shedd Aquarium, Field Museum, Grant Park, the Art Institute, Maggie Daley Park and Millennium Park with an outdoor stage designed by Frank Gehry and Cloud Gate, the shape-bending mirrored art piece better known as The Bean.

Intersecting with the Lakefront Trail, Chicago's Riverwalk extends for over a mile on the south side of the Chicago River. Today, tourists, office workers and residents of The Loop walk, bike, eat, drink, people-watch and relax on the newly re-landscaped banks of a waterway that previously was only noticed once a year when the city dyed it green for St. Patrick's Day.

The south end of the Lakefront Trail is anchored by Jackson Park, site of the 1893 World's Fair, the World's Columbian Exposition. The Exposition's Palace of Fine Arts, the only remaining building from 1893, is now home to the Museum of Science and Industry. The future Barack Obama Presidential Center will be located near the western edge of Jackson Park. A bikeway connects Jackson Park with Washington Park on the Midway Plaisance. This landscaped parkway was home to rides, games and other amusements during the 1893 fair, establishing the term 'midway' for amusement areas in fairgrounds to this day. The Midway Plaisance also links to the extensive bike path network of the 15,000-student University of Chicago.

The Shedd Aquarium, like many other Chicago attractions, can be reached on the Lakefront Trail.

Going north, the Lakefront Trail passes the Navy Pier entertainment complex, beaches, marinas, golf courses and parks including Lincoln Park, home to a museum, a historic theater and the Lincoln Park Zoo. From trail's end, cyclists can use bike lanes to travel to and from 17,000-student Loyola University Chicago.

The Lakefront Trail is reportedly the busiest trail in the United States (Friends of the Lakefront Trail 2013). Summer weekends see 100,000 people using the Lakefront Trail *per day* (Chicago Park District 2018). That's more users than most trails experience in an entire year. To deal with this extraordinary popularity, the Chicago Park District reconstructed the Lakefront Trail, separating the bike trail from the pedestrian pathways (Chicago Park District 2018).

Cloud Gate, AKA The Bean, warps Chicago's skyline in Millennium Park.

Other trails in Illinois have significant economic impact even though they experience much less traffic than Chicago's Lakefront Trail. A 2013 study of the 61-mile Illinois Prairie Path, which attracts 122,000 users per year, found that survey respondents spent an average of $14 during each trail visit (Trails for Illinois 2013). A 2012 survey calculated the following annual trail counts for six other Illinois trails: Fox River Trail: 86,561; MCT Goshen Trail: 67,651; Hennepin Canal State Trail: 9,126; Old Plank Road Trail: 127,637; Rock Island State Trail: 16,838; and Tunnel Hill State Trail: 16,717. Visitors on these six trails spent an average of $30 per person, primarily on restaurants/bars, groceries, vehicle expenses, gear and recreation (Trails for Illinois 2012).

CHAPTER 10

Cockeysville, Maryland – York, Pennsylvania: Torrey C. Brown Rail Trail – Heritage Rail Trail County Park: Cycling through History

Maryland and Pennsylvania offer major historical destinations including Gettysburg, York, Baltimore, Annapolis and Washington, D.C. Now the region is working to complete a planned 250-mile loop called the Grand History Trail, allowing tourists to reach these and other important sites by bicycle. In addition to promoting exercise, recreation and carbon-free transportation options, the existing, two-trail combination of Maryland's Torrey C. Brown Rail Trail and Pennsylvania's Heritage Rail Trail County Park is already proving to be profitable for local economies.

These two trails, with a current combined length of 44 miles, began life as the North Central Railroad (NCR) in the 1830s and were inducted into the Rail-Trail Hall of Fame in 2015. The NCR carried Abraham Lincoln to and from Gettysburg when he made his immortal address and again when the Lincoln funeral procession traveled from Washington DC to Springfield, Illinois following his assassination in 1865 (Stark 2015).

The Torrey C. Brown Rail Trail is managed by the State of Maryland as a unit of Gunpowder Falls State Park. Other units of this state park include Jerusalem Mill Historic Village, an 18th and 19th Century Quaker settlement where living history events play out in a blacksmith shop, general store and a grist mill that operated for over two centuries (Maryland 2020). Monkton Station, roughly eight miles from the southern end of the trail, is home to a restored train station that houses an interpretive center depicting the history of the rail line and the towns it served. In addition to renting bikes here, visitors can also rent inner tubes for a refreshing 3-hour float down the scenic Big Gunpowder Falls River.

A restored 1885 train station is now home to the New Freedom Rail Trail Café

At 19.5 miles from the southern trail end, cyclists enter Pennsylvania at the Mason Dixon Line, the unofficial boundary between the Northern and Southern States that made Charles Mason and Jerimiah Dixon arguably the nation's most famous surveyors. In the Borough of New Freedom, the trail passes a restored 1885 train station that is now home to the New Freedom Rail Trail Café. Here, Steam into History offers variously themed rides on vintage trains powered by steam-driven locomotives. Both cyclists and train riders can stop further up the trail in the Borough of Glen Rock, where an 1832 saw mill has been restored into guest rooms and a restaurant.

Further north, the trail enters the City of York, birthplace of the York Peppermint Pattie. Here the entire downtown is designated as a historic district in the National Register of Historic Places, featuring the Golden Plough Tavern which was built in 1741 and now houses a museum operated by the History Center. Also surrounding the north end of the trail are other historic gems in York's Colonial Complex including the General Horatio Gates House, built in 1751, and the Barnett Bobb Log House, built in 1812 (York County History Center 2020).

Economic studies confirm that these combined trails are good for business. Maryland's Torrey C. Brown Rail Trail attracted over 860,000 users in 2004, generating over $10 million in economic impact in that year (Trail Facts 2005).

In Glen Rock, the trail passes an 1832 sawmill that has been restored into guest rooms and a restaurant.

Pennsylvania's Heritage Rail Trail County Park experiences over 260,000 visitors and contributes from $3.5 to $4.4 million per year to the local economy (Knoch 2017). As another measure of success, plans are moving ahead to complete the last 100 miles of the planned 250-mile Grand History Trail.

CHAPTER 11

Colorado: High on Bicycling

Although Colorado is well known for its altitude, this mountainous state is also determined to become famous for bicycling. Currently, it ranks as the sixth most bicycle friendly state in the nation. It has 24 bicycle friendly communities, 104 bicycle friendly businesses and seven bicycle friendly universities (League of American Bicyclists 2019).

In return for its significant investment in cycle-oriented infrastructure, bicycles annually inject $1.6 billion into the economy of the Rocky Mountain State. Within that total, bicycle tourism, including spending on lodging, food, beverages and transportation, contributes $511 million a year (BBC 2016), a statistic that was apparent in our cross-state trip from Mesa County and Glenwood Springs in Western Colorado to the more urban trails of Denver and Boulder.

The 22-mile Colorado Riverfront Trail intermittently follows the Colorado River from Palisade and Grand Junction through the irrigated farms of Fruita to Loma, where mountain bikers can take the beautiful but demanding 142-mile Kokopelli Trail to Moab, Utah. As a popular detour, a 33-mile loop on Rim Rock Drive offers energetic cyclists spectacular views of the plateaus, cliffs and canyons of the 32-square mile Colorado National Monument. Those who master the 3,200-foot elevation gain on this loop may be lucky enough to see the bighorn sheep that effortlessly navigate this rugged terrain.

Further east, the historic spa town of Glenwood Springs serves as a rail trail hub. The 14-mile Glenwood Canyon Recreation Trail travels upstream along a fast-moving stretch of the Colorado River as it races through a scenic gorge. Heading east, the 42-mile Rio Grande Trail follows the Roaring Fork River, connecting Glenwood Springs with the Village of Aspen by way of Snowmass and Woody Creek. A new bike/pedestrian bridge spans the Colorado River linking downtown Glenwood Springs with the Hotel Colorado, the Glenwood Hot Springs Pool and other historic landmarks as well as the trailhead for the Glenwood Springs Recreation Trail.

Greater Denver boasts 185 miles of regional bicycle trails supporting a growing system of bike lanes and bike-friendly streets that serves as a green network, allowing compact, multi-use development where people can reach jobs, schools, shopping and natural areas by bike or on foot rather than cars (Denver 2019). For decades, Denver has been transforming underutilized industrial land along the South Platte River into a trail-based park credited with sparking $2.5 billion of economic development (Georgia Institute of Technology 2009). Today this trail links the Downtown Aquarium, the Children's Museum and the Denver Broncos Stadium as it follows the river south for 25 miles. In perhaps the best example of this revitalization process, a utility substation adjacent to downtown was relocated to make way for Confluence Park, an expansive civic space that celebrates rather than hides the two watercourses that join at this point. From Confluence Park, the Cherry Creek Regional Trail passes the city center, historic districts, universities, art museums, a medical center and the Colorado Capitol, letting cyclists pedal to Cherry Creek State Park and access jobs anywhere along this 40-mile corridor.

The sandstone Flatirons overlook the trails of Boulder, Colorado.

Heading north from Denver, the cities of Boulder and Ft. Collins have both earned recognition as Platinum Level Bike Friendly Communities (American League of Bicyclists 2019). Boulder's Boulder Creek Path follows the greenway originally proposed by Frederick Law Olmstead, Jr. in 1910. Today, this path links several parks, civic institutions and downtown Boulder with the 27,000-student University of Colorado campus and preserved open spaces with stunning views of the iconic reddish-brown sandstone formations known as the Flatirons. Boulder's investment in bicycle infrastructure has recouped substantial economic benefits. A 2011 survey found that the bicycle industry generates $52 million in sales and employs 330 full time workers in Boulder (Urie 2012).

In 2015, then Governor Hickenlooper vowed to make Colorado the best state in the nation for biking and announced a 4-year, $100 million commitment to bicycle projects and programs (League of American Bicyclists 2019). In 2016, Hickenlooper unveiled the state's 16 highest priority trails including the 900-mile Colorado Front Range Trail from Wyoming to New Mexico and the 65-mile Peaks to Plains Trail linking the Continental Divide at Loveland Pass with the South Platte River Greenway in Denver (Colorado the Beautiful 2019). These 16 trails were selected for several reasons including their support for environmental stewardship, their proximity to underserved communities and their potential to generate economic development opportunities (Hickenlooper 2016).

CHAPTER 12

Covington – Mandeville - Slidell, Louisiana: Tammany Trace Builds Community

On a Thursday evening in April, we joined a few hundred people crowding the bandstand at the Tammany Trace trailhead in Covington, Louisiana. Another hundred revelers or so strolled the surrounding car-free streets, enjoying a beer while chatting with friends and neighbors. The trailhead-adjacent Covington Brewhouse had trouble keeping pace with the demand for their Bayou Bock and Pontchartrain Pilsner. Down the block, people waited for a table at Lola, where a train caboose has been converted into the restaurant's kitchen. Parking was not a problem because most people had walked or biked the Trace to reach the trailhead, which Covington has transformed into its functional town square.

On the following night, we slipped into the stream of folks walking and biking to the Friday evening concert at the Mandeville trailhead, 12 miles down the Tammany Trace from Covington. Before the music started, we had shrimp and grits next to the trailhead at the Old Rail Brew Company, where many home brews have railroad-themes like Cow Catcher Stout and Hobo Helles Lager.

Like many bicyclists, we took a break between Covington and Mandeville at the Abita Brew Pub in Abita Springs. Long ago, travelers flocked to this town for the curative water. Today, the artesian well supplies the secret sauce for Abita beer, once a local favorite and now shipped around the country. What is now the pub originally housed the brewery, but soaring demand for this highly-praised craft beer prompted the founders to build a bigger facility a mile away.

But it's not all about beer. In Covington, bicyclists can soak up some authentic southern atmosphere in the home town of Walker Percy, famously known for his novel *The Moviegoer*. The City of Mandeville features historic homes framed by stately oaks draped with Spanish moss. Many of these mansions were built in a pre-air-conditioned past when wealthy families boated to the North Shore of Lake Pontchartrain to escape the summer heat in New Orleans.

A well-attended concert at the Tammany Trace trailhead, Covington's unofficial town square.

To encourage exploration (and possibly spending), Mandeville hopes to extend a trail spur through its historic neighborhoods, which are studded with unique restaurants and specialty shops (Hammons 2015). East of Mandeville, the Tammany Trace becomes a nature trail, offering the possibility of encountering alligators, wild turkeys and other critters as it bisects Fontainebleau State Park before returning to civilization at the outskirts of the City of Slidell.

This success story did not happen overnight. In 1992, St. Tammany Parish combined funding from the federal Intermodal Surface Transportation Efficiency Act of 1991 with local dollars, including from the non-profit Tammany Trace Foundation, to buy the right of way abandoned by the Illinois Central Railroad, retool its trestles and, over time, create a 31-mile asphalt trail linking Covington and Slidell (Stark 2017). Today the Trace is exceptionally well-maintained and routinely patrolled, earning recognition from the Rails to Trails Conservancy by induction into the Rail Trail Hall of Fame. St. Tammany Parish annually spends just over $1 million on maintenance and administration of the Trace (Hammons 2015). In short, St. Tammany Parish invests in the Trace. However, the Trace returns the favor in the form of economic returns from retail sales and tax revenue as well as health, recreation and alternative transportation benefits.

A spur from the Tammany Trace Trail leads to Mandeville's Historic District.

According to the trail's operations manager, the Trace is St. Tammany Parish's biggest tourist draw, attracting more than 300,000 people every year (Stark 2017). A 2015 study estimated that the Trace annually generated $3.4 million in direct spending plus $3.9 in indirect spending for local and regional economies. This estimate, based on a detailed survey of 120 trail users, found that almost one third of trail users were not local residents. Separate surveys conducted by Trace Rangers suggested that almost three fourths of the trail users who live outside St. Tammany Parish come from outside the state of Louisiana, with many visiting from other countries. By multiplying these survey results by the total trail counts, the study quantified the combined $7.3 million spending estimate by adding expenditures in lodging, meals/refreshments, bike rentals and recreational equipment purchases (Hammons 2015).

The 2015 study also explores benefits of the Tammany Trace that are harder to quantify. Almost all survey respondents reported that the Trace and its trailheads were a valuable community amenity. Detailing this livability benefit in their own words, some respondents volunteered that the Trace was a key reason why they chose to live in St. Tammany Parish. In support of the Trace's health benefits, St. Tammany Parish is routinely ranked as the healthiest parish in Louisiana (Hammons 2015). These lifestyle benefits may be more important to the long-term prosperity of the parish, but the monetary impact mentioned above undoubtedly helps support continued upkeep and expansion of the Tammany Trace.

CHAPTER 13

Dayton – Cincinnati, Ohio: Little Miami Scenic Trail Generates Big Results

In 1892, George Huffman used his sewing machine factory in Dayton, Ohio to produce the first of 100 million Huffy bikes to be manufactured over the next 115 years (Re-Cycle 2019). In that same year, Orville and Wilber Wright opened a bike shop where they designed and built the world's first successful airplanes. Today the Dayton Aviation Heritage National Historical Park preserves that bike shop and a series of bike paths linking downtown Dayton with the National Aviation Hall of Fame and Huffman Prairie Field, where the Wright Brothers tested and demonstrated their aeronautical creations.

In 1965, Horace Huffman, then the president of Huffy Corporation, formed the Greater Dayton Bikeway Committee, which drafted one of the nation's first bikeway plans. That plan was later adopted by the Miami Valley Regional Planning Commission. In 1976, the Miami Conservancy District completed the first 8.2 miles of what is now the 86-mile Great Miami River Trail. With a current count of 15 trails totaling 340 miles, the Miami Valley now boasts the longest paved bicycle trail network in the country (Miami Valley Trails 2019).

The Miami Valley trail network links Dayton with Xenia, population 26,000, which calls itself the Bicycle Capital of the Midwest. Five trails intersect in Xenia including the 29-mile Prairie Grass Trail which joins other trails that ultimately lead to Columbus, Ohio. Also in Xenia, the 78-mile Little Miami Scenic Trail heads south toward Cincinnati. The Little Miami Scenic Trail is part of the Ohio to Erie Trail, which is planned to ultimately connect Cleveland with Cincinnati. The Rails-to-Trails Conservancy also designates the Ohio to Erie Trail as a link in its envisioned 3,700-mile Great American Rail-Trail connecting Washington DC with Seattle, Washington and beyond (Rails-to-Trails Conservancy 2019).

Prosperity Comes in Cycles

The Little Miami Scenic Trail richly deserves its place in the Rail-to-Trails Hall of Fame. Just south of Xenia, the trail begins to follow the twists and turns of the Little Miami River, giving cyclists an enjoyable mix of nature, farmland and rural Americana as it passes through and around a dozen or more towns and villages. There are many opportunities to linger along the trail, like Fort Ancient, the site of 12,000 years of Native American culture, and Loveland Castle, an architectural folly built in the 1920s by an eccentric Notary Public who dubbed himself Sir Harry Andrews (Loveland Castle 2019).

At the southern trail head of the Little Miami Scenic Trail, cyclists can use a completed segment of the Ohio to Erie Trail and the Ohio River Trail to access the bike network serving Cincinnati's riverfront. Here, walkers and bikers can cross into the Kentucky side of the Ohio River on the Purple People Bridge, an 1872 bridge originally owned by the Little Miami Railroad. As its name suggests, the Purple People Bridge is painted purple and was repurposed in 2001 solely for pedestrians. Newport, Kentucky, on the south side of the Ohio River, motivates people to cross the Purple People Bridge with attractions like the Newport Aquarium, the Newport on the Levee entertainment complex and a fleet of riverboats including the 225-foot Belle of Cincinnati.

The Belle of Cincinnati riverboat passes under the Purple People Bridge and heads up the Ohio River.

On the north side of the Ohio River, Cincinnati offers urban rewards for those who complete the Little Miami Scenic Trail. The Over-The Rhine neighborhood preserves many reminders of its German-immigrant heritage, including the 1878 red brick Gothic Revival Cincinnati Music Hall, now the home of the Cincinnati Symphony Orchestra, the Cincinnati Ballet, and the Cincinnati Opera. Further north, the lively Findlay Market has been serving food, entertainment, and community since 1852. A few blocks west, the Cincinnati Museum Center now occupies Union Terminal, an Art Deco landmark in the National Register of Historic Places featuring the largest semi-dome in the Western Hemisphere.

The Little Miami Scenic Trail and four other trails in Ohio's Miami Valley are estimated to generate a total direct economic impact of up to $15.4 million a year (Miami Valley Regional Planning Commission 2017). Considering that the Miami Valley trails represent roughly one fifth of the total bike trail mileage in the state, an analysis of bicycling in Ohio as a whole would likely find economic benefits comparable to those estimated for other Midwestern states. These economic rewards will grow as Ohio continues to build on its bicycling heritage by completing its section of the Great American Rail-Trail, closing the gaps in the Ohio to Erie Trail, and expanding its entire statewide network, which already stretches for almost 1,800 miles.

CHAPTER 14

Delaware and Lehigh Trail, Pennsylvania: A Trail of Two Revolutions

The Delaware and Lehigh (D&L) Trail winds through a region of Eastern Pennsylvania that languished with the decline of coal mines, steel mills, canals, and railroads. But since 2013, the trail has been attracting bicycle tourists and giving local residents more options for transportation, recreation, and healthy exercise. Studies also confirm that the trail is likewise helping the local economy adjust to the realities of the 21st century.

The D&L Canal followed the Delaware and Lehigh rivers, carrying coal, goods and people between the Appalachians and the Atlantic Ocean. In the early 1800s, the canal spurred the development of towns and businesses along its route, particularly sawmills, steel mills, silk mills, and a large tannery. In 1862, a flood wiped out the upper reaches of the canal, and shipments began to transition to railroads (Tomes 2012). But the railroads also faltered and most of the main line was torn up by the early 1980s. Fortunately, most of the right of way was repurposed as the D&L Trail which will be 165 miles long when gaps are closed but currently stretches for 141 miles from Mountain Top to Bristol, Pennsylvania, 23 miles northeast of Philadelphia.

Today, the D&L Trail serves as the spine of the Delaware and Lehigh National Heritage Corridor which was designated by the United States Congress in 1988 in recognition of this region's central role in the Industrial Revolution and the American Revolution. The Heritage Corridor is home to hundreds of properties on the National Register of Historic Places as well as abundant natural beauty. In addition, the corridor has several communities that can benefit from the economic development generated by a destination trail.

On the northern segment of the trail, the town of Jim Thorpe offers historic landmarks, wineries, rafting outfitters, and shuttle services for cyclists seeking a one-way ride. Bikers can ride the Lehigh Gorge Scenic Railroad Bike Train 25 miles to White Haven before hopping off and pedaling the downhill grade back to Jim Thorpe. Pocono Whitewater runs raft trips here on the Lehigh River but has increased its fleet of rental bikes from 20 to 200 thanks to the growing popularity of the D&L Trail (Stark 2018).

The middle segment of the trail passes through Bethlehem and past SteelStacks where the abandoned blast furnaces of Bethlehem Steel dominate a ten-acre complex now used for concerts, festivals, and community events. At the National Canal Museum in Easton, visitors can ride the Joshua White II, a 48-ton canal boat powered by a pair of mules. The museum also screens some of the films that have used this well-preserved stretch of canal for their locations, including *The Farmer Takes a Wife*, Henry Fonda's first movie.

A 1925 steam locomotive powers the New Hope Railroad through scenic Bucks County.

Where the Lehigh River meets the Delaware River, the trail enters Delaware Canal State Park and meanders south to the historic buildings, niche shops, restaurants, inns, and B&Bs in the bustling town of New Hope. Here the New Hope Railroad carries passengers through scenic Bucks County on trains powered by a steam locomotive built in 1925. These trains depart from the charming 1891 station which has become the unofficial symbol of New Hope.

On its way to Bristol, the trail bisects Washington Crossing Historic Park, located where George Washington led the Continental Army across the Delaware on Christmas night 1776 to deliver a morale-boosting surprise to

British forces in Trenton, New Jersey. The Taylorsville historic village here preserves several landmarks including the 1791 Mahlon K. Taylor House, the 1828 Hibbs House, and McConkey's Ferry Inn, where Washington launched his flotilla.

At its current length, the D&L Trail attracted an estimated 283,000 visitors and generated a total economic impact of $19 million in 2012. Roughly $15 million of this total went directly into local economies. Lodging alone accounted for almost half of this amount, indicating that the trail was serving overnight tourists as well as generating expenditures from local residents (Tomes 2012).

The D&L Trail is integral to the Circuit Trails network which is planned to extend and join existing trails in the Greater Philadelphia region to ultimately create an 800-mile system. The D&L Trail also forms a segment of the East Coast Greenway, which is planned to evolve into a 3,000-mile continuous trail linking 15 states from Florida to Maine. The Delaware River Watershed portion of the East Coast Greenway will connect 34 municipalities, eight counties, six state parks, and a national wildlife refuge in parts of Maryland, Pennsylvania, Delaware, and New Jersey. A 2019 study estimated that the 175 miles of East Coast Greenway trails in this region would add $1.77 billion of value to properties within one-quarter mile of the network, save over $45 million in healthcare costs annually, generate $840 million per year in tourism benefits, and produce almost $40 million of ecosystem services including carbon sequestration, water supply/quality, flood mitigation, air quality and wildlife habitat (Econsult 2019).

The Delaware & Lehigh National Heritage Corridor delivered $239 million in economic benefits, 3,325 jobs, and over $22 million in tax revenue in 2013. Non-local and overnight visitors accounted for over 90 percent of this benefit primarily from lodging, restaurants, and transportation. The study recognized the trail as the spine of this corridor, suggesting that even before closing all of its gaps, the D&L trail is already succeeding in helping to revitalize this region (TrippUmbach 2013).

CHAPTER 15

Des Moines, Iowa: It Pays to Make Connections

Iowa offers 1,866 miles of off-road, multi-use trails, including some of the nation's most famous rail trails (Iowa DOT 2018). For example, the Cedar Valley Nature Trail, which meanders for 52 miles along the Cedar River from Waterloo to Hiawatha, was recently named as a gateway trail for the Great American Rail-Trail, the nearly 4,000-mile cross-country bikeway planned by the Rails-to-Trails Conservancy. Likewise, the 62-mile Wabash Trace Nature Trail, once the route of the fabled Wabash Cannonball, mixes rural countryside with iconic trail towns so perfectly that it is honored in the Rail-Trail Hall of Fame.

Not surprisingly, these destination trails have generated meaningful economic benefits at the state as well as the local level. A 2011 study estimated that recreational riders alone contributed $365 million to the Iowa economy. This estimate did not include $52 million in statewide economic activity from bicycle commuters or healthcare cost savings of $87 million estimated for both commuting and recreational riders (Lankford, J. *et al.* 2011).

Central Iowa allows a regional-scale exploration of bicycle trails and their economic impacts. The 676 miles of off-road, multi-use trails form a network linking communities in the 11-county region surrounding Des Moines (Iowa DOT 2018). The 16-mile Great Western Trail travels through five rural towns and merges with the 5-mile Meredith trail which ends at the Principal River Walk in the heart of downtown Des Moines. River Walk is a waterside promenade featuring public art, a skating plaza, and two car-free bridges including the Iowa Women of Achievement Bridge, a curvilinear suspension bridge prominently featured in the logo of the City of Des Moines.

River Walk is also home to the Hub Spot, a café/plaza/rest stop serving as a destination for those bicycling into the city or as a departure point for those traveling to other corners of the region by way of the trails and bike lanes that converge here. Going west on Grand Avenue, cyclists pass the Pappajohn Sculpture Park, an expansive open space and informal picnic area enlivened by works by Plensa, De Kooning, Haring and other famous artists.

Bike lanes lead east from River Walk to the Iowa State Capitol. Heading north, on the 3.4-mile John Pat Dorrian Trail, cyclists pass City Hall, the Simon Estes Amphitheater, the Robert D. Ray Asian Gardens and the Des Moines Botanical Gardens before the trail becomes the Neil Smith Trail and wanders past the northern City Limits, ending 26 miles away at Big Creek State Park in rural Polk County. As an alternative route out of Des Moines, cyclists can access the 27-mile High Trestle Trail, famous for its half-mile-long span over the Des Moines River featuring a hypnotically spiraling art installation. A recent extension took the first step toward closing the gap between the High Trestle Trail and the Raccoon River Valley Trail which offers another 89 miles of peddling around the exurbs and suburbs west of Des Moines.

Cyclists ride the High Trestle Trail just to experience its hypnotically spiraling artwork.

In the City of Des Moines alone, a 2013 study estimated that trails here generated an economic impact of $15 million and produced almost 215 jobs (Fleming *et al.* 2013). Clearly, the communities of Central Iowa are demonstrating that it pays to make connections.

CHAPTER 16

East Bay Bicycle Path, Rhode Island: A Car-Free Way to Get In and Out of Town

The East Bay Bicycle Path links central Providence with picturesque towns that line the eastern shore of Narragansett Bay. It provides some lucky people with an alternative way to commute to work and others with a form of recreation that is healthy and planet-friendly. As a bonus, the trail is also good for business.

At its northern end, the trail starts at India Point Park, the site of Providence's first port and named for a once-thriving center for trade with the East Indies. This point also marks the confluence of the Seekonk and Providence Rivers. A new bicycle/pedestrian bridge over the Providence River completes a loop inviting cyclists and walkers to use the Providence River Greenway to reach the western edge of Brown University and the Roger Williams National Memorial, commemorating the founder of Rhode Island.

From its confluence with the Providence River to Water Place Park, the Woonasquatucket River becomes the stage for WaterFire Providence, a weekend nighttime event involving, well, water and fire, that has been described as a combination public artwork, performance piece, community ritual, and urban festival.

Once it is across the Seekonk River, the East Bay Bicycle Path heads south and soon skirts the Narragansett Bay shoreline, offering outstanding views of greenspace to the east and industrial cargo terminals on the west side of the water. Passing through the Riverside neighborhood of East Providence, a former train station next to the trail has been preserved and repurposed as the Borealis Coffee Company, serving artisanal brews that many cyclists find irresistible. There are many other places to refuel as the trail bisects the towns of Barrington and Warren, which was a whaling port in the 18th century.

A short detour on bike-friendly roads leads to Colt State Park for a visit to Coggeshall Farm Museum. On this preserved salt marsh farm, visitors experience everyday farm activity in the 1790s using a recreated forge, hay barn, and cart shed plus several restored historic structures including a spring house, a 1799 farmhouse, and a late 18th-century cheese house (Coggeshall 2021).

Visitors to Coggeshall Farm step back in time to experience farm life in the 1790s.

The trail returns to the shore in the Town of Bristol, where hungry cyclists can relax at the Beach House, an upscale restaurant with a large deck overlooking both the path and the bay. After recharging, Bristol offers many reasons to linger before pedaling back to Providence. Sailing enthusiasts may want to visit the Herreshoff Marine Museum, home of the America's Cup Hall of Fame as well as a collection of over 60 boats and 500 models. In 1878, Herreshoff Manufacturing began building steamships here and later switched to designing and building yachts, including every winner of the America's Cup Race between 1893 and 1934 (Herreshoff 2021).

Further south, the public is welcome at Blithewold, one of most magnificent and well-preserved estates from the Country Place Era, when wealthy Americans established elaborate gardens to frame their equally-elaborate mansions. The Van Wickles began building this Gilded Age monument in 1894 as a summer home where they could dock their Herreshoff yacht. Today, visitors can tour the 45-room mansion and stroll the 33-acre grounds which feature a rose garden, a water garden, a rock garden, and several other gardens flanking the ten-acre Great Lawn which stretches from the mansion to Narragansett Bay (Blithewold 2021).

In 2014, the East Bay Bicycle Path experienced 2,292 users per day and generated an estimated annual economic impact of $13.9 million. This was greater than the combined economic impact of the other five Rhode Island bike paths examined in a 2014 study (Leonard 2014).

In 2009, the 14-mile East Bay Bicycle Path was inducted into the Rail-Trail Hall of Fame. Today, this trail gets a five-star rating from riders who review it on the Rails-to-Trails Conservancy website (Rail-to-Trails Conservancy 2021). Clearly, Bristol is also pleased with the economic and other benefits generated by the trail given that the town is exploring the feasibility of extending the path even further. Potentially, a lengthened East Bay Bike Path could stretch to the southern end of Bristol, allowing students at Roger Williams University and others a car-free way of getting to Providence and points beyond.

CHAPTER 17

Erie Canal Trail, New York: Transformational Then and Now

The Erie Canal created thousands of jobs when it formed a navigable waterway from the Hudson River in Albany, New York to the Great Lakes in Buffalo, New York in 1825. By connecting the East Coast with the Midwest, the Erie Canal helped fuse isolated regions into a single nation. Today, the multiuse trail that parallels the canal provides countless opportunities for recreation, eco-mobility, and exercise as well as jobs and other economic benefits for the more than 200 communities it connects.

The Erie Canal was accompanied by the building of eight shorter canals connecting with the main canal. After initial success, it was eclipsed by railroads and canal traffic declined, Eventually, communities along the network began constructing trails for multiple benefits including economic development. Various regional and state organizations were enlisted to coordinate these efforts, leading to a plan in the 1970s to develop a 524-mile recreational system including 360 miles along the Erie Canal with the remaining mileage following three of the connecting canals. These efforts were helped in 2000 when the U.S. Congress created the Erie Canalway National Heritage Corridor. As of 2014, 277 miles of the Erie Canal Trail had been completed, or roughly 75 percent of the total (Scipione 2014).

To maximize the economic impact of the trail, the non-profit organization Parks & Trails New York (PTNY) publishes *Bicyclists Bring Business: A Guide for Attracting Bicyclists to New York's Canal Communities*. While this booklet uses the Erie Canal Trail as an example, its advice is applicable to any community seeking to capitalize on trails to build community, strengthen economies, and attract/retain employers and employees. PTNY also maintains a user-friendly web site about the trail, produces *Cycling the Erie Canal*, a guidebook listing the attractions and businesses for each section of the trail, and partners with others in leading *Cycle the Erie Canal*, an end-to-end bike tour held annually since 1999 (Parks & Trails New York).

In the filming of The Gilded Age, *the Central Troy Historic District stands in for 1880s New York City.*

The Erie Canal Trail's eastern end lies in Albany, the capital of the State of New York. The Erie Canal and railroads made Albany an economic powerhouse in the 19th century. After the city languished in the 1950s, then

Governor Nelson Rockefeller championed revitalization of Albany, including construction of the Empire State Plaza, a monumental development across the street from the New York State Capitol that incorporates The Egg, an architecturally-unique performing arts center framed by a series of reflecting pools.

On the east bank of the Hudson River, eight miles north of Albany, the City of Troy is honoring its past while adapting to the present. During the War of 1812, military provisions stamped U.S. from a local meatpacker named Samuel Wilson led to the legend that Troy was the home of Uncle Sam. True or not, the statue of a resolute Uncle Sam now glowers over the Uncle Sam Bus Stop in downtown Troy.

Until the early 20th century, Troy was a prosperous industrial center known for products ranging from steel to shirts. Unlike many other former commercial centers, Troy has been able to survive the flight to the suburbs with help from a strong institutional base including the Emma Willard School, Russell Sage College, and Rensselaer Polytechnic, the nation's oldest private engineering university.

The Egg is arguably the most uniquely shaped building in Albany, New York

Troy's slow growth also allowed nearly 700 properties within several blocks in the middle of the city to become the Central Troy Historic District, arguably the country's best preserved 19th century downtown. The district is a perfect location to film period dramas such as *The Gilded Age*, in which downtown Troy stands in for New York City in the 1880s.

After a 22-mile pedal west of Troy, the Erie Canal Trail enters Schenectady, once known as the City that Lights and Hauls the World. In 1878, Thomas Edison founded the Edison Electric Light Company here, which later became the General Electric Company. Schenectady was also the home of the American Locomotive Company, one of the largest manufacturers of locomotives in the United States. Many of the industrial jobs have since left and the city is in a revitalization period that builds, in part, on its rich trove of historical resources.

Bicyclists entering Schenectady from the Erie Canal Trail can savor that legacy by touring the campus of Union College, established in 1795, making it the nation's first non-denominational institution of higher learning. The 1858 Nott Memorial, listed in the National Register of Historic Places, is now the focal point of the campus and arguably the most recognizable building in Schenectady.

The industrial history of Troy and Schenectady is common to many of the other cities connected by the Erie Canal Trail such as Utica, Rome, Syracuse, Rochester, and Buffalo. The Erie Canalway National Heritage Corridor aims to promote this region as a world-class tourism destination by capitalizing on the recreational opportunities of the canal and the historic significance of these places. The canal itself was a major route on the Underground Railroad used by slaves to reach freedom in Upstate New York and Canada. Frederick Douglass, the famous abolitionist author and orator, lived and worked in Rochester. The First Women's Rights convention convened in Seneca Falls in 1848, launching the long road toward equality that continues to this day. In the early 1800s, places along Erie Canal gave birth to utopian communities, evangelical sects, and new religions like the Church of Jesus Christ of Latter Day Saints and the Seventh-day Adventist Church.

A 2014 study estimated that the Erie Canal Trail alone sees almost 1.6 million visits per year and that spending by trail visitors annually generates roughly $253 million in direct and secondary sales. Each year, the trail contributes 3,440 jobs, $78 million in salaries, and $28.5 million in tax revenues to the regional economy. Lodging accounts for one third of visitor spending followed by restaurant/bar tabs (32 percent), transportation (11 percent), clothing/sporting goods (9 percent), and groceries (8 percent). Overnight visitors account for only 18 percent of total visits yet they generate 84 percent of total spending (Scipione 2014).

The 2014 study recommended marketing the trail as a premier bicycling destination in order to increase the number of bicycle tourists and tourism dollars. Closing the remaining gaps in the trail would help this effort. At a continuous 360 miles from Buffalo to Albany, the Erie Canal Trail would surpass the 335-mile length of the combined Great Allegheny Passage/C&O Canal Trail which currently claims the title of the longest, completed multi-use trail in the nation.

In the race for bike-trail fame, New York State is in the process of connecting the Erie Canal Trail with the Hudson River Valley Greenway between New York City and the Canadian border. Roughly 400 miles of this route currently exist and, upon completion, this network, called the Empire State Trail, will be 750 miles long. Like the Erie Canal in the early 19th century, the Empire State Trail will be transformational in the 21st century.

CHAPTER 18

Farmington Canal Heritage Trail, Connecticut: A Key Link in Two Long-Distance-Trail Chains

The Farmington Canal Heritage Trail will one day connect New Haven, Connecticut with Northampton, Massachusetts. Despite some gaps, the trail already experiences considerable traffic which is improving transportation and health options as well as generating respectable impact for local economies. The prospects for closing the remaining gaps seem good considering that this trail serves as a major segment of both the East Coast Greenway and the New England Rail-Trail Spine Network.

The history of the Farmington Canal Heritage Trail dates back to the 1830s when the Farmington Canal was completed between New Haven, Connecticut and Northampton, Massachusetts, making it at one time the longest canal in New England. Cyclists can appreciate the scale of this engineering accomplishment by stopping for a look at the restoration of Lock 12 in the Town of Cheshire. By 1848, the canal shut down and its right of way was taken over by a railroad line that changed hands many times before ceasing operations entirely in the 1980s. In the 1990s, governments and non-profit organizations began building the rail trail that now extends for almost 50 miles and will be 57 miles long after closing a few remaining gaps (Traillink 2021).

In New Haven, the trail currently starts at Yale University although there are plans to build an extension further south to the Long Wharf Nature Preserve in New Haven Harbor. Traveling north, the trail features outstanding views of the Connecticut countryside as well as glimpses of its canal and railroad eras.

Near the middle of Connecticut, the trail passes through the Town of Farmington, which was such a hotbed of abolitionist activity in the early 19th century that it became known as the "Grand Central Station" of the Underground Railroad. Today, the Farmington Freedom Trail links several sites from that era, including places where the 44 survivors of the rebellion aboard the slave ship *La Amistad* were sheltered after they were declared free people by the US Supreme Court's 1841 decision (The Farmington Historical Society 2021).

Hartford's Riverwalk, a link in the East Coast Greenway, passes the sleekly designed Connecticut Science Center.

In nearby Simsbury, cyclists can refuel at a brew pub located in a restored 1875 railroad station briming with rail era memorabilia. Next door, the Simsbury Historical Society has assembled an assortment of historic buildings including a 1790 school house, a 1795 cottage, and the 1771 Phelps Tavern, listed in the National Register of Historic Places and now home to a museum store, archives, and a research library (Simsbury Historical Society 2021).

At Simsbury, cyclists can stay on the Farmington Canal Heritage Trail and ride to the current end of the trail in Southwick, Massachusetts, perhaps with a well-deserved reward at the Rail Trail Ale House. Alternatively, bike-friendly roads also lead east into Hartford, where various trails link a wide assortment of historical, cultural, and recreational destinations. Fans of Mark Twain will want to tour the house he built here in 1874 and where he wrote many of his most famous works including *The Adventures of Tom Sawyer, The Adventures of Huckleberry Finn,* and *A Connecticut Yankee in King Arthur's Court*. The house is open for tours, events, and programs for writers including classes, workshops, and contests (Mark Twain House 2021).

In the center of Hartford, key segments of the East Coast Greenway follow existing paths linking some of the city's most iconic landmarks. The Victorian Gothic Connecticut State Capitol, built in 1878, sits atop Trinity Hill overlooking a web of multi-use trails crisscrossing Bushnell Park. Nearby, cyclists pass the 1886 Soldiers and Sailors Memorial Arch, honoring the 4,000 Hartford citizens who served in the Civil War including 128 African Americans (Bushnell Park Foundation 2021).

Multi-use paths in Hartford's Bushnell Park pass the 1886 Soldiers and Sailors Memorial Arch.

Further east, cyclists pass the sleekly-designed Connecticut Science Center on the Hartford River Walk, an elevated complex of pedestrian plazas and walkways incorporating Mortensen Riverfront Plaza with a 2,500-seat amphitheater that steps down to a stage at the river's edge. This links with the 16-mile-long Charter Oak Greenway carrying cyclists over Founders Bridge and through greenspace on the east bank of the Connecticut River before turning toward Rhode Island.

In addition to expanding opportunities for recreation, healthy exercise, and planet-friendly transportation, advocates are pointing out the economic benefits of Connecticut bikeways. In a publication entitled *Why Build Multi-Use Trails in Connecticut?*, the Farmington Valley Trails Council estimated that a section of the Farmington Canal Heritage Trail near Simsbury attracts over 154,000 per year and contributes from $4 million to $7 million annually to the local economy (Rails-to-Trails Conservancy 2012).

The East Coast Greenway, which is planned to extend for 3,000 miles through 15 states, includes 200 miles within Connecticut including a major portion of the Farmington Canal Heritage Trail. Almost half of this distance is currently protected and the East Coast Greenway Alliance reports that Connecticut is making terrific progress in closing existing gaps thanks to strong local advocacy (East Coast Greenway Alliance 2021).

Similarly, the Rails-to-Trails Conservancy is working with 20 partners to complete the New England Rail-Trail Spine Network connecting trails in Connecticut, Rhode Island, Massachusetts, New Hampshire, Vermont, and Maine. Half of the system, (over 560 miles), already exists but some of the major trails still have gaps, including the Farmington Canal Heritage Trail (Rails-to-Trails Conservancy 2021). When these gaps are closed, the Farmington Canal Heritage Trail will become even more successful given its position as a key link in two long-distance-trail chains.

CHAPTER 19

Great Allegheny Passage/C&O Canal Trails: Trails and Trail Towns Are Good for Each Other

The Great Allegheny Passage (GAP) Trail and Chesapeake & Ohio (C&O) Canal Trail form an uninterrupted walking/bicycling path from Pittsburgh, Pennsylvania to Washington, DC. These 335 gapless miles represent the longest completed, continuous bike trail in the nation. Every year, over a million people hike or bike either some or all of this distance. The length and great condition of this trail largely explain its popularity. But hikers and bikers also appreciate the towns they pass along the way including several that participate as Trail Towns and Canal Towns, communities that make it easy for hungry, thirsty and tired travelers to find and enjoy local restaurants, pubs, lodging and other trail-related businesses. In turn, these towns benefit from trail-oriented patronage in a region that struggles from the post-industrial age decline of the coal, steel, manufacturing, and railroad industries.

As its name suggests, the Chesapeake & Ohio Canal was supposed to link Washington, DC on Chesapeake Bay, with the Ohio River in Pittsburgh, Pennsylvania. However, it took from 1828 to 1850 to build the canal to Cumberland, Maryland, and stopped there roughly halfway to the originally-planned destination. Progress was slow because the work was done by hand through difficult terrain. In the 22 years of construction, railroads were found to be superior to canals since they could be used year-round while canals were often frozen or flooded from season to season. The C&O nevertheless carried coal and other material until 1924, when a massive flood caused extensive damage and the owners admitted that the canal could not compete with rail lines. In 1971, Congress made the C&O Canal a National Historic Park and the path once used by the mules that pulled the barges up and down the canal became the 185-mile path used by hikers and cyclists today (National Park Service 2020a).

While the canal never reached Pittsburgh, railroads did. Today, after various mergers and abandonments, one rail line remains in operation and the unused rights of way have been transformed into trails for hiking, biking and, in some places, horseback riding. The first trail segment was completed in 1986. A decade later the Allegheny Trail Alliance was formed and ultimately completed the trail, which was honored as the first trail to be inducted into the Rail Trail Hall of Fame in 2007 (Allegheny Trail Alliance 2020; RTC 2020).

The C&O Trail links with the extensive bicycle network of Washington, DC.

Cyclists are attracted by the trail itself as well as the towns that the GAP/C&O connects in its 335-mile journey. To help these towns maximize their economic potential, the Progress Fund launched a Trail Town Program in 2007 that has become a time-tested model for trails throughout the country. Some of the keys to success in the Progress Fund's Trail Town Guide are perhaps obvious such as good trail linkages, welcome centers, branding, marketing, signage and bike racks. But the Trail Town Guide also explains the need for user and business surveys to identify services and amenities that can make a community more attractive and economically healthy. To further promote development, The Progress Fund offers loans and technical assistance to combine economic revitalization with community planning as a way of boosting civic pride as well as attracting bicycle tourists (The Progress Fund 2017).

Pittsburgh, at the northern end of the GAP Trail, is the biggest Trail Town. Over the last three decades, this former steel city has been steadily replacing blast furnaces and industrial plants with a 24-mile network named the Three Rivers Heritage Trail because the system primarily hugs the banks of the Allegheny, Monongahela and Ohio rivers. The Three Rivers Heritage Trail alone generates over $8 million of economic impact annually. Building on that success, plans are now in the works to complete a 261-mile trail between Pittsburgh and Erie, Pennsylvania, which would connect with the GAP/C&O trail to form a 600-mile path from the shores of Lake Erie to Washington, DC (Lynch 2019).

Cooling off at the natural water slides just off the trail in Ohiopyle State Park.

As the GAP Trail travels southeast from Pittsburgh, it passes through the Rivers of Steel National Heritage Area. Located on the GAP Trail, Rivers of Steel maintains the Homestead Steel Works Pump House, the site of a bloody 1892 battle between striking union workers and Pinkerton agents that left ten dead. On the opposite shore of the Monongahela River, the massive, rusted towers of the Carrie Blast Furnaces are preserved as the most prominent industrial landmark from the era when this region produced over half of the nation's entire steel output (Rivers of Steel 2020). The GAP trail then twists further through the National Heritage Area linking towns like McKeesport and Connellsville that are looking to the GAP Trail to help reverse the decline of the regional coal and steel industries.

Before passing out of the National Heritage Area, the GAP trail enters 20,500-acre Ohiopyle State Park, where the rapids and waterfalls of the Youghiogheny River attract whitewater enthusiasts as well as photographers. This town hosts over 1.5 million visitors annually with a combination of outdoor recreation and an array of restaurants, lodging and equipment stores that likely serve as a Trail Town model (Trail Town Program 2015). Shuttles also travel from Ohiopyle to Fallingwater, the house designed by Frank Lloyd Wright that is designated as a UNESCO World Heritage Site and voted by members of the American Institute of Architects as the best all-time work of American architecture (Fallingwater 2020).

Fallingwater, the Frank Lloyd Wright masterpiece voted best all-time work of American architecture

After 73 more miles and four more Trail Towns, cyclists roll into Cumberland, Maryland, where the GAP Trail meets the C&O Canal Trail. Cumberland's Downtown Historic District is anchored by a pedestrian mall, allowing car-free contemplation of over 100 commercial buildings with a wide range of architectural styles including Italianate, Art Deco, Beaux Arts, Romanesque and Georgian Revival (National Park Service 2020b). At the end of the historic district, train buffs can take the Western Maryland Scenic Railroad from Cumberland to Frostburg through the Cumberland Narrows on tracks that parallel the GAP Trail. Across the tracks, the Daughters of the American Revolution maintain a log cabin used as the headquarters of

George Washington when he was a colonel during the French and Indian War and again in 1794 when then President Washington personally led troops against the Whiskey Rebellion (Allegany County 2020).

As background to the next 185 miles of trail, a museum in the Western Maryland Railway Station tells the story of the C&O Canal complete with explanations of the locks and lock keepers houses that cyclists pass on the trail as well as a life-size section of a canal boat and a model of the Paw Paw Tunnel, which took so much time and money to build that it is often cited as the reason the C&O Canal only got to Cumberland.

As a counterpart to the Trail Towns on the GAP Trail, the C&O Canal Trail has Canal Towns that improve their economies by welcoming hikers and bicyclists. In the Canal Town of Williamsport, 85 miles down the trail from Cumberland, a National Park Service boat tour explores a restored section of the canal illustrating features of the original infrastructure including a lock, lift bridge, and navigable aqueduct (National Park Service 2019). After another 33 miles, cyclists are at the Canal Town of Harpers Ferry, made famous by John Brown's 1859 raid that helped to trigger the Civil War.

Although it is not officially a Canal Town, the Washington, DC neighborhood of Georgetown ably anchors the eastern end of the C&O Canal. In addition to a historic district on the National Register of Historic Places, Georgetown is home to newly-restored locks and a section of canal ready for the return of rides on a replica canal barge. At Georgetown, the C&O Canal Trail links with DC's Rock Creek Trail and the Capital City Crescent Trail, just two segments of this region's extensive trail network. There are already 436 miles of bicycle trails in the region plus a robust system of bike lanes reaching to numerous destinations including the National Mall, the Smithsonian Institution, and the US Capitol Building itself. In addition, 302 more miles of trails are planned including gap closures in the Anacostia Riverwalk and the Mt. Vernon Trail which leads to the restored home of George Washington (Glambrone 2018).

The GAP Trail alone was estimated to generate $40 million in direct spending and $7.5 million in wages during 2008. In response to a survey of Trail Towns, business owners reported that the trail produced almost one quarter of their gross revenue on average and roughly two-thirds of respondents reported an increase in business due to their proximity to the trail (The Progress Fund 2009). Notably, this study was conducted at the start of the Great Recession and before the last gaps in the two trails were closed in 2013. A 2016 study estimated well over 1 million total users on the GAP Trail alone that year (Herr 2017) and a 2015 study confirmed that economic impacts had also increased since the previous studies were conducted (The Progress Fund 2015). These studies confirm that trails and trail towns are good for each other.

CHAPTER 20

Greenbrier River Trail; West Virginia: Boom Towns, Ghost Towns, and Bike Towns

The Greenbrier River Trail features two tunnels, 35 bridges and 77 miles of natural beauty as it follows a former rail corridor through rural West Virginia. The trail cannot single-handedly resurrect the rail-based economy that once powered the mill towns of this valley. But it has introduced a more sustainable and enjoyable way of generating income, jobs and tax revenues for a region in transition.

In the late 1800s, the Chesapeake & Ohio Railroad constructed a rail line on the banks of the Greenbrier River to haul timber to distant markets. Mill towns sprouted along this line to convert the trees into lumber. In the early 20th century, this rail line served over 40 sawmills with the largest being the West Virginia Pulp and Paper Company in Cass. But even after the line added passengers and other freight, rail traffic dwindled and the State of West Virginia ultimately converted the abandoned right of way into the Greenbrier River Trail. Some of the former towns along this line have shrunk or disappeared along with the trains. But the survivors are experiencing some economic help from the Greenbrier River Trail, an inductee into the Rail Trail Hall of Fame (Rails-to-Trails Conservancy 2020).

At the northern end of the trail, railroad heritage is preserved in Cass, a town built by and for the West Virginia Pulp and Paper Company, which at one time produced 60,000 board feet of lumber per day. Now listed in the National Register of Historic Places, the Cass Historic District showcases the Cass Historic Theater, the Cass Historic Museum, the Last Run Restaurant and Soda Fountain and a gift shop located in what was once the company store. The company houses are available for overnight stays and a restored steam-powered locomotive pulls a tourist train 11 miles from Cass to the top of Bald Knob, the third highest point in West Virginia, for a spectacular view of the countryside (West Virginia State Parks 2020).

From Cass, cyclists follow the river through the most untouched section of the trail. Quiet riders may surprise deer and other wildlife on the gradual downhill cruise. Anglers may also be seen along the banks since smallmouth bass and the occasional trout inhabit the Greenbrier River. Just before the tiny community of Harter, anyone with a camera or a smart phone will stop to photograph the trail as it emerges from Sharps Tunnel and immediately crosses a 230-foot-long curving bridge over the Greenbrier River (Lynch 2012).

Near the Town of Marlinton, the trail passes a restored 1923 railroad water tank and the remnants of the C&O turntable. Marlinton is the county seat of Pocahontas County and a great cycling base camp. Appalachian Sport rents bicycles as well as kayaks and canoes and offers a shuttle service to cyclists who prefer to ride back to their cars from the trail's highest point at Cass. The Dirtbean Café and Bike Shop also rents bikes and, importantly, opens at 7AM for cyclists looking to get out on the trail early. At the end of the day, experienced riders recommend the incredible view from the outdoor deck at Marlinton's Greenbrier Grille and River Pub (Rails-to-Trails Conservancy 2020).

Downstream from Marlinton, the trail passes Old Watoga, a ghost town originally built around the Watoga Lumber Company's sawmill and kindling wood factory in the early 1900s. In the 1920s, an African-American organization called the Watoga Land Association bought the town site and struggled to rebuild it for a few decades before the community was finally abandoned in the 1950s. Today, a portion of the Land Association's 10,000-acre purchase has been repurposed as Watoga State Park and the only reminders of this former boom town are remnants of the company store and other assorted ruins (Schultz 2014; Rails-to-Trails Conservancy 2020).

A 2015 study estimated that West Virginia's Greenbrier River and North Bend rail trails together generate $6.6 million of economic impact per year. The Greenbrier Trail alone created an economic impact of $3.1 million in 2015. The Cass Scenic Railroad State Park at the north end of the Greenbrier Trail separately generated another $3.1 million of economic impact (Magnini and Uysal 2015). Although it's not comparable to the valley's heyday, the growing success of the Greenbrier River Trail proves that it is possible to generate meaningful sales, jobs, salaries and tax revenues from activities that promote healthy lifestyles, carbon-free recreation and environmental protection.

CHAPTER 21

Greenville, South Carolina: The Swamp Rabbit Inspires More Trail Reproduction

Greenville replaced an eyesore with the graceful Liberty Bridge

Over the past four decades, Greenville, South Carolina transformed its declining core into a vibrant downtown encircling a park complex created from an abandoned industrial zone. The city wisely threaded this park with multi-use pathways and eventually linked this network to the 17-mile Swamp Rabbit trail plus several other greenways. Today, this system connects residential neighborhoods with schools, parks and cultural attractions throughout the city and its suburbs. Although the

Greenville Health System supported this trail primarily to promote active transportation and healthy lifestyles, the Swamp Rabbit Trail is also good for business.

The revitalization process began when Greenville put its Main Street on a diet, reducing the roadway to two lanes and expanding the sidewalks to create a more pedestrian-friendly environment and accommodate outdoor dining. Next door, the city reimagined the Reedy River, replacing a concrete vehicular bridge with the sleek Liberty Bridge, a curved 355-foot suspension bridge for cyclists and pedestrians. The surrounding area opened as Falls Park on the Reedy in 2004 and quickly became the recreational/cultural heart of the city. On the east bank of the river, a public-private partnership built the theater/concert hall complex known as the Peace Center. Next door, an upscale restaurant moved into a retooled industrial building dating from the Civil War (Greenville 2018).

New development lines the trail in downtown Greenville.

Heading south and east from Liberty Bridge, the Swamp Rabbit hugs the bank of the Reedy River and passes a jet on display at the war memorial honoring Rudolf Anderson, a Greenville native whose spy jet was downed during the Cuban Missile Crisis in 1962 (Greenville 2018b). Entering Cleveland Park, cyclists can break for a walk around the Greenville Zoo, which is relatively small but nevertheless features all the favorites including lions, monkeys and giraffes. Heading further south, the Swamp Rabbit reaches 13,000-student Greenville Technical College and ends, for the time being.

Across the Reedy River from the Peace Center, developers converted a parking lot into RiverPlace, a complex that mixes residences, hotel rooms, offices and restaurants overlooking the park, the Liberty Bridge and the waterfall that was the birthplace of Greenville (Greenville 2018). Within this complex, visitors can rent a bike from Pedal Chic and use the Swamp Rabbit Trail's underpasses to avoid downtown streets. Before long, many cyclists take a break at the Swamp Rabbit Café and Grocery, which specializes in locally-sourced food. This is just one of several businesses that have not only located along the trail but also named themselves after the trail including the Swamp Rabbit Brewery, the Swamp Rabbit Inn and even Swamp Rabbit CrossFit. A bike lane also takes fans close to the home stadium of the Swamp Rabbits, Greenville's professional hockey team.

Seven miles from downtown, the Swamp Rabbit skirts the campus of Furman University. Many cyclists choose to detour onto Furman's pathways to explore the 800-acre grounds, recognized for outstanding landscape architecture. The curious can check out a replica of the cabin where Henry David Thoreau lived for two years and wrote his classic book *Walden*. The hungry can patronize any of four different restaurants in the student center overlooking the bell tower surrounded by Furman's Swan Lake.

Outdoor restaurant overlooking the Swamp Rabbit Trail.

Further north, the Swamp Rabbit enters the City of Travelers Rest, which got its name in the early 19th century when people needed to prepare for ascending or to recover from descending the Blue Ridge Mountains (Traillink 2018). By the mid-2000s, this city of 4,500 people had become a little too restful, with vacant buildings indicating a languishing economy. After the Swamp Rabbit opened, entrepreneurs soon realized that the trail was a hit and that growing numbers of cyclists, joggers and walkers were working up an appetite on their way to Travelers Rest. Today this stretch of the trail is home to more than a dozen restaurants and brewpubs serving everything from sushi and pizza to crepes and tacos. Establishments that predated the trail also renovated, like the Whistle-Stop at the American Café which serves its railroad themed goodies in an actual 1932 whistle stop crammed with railroad memorabilia. As one of the owners of The Café at Williams Hardware stated about the Swamp Rabbit: "It has really been an economic boon, not just to Greenville and Travelers Rest but to the whole county" (Stark 2016).

In 2014, a study conducted by a Furman University professor documented some of the economic benefits generated by the over 500,000 people who used the trail in the prior year. Entrepreneurs opened seven new businesses because of the trail. Bike shops and restaurants near the trail saw revenue rise between 10 to 85 percent, with some stores reporting income growth as high as $400,000 (Reed 2014). Of the total number of people on the trail, one quarter were tourists and injected $6.7 million into the local economy in 2013 (Maxwell 2014).

Communities surrounding Greenville are eager to connect to Greenville's trail network. The Swamp Rabbit already extends a mile north of Travelers Rest on its way to Slater-Marietta. To the southeast, the communities of Maudlin, Simpson and Fountain Inn are planning extensions to Greenville that would also link to the existing six-mile trail that winds through the Conestee Lake Nature Park. These are all indications that the success of the Swamp Rabbit Trail is inspiring a trail building boom in the Blue Ridge Mountains of South Carolina (Stark 2016).

CHAPTER 22

Gulf Coast, Alabama: Snow Birds Flock Here

We probably spent more time watching wildlife than bicycling during our two days on the Gulf Coast of Alabama. The multi-use trail network within Gulf State Park has extensive elevated boardwalks, allowing us to view alligators from a safe perspective. There was nothing to worry about as the armadillos and gopher tortoises crossed the trails here, oblivious to bicyclists as they focused on their next meal.

Gulf State Park lies between the cities of Gulf Shores and Orange Beach, roughly 25 miles southeast of the City of Mobile, Alabama and 25 miles west of Pensacola, Florida. This 6,150-acre park protects nine ecosystems: evergreen forest, pine savannah, maritime forest, dune ridge/sand scrub, freshwater/saltwater marshes, coastal ponds, coastal swales, dunes, beaches and the Gulf of Mexico itself. These habitats are home to migratory birds and butterflies as well as rare residents like the Alabama beach mouse, a federally endangered species (Alabama State Parks 2016).

Inside Gulf Park, bicyclists can wander for 27 miles on 15 intersecting trails with names like Rattlesnake Ridge, Cotton Bayou, Rosemary Dunes, Gulf Oak Ridge, Beach Mouse Bypass, Live Oak Trail, Bobcat Branch, and Alligator Marsh (Smithsonian 2018). The park's trail network also links to destinations within the two adjacent cities. As the Catman Road Trail exits the eastern border of the park, bicyclists can continue pedaling to the Orange Beach Marina on bike-friendly Marina Road. Similarly, as the Coyote Crossing Trail leaves the western park boundary, it connects with the Fort Morgan Road Trail, a multi-use path that extends almost to the western city limits of Gulf Shores. From that point, bicyclists can continue west on a bike lane to Fort Morgan State Historical Site, home to a well-preserved Civil War coastal fortification. By taking the intersecting Pine Beach Trail, nature lovers can also reach the hiking paths and kayaking routes of the Bon Secour National Wildlife Refuge.

Two million people visit Gulf State Park every year. While the beach and the campgrounds are the main attractions, almost one third of those responding to a survey cited the trails as one of their top reasons for visiting (Alabama State Parks 2016). If one third of the two million visitors use the park trails, a completely unofficial assumption is that these trails see over 600,000 users annually, a volume that is comparable to many of the country's most popular rail trails.

Bicyclists share Alabama's gulf coast with lots of alligators.

The park and the abutting cities of Gulf Shores and Orange Beach lie within Baldwin County, where the economy is heavily dependent on tourism. Retail, lodging, food and other service industries account for over 80 percent of the jobs in Baldwin County. Visitors spent over $3.2 billion here in 2013, supporting 45,000 workers in travel-related jobs (Alabama State Parks 2016). Tourists drawn to the trails of Gulf State Park and its neighbors logically account for a substantial portion of that revenue.

Alabama's bike and pedestrian plan reports that leisure and tourism bicycle trips have become increasingly important to economies at the local, regional, and statewide levels (Alabama 2017). Similarly, the 2016 Gulf State Park Master Plan aims to increase economic activity, create local jobs, add tax receipts and increase the revenue from the user fees that largely fund the Alabama park system. The survey for the plan found that bicycle and pedestrian improvements were ranked as the number one priority for local residents and the number 2 priority for visitors (Alabama State Parks 2016).

In response to public feedback, major bikeway and pedestrian improvements are proposed for all three implementation phases of the Gulf State Park Master Plan. Phase I calls for 9.5 miles of new trails and 3.5 miles of trail enhancements including differentiating existing trails for walkers and bicyclists. Phase II involves completing trail loops, adding educational features and building more "pause places" where people can catch their breath and actually study nature. Several of the plan's 34 pause places would facilitate viewing of the park's diverse wildlife including alligators, gopher tortoises, osprey, herons, hawks and kestrels. Finally, Phase III includes specific enhancements like widening some multi-use trails (Alabama State Parks 2016).

Certain penalties paid by parties responsible for the Deepwater Horizon disaster can be used to fund restoration and improvement projects on Alabama's Gulf Coast, which was severely impacted by that 2010 drilling rig explosion and the subsequent oil spill. The 2018 draft plan for spending some of this money includes $4.4 million to complete the multi-use trail from the City of Gulf Shores to Fort Morgan State Historical Site, which would result in a continuous 30-mile recreational trail from the tip of Fort Morgan Point to the City of Orange Beach (Orange Beach Alabama Community Website 2018; Alabama Gulf Coast Recovery Council 2018).

The trails of Alabama's Gulf Coast are already providing economic development, mobility, recreation, and exercise options for year-round residents as well as winter visitors. Further extension of this network may also encourage snowbirds to arrive earlier in the season and perhaps stay a little longer.

CHAPTER 23

Harmony – Preston – Lanesboro - Houston, Minnesota: Linking Art and Crafts

Minnesota was an early adopter of paved, long-distance, off-road bike trails. The 49-mile Heartland State Trail debuted in 1974, making it one of the first rail trails in the nation. As expected in the *Land of 10,000 Lakes*, this trail offers abundant opportunities for fishing and swimming. Similarly, the 116-mile Paul Bunyan Trail, a Rail-Trail Hall of Fame honoree, passes 21 lakes as it meanders through 116 miles of spectacular north woods scenery. Today, the Department of Natural Resources manages almost 600 miles of state-owned and operated paved trails (Parks and Trails Council 2017).

In 2007-08, average users of the Heartland Trail lived 125 miles from the trail and spent over $1 million. Likewise, riders on the Paul Bunyan Trail traveled 120 miles on average and spent over $1.2 million in 2007 (Kelly 2010). The third tourist-oriented trail in that study, published in 2010, was the Root River- Harmony Preston Valley Trail, which we visited in June of 2019 for a first-hand look.

As its name suggests, the Root River – Harmony Preston Valley Trail is a mash-up of two trails. The eastern end of the 42-mile Root River Trail lies in the City of Houston, population 979, 15 miles from the Mississippi River in southeastern Minnesota. This trail largely follows the twisting Root River for 36 miles before veering off to its western end in the City of Fountain, population 410. The 18-mile Harmony - Preston Valley Trail bisects the City of Preston, population 1,325, and reaches its southern end in the City of Harmony, population 1,020. Along the way, this trail complex passes through four other trail towns including the City of Lanesboro, population 754, and the City of Whalan, population 63.

Some of these tiny trail towns use the trail system to leverage other attractions. Harmony and environs are home to Minnesota's largest Amish population. Amish furniture outlets here use their highway frontage to display colorful chairs and other handicrafts. The City's welcome center complex features an Amish quilt store. Horse drawn buggies are a common sight on roads with extra wide shoulders designed for slow vehicles. The curious can take buses or rent a CD for self-guided tours of Amish farms that welcome visitors to shop at on-site gift stores for home-grown foods and hand-made furnishings.

Tourists visit Harmony to experience Amish culture as well as ride the trail.

Further north, Lanesboro seems to be thriving on a mix of trail riding, river rafting and art. In 2014, the City Council declared the entire town as an Art Campus. An organization called Lanesboro Arts sponsors art fairs, artist residencies, educational programs, events at the St. Mane Theater, and an art gallery (Lanesboro Arts 2019). Next door, the Commonweal Theater has been mounting multi-play seasons of live professional theater for 30 years (Commonweal Theater 2019). Lanesboro is home to ten restaurants and 14 inns or B&Bs, which is unusual for a community of 754 inhabitants. Perhaps as an indication of the demand for tourist accommodations, some of this lodging can be found in repurposed buildings, including a former feed mill.

Similarly odd conversions can be found in Preston, notably the Jail House Inn which was retooled from the old county jail. In addition to the trail, fishing lures visitors to Preston. This town is home to the National Trout

Center, devoted to habitat restoration, research, education and, of course, fishing. The Center has designed a nine-hole fishing course along a mile or so of the Root River as it bends around the city. The trout obsession here is supported by like-minded businesses like the Driftless Fly Fishing Company, offering guides, canoe/kayak rentals, gear, and priceless fishing tips.

Riding the trail gives cyclists a great excuse to indulge themselves at the Aroma Pie Shoppe in tiny Whalan. On the day we visited, parked bikes surrounded the shop. We waited in line behind a dozen hungry bikers only to be told that they had run out of pie and that we would have to pedal back the next day, which we did.

In 2010, 70 percent of the riders on the Root River/Harmony-Preston Valley Trail lived over 50 miles away. The median distance traveled to reach the trail was 120 miles, which is roughly the distance to Minneapolis-St. Paul. The predominance of tourist bicyclists largely explains the proliferation of restaurants and lodging near the trail. In total, this study estimated that the trail was responsible for trip spending of over $2.2 million (Kelly 2010).

In 2008, Minnesota trails as a whole were estimated to experience 30 million person-days of bicycle riding. A 2009 study calculated that trail bicycle riding generated $427 million in total spending, supporting 3,736 jobs with employee compensation of $87 million and state and local tax revenues of over $35 million (Venegas 2009). At the statewide and local levels, these studies demonstrate that bike trails make a significant contribution to economic development, particularly when they connect other things tourists like, including cute towns featuring restaurants, art, and crafts.

CHAPTER 24

Hattiesburg - Prentiss, Mississippi: Adding Spokes to Hub City

There are more cyclists in downtown Hattiesburg, Mississippi these days. That was the unofficial opinion of our waiter at The Porter Public House, a brewpub/comedy club/live music venue, when asked about the impact of the Longleaf Trace Rail Trail. In 2017, a two-mile extension of the Trace into the center of town greatly increased access to the trail and linked two important economic engines: the historic heart of the city and the University of Southern Mississippi.

In 1912, Hattiesburg was nicknamed Hub City because it was at the center of several key railroad lines. Landmarks from its heyday can still be found around every corner in the downtown. The National Register of Historic Places lists over 200 contributing buildings in the Hub City Historic District. The Historic Hattiesburg Downtown Association uses this authentic sense of place to reinforce downtown as a center of art, culture and heritage (HHDA 2018). Highlighting this effort are the Hattiesburg Cultural Center and the Saenger Theater, a Neo-Classical/Art Deco movie palace built in 1929 and recently restored for live performances including concerts on the original silent-film era pipe organ (Saenger 2018).

The Hattiesburg Tourism Commission encourages visitors to join their walking tours of downtown. The Commission also offers its '64 Freedom Summer Trail, with stops at key sites from the civil rights movement including the Forrest County Courthouse, where peaceful demonstrators picketed non-stop for several months beginning on Freedom Day, January 22, 1964.

For over a decade, the 14,500 students at the University of Southern Mississippi have been able to bicycle the Trace from an on-campus trailhead to the town of Prentiss, 41 miles to the west. Long ago, the old growth forest here was hauled away by the Mississippi Central Railroad using the right of way now enjoyed by bicyclists, walkers, skaters and equestrians. But new pines have replaced the old-growth forest, making a home for various critters and offering a quiet, contemplative ride accompanied by cardinal warbles and other bird songs.

The Forrest County Courthouse is one of the key sites on Hattiesburg's '64 Freedom Summer Trail.

As of 2017, a trail extension links the USM campus with downtown Hattiesburg, making it easier for students to pedal to cultural and culinary attractions there while allowing city residents to bike directly from urban neighborhoods out into the countryside. The extension connects to the recently-restored 1910 Hattiesburg depot, which is a historic icon as well as a multimodal transportation hub providing bus, taxi and rail service.

The Longleaf Trace annually attracts over 100,000 people (Mussiett 2015). Visitors have come from all 50 states and several other countries. In a typical week, trail users come from five or more states (Pearl and Leaf Rivers Rails to Trails Recreational District, undated a). The Trace has received well-deserved attention, including induction into the Rail-Trail Hall of Fame and designation as a National Recreation Trail. The trail has also been cited as an economic development tool. This recognition likely adds ongoing support for the Pearl and Leaf Rivers Rails to Trails Recreational District, the partnership of the four cities and three counties that maintains the Trace using a ¼ mill tax on property.

Economic benefits also add support for the Trace. The Pearl and Leaf Rivers Rails to Trails Recreational District lists dozens of businesses that cater to trail users and some that deliberately located close to the Trace including bed and breakfasts, restaurants and other food/refreshment outlets (Pearl and Leaf Rivers Rail to Trails Recreational District undated b). On our ride, we lunched at Lau-Tori's Fine Foods in the bike-friendly town of Sumrall, where Trace ridership can be gauged by the number of bicycles outside (McNeill 2005).

The Hub City Historic District boasts over 200 buildings on the National Register of Historic Places.

Putting a single business under the microscope, the owner of one local bike store reports that, by 2014, the opening of the Trace generated significant increases in his revenue and workforce, specifically adding $900,000 in payroll, $96,000 in property taxes and over $265,000 in sales tax revenue (Exploring by Bicycle 2017; Moore 2011).

According to the Pearl and Leaf Rivers Rails to Trails Recreational District, the Longleaf Trace annually accounts for more than 500 motel room stays, 1,000 bicycle rentals and 5,000 restaurant visits. As evidence or the Trace's attraction, subdivisions and housing complexes have been built along the Trace that highlight proximity to the trail in their marketing campaigns.

In addition to economic benefits, the district reports improved health from increased exercise, reduced need for motorized vehicles, and a corresponding increase in active transportation modes to reach the USM campus and other destinations along the Trace (Pearl and Leaf Rivers Rail to Trails Recreational District undated a).

As perhaps the most reliable indicator of satisfaction, Hattiesburg continues to look for further extensions of the Longleaf Trace. In commemorating the link to Chain Park, Toby Barker, Mayor of Hattiesburg, stated that the city intends to pursue additional connectivity: "Our goal is to have neighborhoods and pathways lead to the Trace, so no matter where you live in Hattiesburg, there's a way for you to get here by bike or by foot" (Bunch 2018).

CHAPTER 25

Indianapolis - Carmel, Indiana: Slowing Down Pays Off

Indianapolis is famous for cars racing around its Speedway every Memorial Day Weekend. But this city has also recognized the many benefits of bicycling, as demonstrated by an impressive regional trail system and the 8-mile, multi-use Indianapolis Cultural Trail connecting parks, waterways, landmarks and other community destinations throughout the heart of the city.

The Monon Trail, an inductee in the Rail-Trail Hall of Fame, links downtown Indianapolis with the town of Sheridan, 23 miles to the north. Located at the trail's midpoint, the City of Carmel has been named as a silver level Bicycle Friendly Community by the League of American Bicyclists. To maximize people-powered mobility, Carmel is concentrating commercial, residential and community buildings along the Monon Trail, including Carmel's Center for the Performing Arts and the Booth Tarkington Civic Theater, named for Indianapolis's own Pulitzer Prize-winning writer. Further north on the Monon Trail, cyclists enter Carmel's Arts and Design District, home to galleries, design centers, specialty shops and restaurants.

The Monon Trail also forms the spine of the Carmel Caffeine Trail, this city's variation on the more-commonly found wine, brewery and distillery trails. Here, cyclists can recharge at any of 19 shops and cafes serving gourmet coffees and teas. Other attractions on the Monon Trail include the Indiana State Fairgrounds and the Broad Ripple Cultural District with trail-friendly restaurants and cafes like Brics, located in a former train depot. With this impressive connectivity, it's not surprising that the Monon Trail attracts 1.3 million visitors a year (Rails to Trails Conservancy 2009). In addition to the businesses that benefit from proximity, real estate values are 11 percent higher near the Monon Trail (Flusche 2012).

At Broad Ripple, cyclists can switch to the Central Canal Trail, pedal past

Butler University and visit the many attractions in Newfields Park including a beer garden, the Indianapolis Museum of Art, the 100-acre Virginia B. Fairbanks Art and Nature Park plus the home and surrounding formal gardens of the late businessman/philanthropist J.K. Lilly Jr. Further south, the Central Canal Trail becomes the White River Trail, leading to many parks and the Indianapolis Zoo.

At Newfields, cyclists can visit the home of the late businessman/philanthropist J.K. Lilly Jr.

The White River Trail crosses White River State Park, the site of the Indiana State Museum, the NCAA Hall of Champions and the Eiteljorg Museum, featuring Native American/western art, culture and history. From here, pedestrians and cyclists can navigate trails flanking Indianapolis's restored 19th century downtown canals. In addition to walking or biking the 3-mile Canal Walk loop, visitors can also explore these quiet canals by kayak, pedal boat or Venetian-style gondola, complete with singing gondolier.

White River State Park and the canals are one of six districts in the Indianapolis Cultural Trail, an 8-mile pedestrian/bike path connecting parks, plazas and other key downtown destinations including the historically-significant Old National Centre, the Indianapolis City Market, and the Glick Peace Walk featuring luminescent art pieces that celebrate extraordinary individuals including Jonas Salk, Martin Luther King, Jr., and Susan B. Anthony.

The Indianapolis Cultural Trail has been good for businesses and property values. Over half of the owners of businesses on the trail reported an increase in customers with anticipated spending in some trail segments estimated to be as high as $3.2 million. New establishments and additional jobs have been attracted to the trail, with 25 percent of these new businesses choosing their locations because of the trail. Between 2008 and 2014, assessed value of properties within 500 feet of the trail rose by over $1 billion (Indiana State University Public Policy Institute 2015).

The Indianapolis Cultural Trail incorporates the Canal Walk, a 3-mile loop linking downtown parks, museums, landmarks and businesses.

This city is best known for cars that average over 200 miles per hour as they race around the Indianapolis Speedway one day a year. Ironically, the Indianapolis Cultural Trail demonstrates that people are also attracted throughout the year to places where they can slow down and savor the sights of a city by traveling at leisurely, human-powered speeds (Rails-to-Trails Conservancy 2019).

CHAPTER 26

La Crosse — Madison - Milwaukee, Wisconsin: The Route of the Badger

Wisconsin has earned its title as a bicycle trail blazer. In 1965, the Badger State opened the Elroy Sparta Trail, becoming the first rail trail in the United States. As early as 1998, this trail alone was generating over $2 million in economic benefit annually (Wisconsin DOT 1998). At the western end of this iconic trail, the City of Sparta, the self-proclaimed Bicycling Capital of America, has developed into a bicycle trail hub, making residents as well as business owners happy (Wisconsin Bike Fed 2019). Over time, Wisconsin has built on its recognition that bike trails are good for business, which partly explains why the state alone manages 35 trails with over 748 miles of asphalt or limestone pavement (Wisconsin DNR 2019).

Wisconsin continues to have ambitious plans for its state-wide trail network. The Rails-to-Trails Conservancy and Wisconsin Bike Federation are leading an effort to complete a network of trails, called the Route of the Badger, across the state from the shores of Lake Michigan to the crossing of the Mississippi River into Minnesota. When complete, this route will become one of the country's premier destination trail networks with a total length of 500-plus miles (Kapp 2016).

Fortunately, the Route of the Badger can become a reality largely by closing gaps in a series of trails that already cross southern Wisconsin. The 24-mile Great River State Trail forms a segment of the Mississippi River Trail, a 3,000-mile route linking Itasca, Minnesota with the Gulf of Mexico. Turning east, the 21-mile La Crosse River Trail connects with the 34-mile Elroy-Sparta Trail, which in turn links with the 22-mile 400 Trail, creating an existing 101-mile chain of trails collectively known as the Bike 4 Trails.

At the end of the 400 Trail, plans show the Route of the Badger closing a gap to Baraboo, the birthplace of the Ringling Brothers Circus and now home to Circus World Museum, which restores ornate circus memorabilia and presents daily circuses in a big top. The route then passes Devil's Lake State Park, which annually attracts over 2.5 million visitors including many who hike to the Devil's Doorway rock formation and other geological curiosities.

Madison transformed State Street into a car-free pedestrian/cyclist zone.

The proposed Route of the Badger enters the City of Madison and passes the 44,000-student University of Wisconsin. Here, a pedestrian/bicycle/bus mall links the UW campus with the State Capitol, which serves as the hub of a 413-mile bicycle path/lane network that has earned Platinum level recognition from the League of American Bicyclists. The 40-mile Badger State Trail takes cyclists from Madison to Monroe, the Swiss Cheese Capital of the USA and then becomes the 47-mile Cheese Country Recreation Trail. Alternatively, cyclists can take the 40-mile Military Ridge Trail to Dodgeville, one of Wisconsin's oldest cities, or take the 23-mile Sugar River State Trail to New Glarus, which celebrates its Swiss heritage with alpine architecture and events like the Wilhelm Tell Festival.

Heading east from Madison, cyclists are treated to the 53-mile Glacial Drumlin Trail which passes farms, lakes, wetlands and glacially-formed topography while linking several classic trail towns before ending in the City of Waukesha. East of Waukesha, the New Berlin Trail connects with Milwaukee County's 125-mile Oak Leaf Trail which connects dozens of parks with the shores of Lake Michigan, dominated by the Milwaukee Art Museum designed by starchitect Santiago Calatrava.

The Calatrava-designed Art Museum creates a spectacular rest stop on Milwaukee's 125-mile Oak Leaf Trail.

The trail network in Southeastern Wisconsin puts 90 percent of this region's population within three miles of a trail (Lewis 2016). Trails that radiate from Milwaukee County include the 30-mile Ozaukee Interurban Trail, which offers a pleasant day trip to the well-preserved mill town of Cedarburg. The 18-mile Sheboygan Interurban Trail ends in the City of Sheboygan, the Bratwurst Capital of the World. The 15-mile Hank Aaron State Trail, named for the baseball slugger who beat Babe Ruth's homerun record, leads appropriately to Miller Park, home of the Milwaukee Brewers.

At its eastern end, the Hank Aaron Trail meets Lake Michigan at Lakeshore State Park and Festival Park, home of Summerfest, the nation's largest music festival. Here, bike trails and lanes wander through the Historic Third Ward, where 19th Century factories and warehouses were thankfully forgotten rather than demolished, making way for a now-thriving arts, entertainment and residential district. These trails intersect with Riverwalk, a pedestrian promenade that is transforming the previously-ignored Milwaukee River into one of the City's most beloved destinations. In the downtown,

Riverwalk bisects Milwaukee's Theater District and crosses the river on a bike/pedestrian bridge leading to Old World Third Street, offering a taste of the city's German heritage including a sausage factory and beer hall. Speaking of beer, the Beerline B neighborhood just upstream takes its name from the rail line that used to bring supplies into Milwaukee's famous breweries. Portions of that corridor have become the Beerline B rail trail, another amenity that partly explains the construction frenzy occurring in this neighborhood as Milwaukee adds both pedestrian and bicycle options for reaching downtown jobs (Milwaukee 2019).

Studies indicate that even individual trails here can generate meaningful economic benefits. For example, the 47-mile Gandy Dancer Trail, linking St. Croix Falls and Danbury in northwestern Wisconsin, annually contributes $3.3 million to local businesses (Kazmierski et al. 2009). Statewide, a 2010 study concluded that bicycle recreation in Wisconsin generated $924 million in economic impacts and supported 13,191 full-time-equivalent jobs (Grabow, Hahn & Whited 2010). Early adoption dating to the opening of the first rail trail in the US explains part of this success. But another component is Wisconsin's ongoing drive to extend and connect its many trail networks, including the Route of the Badger.

CHAPTER 27

Lackawanna River Heritage Trail, Pennsylvania: From Electric City to Coal Country

The Lackawanna River Heritage Trail joins over 30 communities in four counties in northeastern Pennsylvania. It meanders for over 70 miles through the heart of the Lackawanna Heritage Valley National and State Heritage Area established in 2000 by the U.S. Congress to recognize this area's central role in American history. The Lackawanna Heritage Valley Authority aims to renew the economy, restore the environment, and promote a sense of pride in a region that was essential to the nation's growth as an industrial powerhouse. The trail is important to that mission and is also an economic engine in its own right.

Scranton, the biggest city on the trail, is a major center of railroad history. Lackawanna Station was built here in 1908 as the regional headquarters of the Delaware, Lackawanna and Western (DL&W) Railroad which was initially formed to serve Pennsylvania's Coal Region. In 1977, the six-story landmark was placed in the National Register of Historic Places. It was restored in 1983 as the Lackawanna Station Hotel and today retains original features that recall the golden age of rail including a two and a half story lobby with a Tiffany stained-glass ceiling and 36 tile murals depicting scenes along the rail line's route.

On the other side of downtown Scranton, the former rail yard of the DL&W has been transformed into the Steamtown National Historic Site, complete with a working turntable and roundhouse that largely replicate the original facilities. The site preserves vintage rolling stock including 29 steam locomotives like the Rahway Valley Railroad Number 15 built in 1916. Today, rail enthusiasts can board the "Scranton Limited" for a three-mile ride past the Lackawanna Station Hotel and back. For an even more limited ride, visitors can ride in a caboose around the 40-acre park.

Within Steamtown, The Electric City Trolley Museum, with a collection of over 25 historic vehicles, also offers trolley rides including game-day trips to PNC Field to watch minor-league baseball played by the hometown team, the Scranton/Wilkes-Barre RailRiders.

Scranton's nickname, Electric City, began in 1880, when electric lights were installed in the Dickson Manufacturing Company here. In 1886, Scranton launched the first successful streetcars in the U.S. powered entirely by electricity. These electrifying firsts were memorialized in a 1,200-bulb electric sign that still towers above downtown atop the Scranton Electric Building. After being on and off repeatedly since the 1930s, the original incandescent bulbs were replaced in 2014 by one-watt LEDs and the sign may now be a permanent fixture of Scranton.

The Starrucca Viaduct, a thousand-foot-long stone arch bridge built in 1848, is still in use today.

In addition to railroad buffs, Electric City attracts fans of *The Office*, the TV sitcom about the fictional Dunder Mifflin Paper Company which was fictionally located in Scranton. Although the show was not filmed here, dedicated fans can visit several real places mentioned in the show including Cooper's, a seafood house resembling a pirate ship, the Anthracite Heritage Museum, and Steamtown Mall, a real mall that has embraced its mission as headquarters for Dunder Mifflin memorabilia.

The Delaware and Hudson (D&H) Trail portion of the Lackawanna River Heritage Trail begins in the former coal town of Simpson and meanders north for 38 miles to within a few miles of the Pennsylvania-New York State

Line. Hauling coal over Ararat Summit required three pusher engines to assist the lead locomotive. Now that the D&H is a rail trail, many cyclists push themselves to reach this high point and then reward themselves by coasting back down to any of several restaurants in Forest City, Simpson, or Carbondale.

Those who choose to pedal north of Ararat Summit can stop at an ice cream shop located in the original rail depot in Thompson. At the northern trailhead in Lanesboro, cyclists get a feeling of accomplishment when passing beneath the 110-foot-tall bluestone arches of the Starrucca Viaduct, a 1,040-foot-long stone arch bridge which became the longest stone arch railroad bridge in the world when the New York and Erie Railroad built it in 1848. Still in use today, the Starrucca Viaduct is listed on the National Register of Historic Places and designated as a National Historic Civil Engineering Landmark.

In 2016, the Lackawanna River Heritage Trail attracted 315,000 visits, a 145 percent increase over the 128,000 visits recorded in 2009. These visits generated a total economic impact of $91.9 million in 2016, of which $72 million occurred within Lackawanna County, the county surrounding Scranton (Lackawanna Heritage Valley 2017).

As another indication of success, a 2015 study prepared for the National Park Service reported that the towns served by the trail use it as a linear park, with many educational, recreational, and community events held on the trail itself. The Lackawanna River Heritage Trail is "… an important economic and community resource to the entire region, especially the smaller or less prominent localities in the LHV who do not have the populations or historic assets to match Scranton's" (Jones *et.al.* 2015, p7).

CHAPTER 28

Louisville, Kentucky: Getting Everyone in The Loop

For over a century, Louisville, Kentucky has reaped the benefits of an Olmstead-designed park system connecting citizens with recreational, cultural and natural destinations. In 2017, this city of 766,000 people burnished its legacy, opening a natural greenbelt that wraps around the southeastern corner of the metro area. And to maximize human-powered access between downtown and this rural oasis, Louisville is now completing the Louisville Loop, a 100-mile multi-use trail planned to encircle the entire consolidated city-county.

Frederick Law Olmstead, the father of American landscape design as well as the architect of New York's Central Park and the US Capitol Grounds, was hired in 1891 to envision a park system for Louisville. Over the next 30 years, Olmstead and his two sons developed a plan that ultimately protected three large natural parks, 15 neighborhood parks/squares/playgrounds and 15 miles of parkways linking residents with open space throughout the city. The Louisville system is one of only four completed Olmstead park system plans in the world. In 1982, the Louisville Park System was listed in the National Register of Historic Places (Olmstead Parks Conservancy 2019; The Cultural Landscape Foundation 2019).

In the spirit of Olmstead, Metro Louisville and its partners are now completing the 3,700-acre Parklands of Floyds Fork, a network of four major parks linked by a scenic drive, a multi-use trail system and a water trail following Floyds Fork Creek as it meanders through newly created Broad Run Park, Turkey Run Park, Pope Lick Park, Beckley Creek Park and The Strand. In 2017 alone, its first year as a fully open park, The Parklands of Floyds Fork experienced over 3 million visits and registered a substantial number of bike and canoe rentals (The Parklands of Floyds Fork 2018). In 2018, attendance almost doubled to 5.5 million visits (The Parklands of

Floyds Fork 2019).

To further connect people with parks, businesses, institutions and other everyday destinations, Louisville is now in the process of building the Louisville Loop, over 100 miles of planned multi-use paths of which 50 miles are already in existence. When completed, the Loop will reach within one mile of 66 percent of the residents of Louisville, within a half mile of public transit and within a mile of almost half of the city's public schools (Rails-to-Trails 2019).

The Louisville's Riverwalk passes the Muhammad Ali Center.

The 19 miles of multiuse trails through The Parklands of Floyds Fork is one of five sections in the Loop. Three others are named for the topography and geology they traverse: Limestone Belt, Shale Lowlands and The Knobs. At 25 miles, the Ohio River Valley is the longest continuous section of the Loop. The Loop's mile markers begin at the Big Four Bridge, originally built as a rail crossing of the Ohio River in 1895. Today, only pedestrians and cyclists can use this bridge to travel between Jeffersonville, Indiana and Waterfront Park in Louisville (Ahn 2018).

The Riverwalk portion of the Loop takes cyclists past the Belle of Louisville, a riverboat first launched in 1914 as a working ferry and now used for dinner cruises, weddings and sightseeing. Further west, cyclists can visit the Muhammad Ali Center, a museum devoted to the life and times of this

Louisville native, arguably the most famous boxer in history. At 120 feet in height, the world's biggest baseball bat welcomes fans to the Louisville Slugger Factory and Museum where they can buy a personalized bat or just soak in baseball nostalgia dating back to 1884.

In downtown Louisville, cyclists can take a well-deserved break at Fourth Street Live, a car-free block of restaurants, bars, entertainment venues and performance stages cleverly protected from the elements by a jaunty, angled roof. The nearby Louisville Visitors Center issues passports to the Urban Bourbon Trail, encouraging tourists to responsibly sample America's only native spirit at 44 participating downtown restaurants and bars, including the Brown Hotel, a National Register landmark that has served as a center of social and business life since 1923.

Louisville views the Loop as an economic development tool as well as a means of promoting healthy lifestyles, environmental quality and human-powered mobility between parks, work, schools and businesses. The Loop's connectivity builds on the legacy of the Olmstead park plan. In short, the Loop is seen as a means of transforming Louisville into one of the most livable cities in the US, helping to attract outdoor tourism and new businesses to the region. As Greg Fischer, former Louisville Mayor put it: "The Louisville Loop will not only set us apart as a desirable city…it will bring us together as a community … it will be a wedding ring for our city … joining neighborhoods … helping connect people to recreation, to their work and to the place they do business" (Rails-to-Trails 2019).

CHAPTER 29

Maine: Seeing the Light

Maine is realizing the power of bicycle trails. The state currently offers over 400 miles of rail trails and in 2001 released a study documenting the sizeable benefits of bicycle tourism to Maine and its local economies. Various agencies and organizations are building on this success with plans to expand the network, including efforts to further develop 367 miles within Maine of the East Coast Greenway, the 3,000-mile trail planned to link 450 communities in 15 states from Florida to Maine.

The 29-mile Eastern Trail, currently links 12 communities between Kennebunk and South Portland using both on- and off-road segments. This trail and others form the route for the annual Maine Lighthouse Ride which offers four optional rides such as a 100-mile route with views of nine lighthouses including six near the Eastern Trail. The Portland Head Light, first lit in 1791, presents an irresistible photo opportunity hugging the end of a rugged point and framed by a former keepers' quarters that now serves as a lighthouse museum. Cape Elizabeth is another favorite, partly because it has two separate lighthouses and partly because of the wildly-popular restaurant, Lobster Shack at Two Lights.

This region has more to offer than charming, historic lighthouses. Near Kennebunk, at the current southern end of the Eastern Trail, the U.S. Fish & Wildlife Service manages a national wildlife refuge named for Rachel Carson, the marine biologist and author of *Silent Spring*, the book often credited with sparking the modern environmental movement. The refuge protects 50 miles of undulating coastline containing barrier beaches, dunes, meadows, salt marshes, and estuaries essential to migratory birds.

Further north, Old Orchard Beach offers less contemplative recreation such as Palace Playland, a classic ocean amusement park with a carousel, arcade, roller coaster, thrill rides, and, of course, a Ferris wheel.

The bike lanes into Portland guide cyclists to Commercial Street, the main artery of the Portland's Working Waterfront, home to more than a dozen piers and wharves teaming with boats, fishing businesses, and restaurants specializing in seafood, especially lobster.

As the harbor bustle ends, cyclists can continue onto the Eastern Promenade Trail and arrive at East End Beach, where they can switch from pedaling a bike to paddling a kayak. The trail here passes the Maine Narrow Gauge Railroad Museum and parallels closely-spaced tracks offering rides on diminutive trains that were once a common form of transportation throughout Maine.

Portland Head Light, dating from 1791, can be seen on the annual Maine Lighthouse Ride

The Eastern Promenade Trail becomes the Bayside Trail, which ducks under the I-295 bridge, allowing cyclists to enjoy a pleasant spin around Portland's Back Cove. From there, cyclists can use bike-friendly streets to circle back through downtown Portland and the old port district, which is loaded with historic buildings repurposed as brewpubs, ice cream shops, coffee joints, and even more places to eat lobster.

When indirect effects as well as direct spending are calculated, bicycle tourism in Maine as a whole was estimated to generate an economic impact of over $68.8 million and support 1,200 jobs. Despite that respectable total, the 2001 study that came up with that estimate also offered recommendations for increasing ridership and revenue by improving roadways and shared use pathways, particularly three trails of statewide significance including the Eastern Trail (Wilber Smith 2001).

Estimates for the Eastern Trail alone have been prepared by the Eastern

Trail Alliance, the non-profit organization that organizes the annual Maine Lighthouse Ride mentioned above. In 2018, with ridership capped at 1,200 registrants, 70 percent of Maine Lighthouse Ride participants came from out of state, 44 percent used local hotels and B&Bs for overnight stays, and many stayed in Maine for several days before and after the event. In 2014, the Maine Lighthouse Ride alone generated $354,000 in direct local spending (Andrews 2018). In 2018 as a whole, the off-road portions of the Eastern Trail saw 251,000 visitors and generated roughly $3 million in sales and rentals (Eastern Trail Alliance 2021).

The Alliance notes that the Eastern Trail increases the value of nearby property and, consequently, local property tax revenues. In Scarborough alone, one of the 12 communities on the trail, the Eastern Trail is credited with increasing the value of houses within one-half mile of the Eastern Trail by five percent, or over $13 million, which contributes an additional $192,322 of property tax revenue to Scarborough every year (Andrews 2018).

Real estate agents report that homes near the Eastern Trail sell faster than those further from the trail, providing further evidence that trails are a big factor in the decisions of home buyers. Developers are also eager to build near the trail and seek direct access to the trail from their projects. To advertise this feature, the developers of a subdivision bordering the trail in Old Orchard Beach have named their project "Eastern Trail Estates" (Andrews 2018).

The Eastern Trail Alliance is spearheading efforts to build a 3.1-mile off-road section of the trail between and through Saco and Biddeford which, when completed, would create a gap-free trail of over 25 miles. This non-profit organization is also working to close the gap between South Portland and Scarborough and build an off-road trail south from Kennebunk to South Berwick on the border between Maine and New Hampshire (Eastern Trail Alliance 2021). The economic as well as health, mobility, and recreational benefits demonstrated by these studies of the Eastern Trail should help secure the funding and the public support needed to make these visions a reality.

CHAPTER 30

Minneapolis, Minnesota: Learning from the Grand Rounds

In the 1880s, Minneapolis launched the Grand Rounds, a 50-mile greenway linking parks, lakes, and recreational/cultural centers, forming the spine of what is now considered one of the best park systems in the nation. Building on that success, this city of 425,000 now has one of most extensive and heavily-used trail systems in the US and a reputation as a bike-friendly community with remarkably high percentages of commuting by bicycle. In return, Minneapolis and the entire Twin Cities Metro Area today enjoys a considerable economic benefit from believing in bicycles.

The Grand Rounds was the brainchild of Horace Cleveland, a pioneer landscape architect who articulated his goal of making "...the city itself a work of art..." (Cleveland 1888). On a more practical note, Cleveland observed that parkland enhances property values, defends against wildfires like the 1871 conflagration that destroyed Chicago, and preserves natural spaces that are difficult to save once real estate speculation makes them unaffordable. It also helped that Minneapolis elites had a rivalry with adjacent St. Paul, which was already protecting the east banks of the Mississippi River. By 1891, the vision focused on the Grand Rounds, a greenbelt encircling the entire city and creating the organizational framework for a park system that now includes over 6,800 acres of green/blue space, 55 miles of parkways, 102 miles of Grand Rounds walking and biking paths, 22 lakes, 12 formal gardens, 49 recreation centers and 23 million visits per year. Today, experts often credit Minneapolis as having the best park system in the nation and the American Planning Association recognized the Grand Rounds specifically as one of its Great Places in America (Minneapolis Parks & Recreation Board 2019; Pruetz, 2012).

The Stone Arch Bridge offers a car-free, ultra-scenic crossing of the Mississippi River.

The Stone Arch Bridge is arguably the most dramatic link in the Grand Rounds. Originally built in 1883, it stands as the second oldest crossing of the Mississippi River still in use. In 1994, the Minnesota Department of Transportation refurbished this engineering marvel and the Minneapolis Parks & Recreation Board now maintains the bridge as a bike and pedestrian trail. Cyclists often stop here to contemplate St. Anthony Falls and the remnants of structures built in the days when Minneapolis flour mills together with their canals and raceways constituted the largest water-powered industrial complex in the world (Pruetz 2012).

At the west end of Stone Arch Bridge, cyclists encounter Mill Ruins Park and Mill City Museum, located in a National Register building that was once the largest flour mill on earth. Here visitors can learn about Minneapolis' industrial heyday and enjoy live music in the Charles Bell Ruin Courtyard. Throughout the historic mill district, the city is transforming sturdy brick warehouses into unique residential, office and retail spaces. Cultural attractions are also gravitating to this area including the MacPhail Center for Music and the acclaimed Guthrie Theater, housed in a bright blue, distinctly non-historic structure designed by starchitect Jean Nouvel.

Cyclists wanting to travel the entire Grand Rounds loop can pedal southeast through another cultural/educational complex formed by a part of the University of Minnesota located on the west bank of the Mississippi River. Heading further downstream, the path offers endless views of the river before veering southwest to pass Minnehaha Falls, immortalized in *The Song of Hiawatha*, Henry Wadsworth Longfellow's 1855 epic poem. For good measure, Minnehaha Park, which is on the National Register of Historic Places, also features a slightly shrunken replica of Longfellow's House in Cambridge, Massachusetts. Further west, the trail meanders along Minnehaha Creek past Lake Hiawatha and Lake Nokomis, which features a beach with a floating swimming dock.

Minneapolis's Historic Mill District has attracted cultural destinations like the Guthrie Theater.

The next district of the Grand Rounds winds through and around a chain of lakes that are hugely popular for boating, canoeing, windsurfing, kayaking and sail boating as well as swimming in summer and ice skating in winter. At the south end of the chain, Lake Harriet features a fancifully-designed band shell reminiscent of its predecessor built in 1891 (Koutsky 2016).

Between Bde Maka Ska Lake and Lake of the Isles, the Grand Rounds Trail intersects the Midtown Greenway, an example of how Minneapolis uses bicycle infrastructure for economic development and alternative transportation as well as recreation and health. Often referred to as a 'bicycle freeway', the Midtown Greenway links with trails extending into the western suburbs and uses primarily grade-separated infrastructure into downtown Minneapolis. It also connects with the eastern as well as the western loop of the Grand Rounds and several intersecting lanes and paths including the Hiawatha Trails and the paths along the Mississippi River. The Midtown Greenway has sparked more than $750 million in new housing development including the Midtown Exchange, a redeveloped 1.2 million square-foot, former Sears distribution center. The Midtown Greenway also attracts office and retail construction such as MoZaic, a mixed-use building featuring a ramp and pedestrian bridge connecting with the trail. Annually accommodating over 1.5 million users, the Midtown Greenway was inducted into the Rail-Trail Hall of Fame in 2015 (Stark 2015; Urban Land Institute 2016).

Today's Lake Harriet Band Shell reimagines one built on the site in 1891.

As of 2016, Minneapolis had over 200 miles of bikeways. Cyclists of all stripes have responded, with bicycle commuting alone increasing by more than 186 percent between 1990 and 2014. Proximity to bike trails boosts median home values here. The League of American Bicyclists has rated the city as a Gold Level Bicycle Friendly Community and ranks Minnesota as the second most bike friendly state in the nation (League of American Bicyclists 2019; Urban Land Institute 2016).

The bicycle infrastructure of Minneapolis is ably supported by a regional network of over 40 trails with a combined length of more than 400 miles including the trail system along the Mississippi River that is part of the 10-state, 3000-mile long Great River Road complex (Rails-to-Trails Conservancy 2019). At the western edge of the region, the 73-mile Luce Line Trail passes or crosses more than a dozen lakes before connecting with the Grand Rounds in Minneapolis. Together, trails in the seven-county metro area were estimated to experience almost 86 million person-days of walking, bicycling, running and inline skating in 2008, generating over $487 million in trail spending, or roughly one quarter of the $2 billion of spending generated by these four activities throughout all of Minnesota (Venegas 2009).

In the 1890s, Minneapolis planned the Grand Rounds and within ten years built over 40 miles of bicycle paths, including trails along Harriet Lake and Minnehaha Creek. By 1903, 30,000 bicycles were licensed in the city. As in most US cities, cars gradually overran Minneapolis in the middle of the 20th Century. But since the 1970s, people here have been rediscovering the health, recreational and mobility advantages of bicycling (Minneapolis 2011). In turn, the city has been supplying bicycling infrastructure to both meet and stimulate demand, often building on the award-winning foundation of the Grand Rounds plan developed over 125 years ago. Consequently, Minneapolis is now consistently in the top tier of bicycle friendly cities in the nation and profiting from the resulting economic impact.

CHAPTER 31

Minuteman Commuter Bikeway, Greater Boston, Massachusetts: Declaring Independence from the Automobile

The Minuteman Commuter Bikeway, which approximates part of Paul Revere's famous 1775 midnight ride, is just one of many trails in Massachusetts where cyclists can experience community character and places of historic significance at a more contemplative and enjoyable pace than is possible through the windshield of a car. In addition, the Bay State is recognizing that bike trails create benefits for health, mobility, clean air, and local economies as well as recreation. True to the virtuous cycle, these impacts are prompting the addition of even more trails.

As most Americans recall, Paul Revere rode his horse from Charlestown to Lexington to warn colonists that British troops were advancing from Boston. Enroute, Revere passed near what is now the Alewife Subway Station in Cambridge, which is also the eastern end of the Minuteman Commuter Bikeway. Near the start of the 10-mile journey on the Minuteman, cyclists can stoke up or recharge at the wildly-popular Kickstand Café in nearby Arlington.

Like Revere, cyclists soon pass the Lexington Green, the town common where British soldiers, on the morning of April 19, 1775, fired on a group of colonial minutemen, named for their ability to assemble at a minute's notice. Lexington Green, now a National Historic Landmark, forms the backdrop for the Lexington Minuteman Statue, a life-size bronze monument of a farmer with musket at the ready. Buckman Tavern, built in 1710, sits opposite the Lexington Green and is also preserved as a U.S. Historic Landmark for its role as a gathering place for the militia. At the north end of Lexington

Green, a meeting house where Reverend Jonas Clarke urged parishioners to resist British rule has been replaced by a classic, white Unitarian Universalist church built in 1847.

From Lexington, the trail heads north and ends at Bedford Depot Park, where the 1877 Freight House of the Boston & Maine Railroad has been restored and repurposed as a snack shop and mini-museum of railroad history. From here, cyclists can use bike-friendly streets and the Reformatory Branch Trail to reach the charming town of Concord, home to Transcendentalist writers including Henry David Thoreau, who transformed a nearby pond into a shrine for environmentalists with his book about living a simple life in the woods called *Walden*.

Lexington Common provides a green backdrop for this statue of a musket-toting Minuteman.

On the way, history buffs will want to stop at the Old North Bridge over the Concord River, where the colonial militia "fired the shot heard round the world", forcing the British to retreat and signaling the start of the American Revolutionary War. Today, the bridge offers a serene spot for contemplation while watching kayakers navigate the placid Concord River.

Uphill from the Old North Bridge, Old Manse was once occupied by Ralph Waldo Emerson and Nathaniel Hawthorne. Further east, bike-friendly roads pass more Emerson and Hawthorne homes as well as that of Louisa May Alcott, author of the beloved novel *Little Women*. Within the Battle Road Unit of Minute Man National Historic Park, cyclists and pedestrians can use the car-free Battle Road to imagine the eight-hour skirmish that took place here on the afternoon of April 19, 1775, as the colonials chased the British back to Boston.

The Minuteman and other bikeways are good for business, health, and mobility as well as facilitating an appreciation of American history. In a 2021 study of four shared-use paths in Massachusetts, MassTrails found that the Minuteman Bikeway produced $2.6 million in total economic impact, supporting 25 jobs and generating $363,000 in state and local taxes. Although the Cape Cod Trail saw fewer trips than the Minuteman, it generated more total economic impact ($9.2 million) likely because the Cape Cod Trail sees a higher percentage of bicycle tourists. The four multiuse trails in this study produce a combined total of $2.8 million in healthcare savings annually with the Minuteman alone contributing $1.4 million every year. By substituting active transportation for motor vehicles, the four trails eliminated 170,638 of vehicle miles traveled (VMT) during a four-month study period in 2019, with the Minuteman alone accounting for a 74,834-mile reduction in VMT. The switch from motor vehicles to active transportation on the four trails was estimated to reduce $23,000 worth of greenhouse gas emissions per average weekday (MassTrails 2021).

Following the success of the Minuteman and other bikeways, Massachusetts has seen a flurry of plans to build more bike trails. Boston aims to more than double bicycle infrastructure within the city limits by 2043, completing a 356-mile system of which over 100 miles will be off-street paths (Boston 2013). The East Coast Greenway envisions a 138-mile spine through Massachusetts from Rhode Island to New Hampshire including the existing 23-mile Charles River Bike Path that follows the Charles River between Waltham and Boston (East Coast Greenway 2021). The Bay State as a whole already offers 412 miles of cycling on 73 rail trails and there are plans to significantly extend that network (Rails-to-Trails Conservancy 2021). These greatly expanded bike networks will create additional opportunities in the Greater Boston Region and all of Massachusetts for more people to declare their independence from the automobile.

CHAPTER 32

Montreal - Quebec, Quebec, Canada: *Route verte* - Green in Many Ways

Quebec's *Route verte*, or green way, is a 5,000-kilometer network of fully-signposted bike lanes and off-road paths, the longest network in North America. *Route verte* clearly earns its name through recreation and mobility powered by human energy rather than climate-altering fossil fuels. In addition, *Route verte* is greening the economy of this Canadian province through the spending, jobs and tax revenues generated by this world-class example of bicycle tourism.

In 1956, a priest named Gabriel Lupien founded a bicycle tourism school that by 1967 became the cycling organization now known as Velo Quebec. In 1992, Velo Quebec presented the concept of a province-wide network of bike paths and routes at the World Cycling Conference in Montreal. The Quebec government authorized Velo Quebec to develop this concept and by 2012, the *Route verte* encompassed 5,000 kilometers stretching from Quebec's western border with Ontario to the Madeleine Island's on the Atlantic coast (Velo Quebec 2017).

Velo Quebec organizes *Route verte* in 12 regions. In Abitibi-Temiscamingue, *Route verte* uses paved road shoulders to carry cyclists through forests dotted with lakes and historic mining towns like Val-d'Or. At Mont-Laurier, cyclists, hikers and cross-country skiers can take the P'tit Train du Nord off-road trail through 232 kilometers of the Laurentian region to Sainte-Jerome before linking to other off-road trails leading to the northern suburbs of Montreal. In a third region, on- and off-road segments connect a dozen towns along the banks of the Ottawa River and approach Montreal from the west (Velo Quebec 2010).

Montreal serves as a major hub of *Route verte*. Here, bikeways branching off from trails along canals and the Saint Lawrence River connect popular destinations including Mount Royal Park, McGill University, the old port and several other historic districts. On St. Helen's Island, a network of bike paths allows exploration of sights remaining from the 1967 World's Fair including a geodesic dome designed by Buckminster Fuller and a sculpture park featuring work by Alexander Calder and other artists. On adjacent Notre Dame Island, cyclists can visit the Montreal Casino and other attractions including a NASCAR race track. Bike trails also lead past Habitat 67, a model housing complex designed for the World's Fair by Moshe Safdie which has become one of Canada's most recognizable architectural landmarks.

Montreal's bike trail network passes this geodesic dome built for the 1967 World's Fair.

Montreal has earned widespread recognition as a bicycle-friendly city in its own right. Montreal and Vancouver, British Columbia are the only two cities in North America to be listed in the top 20 cities worldwide according to the 2019 Copenhagenize Index, which calls itself the most comprehensive and holistic ranking of bicycle-friendly cities on the planet. Not resting on its laurels, Montreal is now adding 184 kilometers of protected, one-way, express cycle tracks to its existing 80-kilometer network (Copenhagenize 2020).

Route verte offers various ways of riding between Montreal and Quebec City. The most direct option combines off-road trails with bike lanes on the historic Chemin du Roy, a centuries-old highway along the northern banks of the St. Lawrence River. A lengthier southern loop follows the Richelieu River past the remnants of forts originally built in the 17th Century and fought over by the French, British, Native Americans and colonists during numerous conflicts including the American Revolutionary War. Rail trails provide off-road cycling for most of this 400km ride, which also doubles as a major segment of the Great Trail that will eventually cross Canada from the Atlantic to the Pacific (The Great Trail, 2020; Velo Quebec 2010).

The City of Quebec forms another unofficial hub for the *Route verte*, with trails radiating north to Pointe-Taillon National Park, south to the US border and east to the classic seascapes of the Gaspe Peninsula and Magdalen Islands (Velo Quebec 2010). Of course, Quebec City itself is also a bicycle tourist magnet. The neighborhood of Old Quebec is a UNESCO World Heritage Site. Here, the Upper Town is dominated by the 19th Century Chateau Frontenac, a classic hotel originally built by the Canadian Pacific Railway company. The Lower Town can be reached by a funicular and offers a maze of cobblestone lanes lined with shops and restaurants.

Along the 5,000-kilometer system, Velo Quebec has certified 500 bicycle-friendly establishments under its *Bienvenue cyclistes!* program including 400 hotels and bed-and-breakfasts as well as 100 campgrounds (Velo Quebec 2016). When other businesses are added to the mix, the economic benefits are significant. In 2000, cyclists on *Route verte* spent $95.4 million CAD, ($64.6 million USD), supporting 2,000 jobs and generating $15.1 million in tax revenues for the Quebec government as well as $11.9 million for the government of Canada (Velo Quebec 2003).

When considering all of Quebec as well as *Route verte*, the economic impact is even greater. Bicycle tourism in the province generated $700 million in spending in 2015, creating 6,800 jobs and generating $100 million in tax revenues for the Quebec government as well as $38 million for the Canadian government, illustrating that it pays to go the green way (Velo Quebec 2016).

CHAPTER 33

New Hampshire: Bridging the Old and the New

New Hampshire has a relatively large bicycle trail system for a small state and the multiple benefits have not gone unnoticed. Efforts are underway to expand this network as an economic development tool as well as a path toward improving mobility, health, and quality of life.

The college town of Keene, New Hampshire sits at the intersection of two sizable rail trails, making it an ideal base camp for multiday excursions through the surrounding New England countryside. The 22-mile Ashuelot Recreational Rail Trail, featuring four 19th-century covered bridges, begins at its intersection with the Cheshire Rail Trail in downtown Keene. It heads south and passes the campus of Keene State College before crossing the Ashuelot River and reaching the farms and forests of Cheshire County. Curving west to link with another trail at the Connecticut River, the trail passes the 1859 Cresson Covered Bridge, the 1832 Thompson Covered Bridge, the 1862 Slate Covered Bridge, and the 169-foot-long Ashelot Covered Bridge which was built in 1864 and still carries motor vehicles (and bikes) to this day.

In 2017, the Industrial Heritage Trail joined the northern and southern segments of the 33-mile Cheshire Rail Trail in Keene. The northern section is occasionally steep and rocky but, from August through October, cyclists can fortify themselves with apples, bakery, and other local goodies at Alyson's Orchard or stop in for a tasting at the Summit Winery. As the trail nears Keene, Stonewall Farm runs a store featuring hand-made ice cream and organic foods produced using the regenerative practices taught here.

The Cheshire Rail Trail enters Keene near the Colony Mill, which started life in 1815 as the Faulkner & Colony Woolen Mill and remained in operation until 1954. Today, the mill has been restored, placed in the National Register of Historic Places, and converted primarily into loft apartments. However, the retooled complex is also home to the Elm City Brewing Company, which features beers with locally-flavored names like Keene Kolsch and Peachy Keene.

The Cheshire Rail Trail then travels through the heart of Keene, where cyclists have many additional options for food, drink, and lodging. Keene is home to 16 landmarks in the National Register of Historic Places, including a classic white 1786 church with a tall white steeple that adds a perfect focal point to the town's classic New England Central Square.

The 1847 Cheshire Railroad Stone Arch Bridge, now part of the Cheshire Rail Trail, is one the best-preserved stone arch bridges of its era.

As the trail crosses Main Street, a mural depicts three generations of locomotives that helped make Keene a regional industrial center back in the day. This is one of 16 murals painted on the sides of buildings here by The Walldogs, an organization of artists that swoop into a town and complete several murals during a 3- to 5-day creative festival. The Walldogs artworks illustrate historic themes like the Keene Base Ball Club launched in 1860, the Trinity Bicycle Works founded in here in 1897, and the Keene Evening Sentinel which published its first newspaper in 1799.

Heading south out of Keene, the trail passes over the Branch River on the Cheshire Railroad Stone Arch Bridge built in 1847 and considered one the best-preserved stone arch bridges of its era. After pedaling for a few miles, cyclists can have a brew or two while listening to live music in the beer garden at Granite Roots Brewing in the Town of Troy. Just outside of Troy, hikers flock to climb the 3,000+ foot summit of Mount Monadnock partly because of its unrivaled view and partly because of its association with famous authors, including Ralph Waldo Emerson, Henry David Thoreau, and Mark Twain. Further south, the trail passes Rhododendron State Park before reaching its end near the Massachusetts border.

Over $35 million is spent every year in New Hampshire on bicycles and other gear for walkers, runners, and cyclists. The multiplier effect increases that amount to a total annual impact of over $48 million in sales, supporting 335 jobs. In addition, more than $28 million is generated by out-of-state bicycle tourists paying for lodging (45%), food/beverage (24%), retail (17%), transportation (9%), and entertainment (5%). When secondary impacts are added, bicycle tourism produces $43 million in sales, almost 400 jobs, $14 million in labor income, and almost $24 million in value added (Alta 2020).

New Hampshire recognizes the positive return on investments in bicycling infrastructure. The Granite State already has 75 bike trails totaling 562 miles (Rails-to-Trails Conservancy 2021). Considering New Hampshire's 2020 population of 1,377,529 residents, the state already has one of the highest, if not the highest mileage-per-capita ratio in the country. In 2002, it was estimated that the state had 1,200 miles of abandoned corridors, mostly from old logging railroads, creating many opportunities to expand the current network (Penna 2002).

Not surprisingly, trail network expansion is on the minds of many advocates in New Hampshire. The Rails-to-Trails Conservancy is working on 21 projects that would add another 286 miles to the system (Rails-to-Trails Conservancy 2021). In fact, New Hampshire may become the first state to complete its portion of the East Coast Greenway envisioned to link 450 communities in 15 states with a 3,000-mile trail from Florida to Maine (East Coast Greenway 2019).

CHAPTER 34

New Jersey: Cultivating the Garden State

New Jersey occupies the center of America's Mid-Atlantic megalopolis, the conurbation stretching from Boston to Washington, D.C. with a population of over 50 million people. The Garden State already has a sizeable number of multi-use trails, including the 72-mile Delaware and Raritan Canal State Park. In addition, supporters of the East Coast Greenway and other organizations are working to build a fully-connected trail network providing millions of people with alternative transportation options, more places for healthful exercise, property value increases, and a proven catalyst for economic development.

New Jersey currently offers 81 bike trails with a combined length of roughly 435 miles (Traillink 2021). These trails are one of many reasons why active transportation-related infrastructure, businesses, and events added over $497 million to the economy of New Jersey in 2011 and supported 4,018 jobs with a payroll of more than $153 million. This activity was estimated to add $278 million to New Jersey's GDP in 2011 and contribute $49 million in tax revenues (Brown *et. al* 2011).

New Jersey is also integral to the plans for various trail networks including the East Coast Greenway envisioned to ultimately link 450 communities in 15 states from Florida to Maine with a 3,000-mile trail system. The Delaware River Watershed portion of the East Coast Greenway planned for parts of Maryland, Pennsylvania, Delaware, and New Jersey in the Delaware River Watershed will connect 34 municipalities, eight counties, six state parks and a national wildlife refuge. This planned network includes nine significant trail systems, including the Circuit Trails network described in the chapter on Philadelphia. The greenway will also incorporate the existing Delaware and Lehigh Trail on the Pennsylvania side of the Delaware River and a planned trail on the New Jersey side of the river between Philadelphia and Trenton, New Jersey (Econsult 2019).

In New Jersey, the East Coast Greenway is planned to head east from Trenton and cross over into New York at Jersey City. Fortunately, a portion of the existing 72-mile Delaware and Raritan (D&R) Canal State Park Trail already provides over half of the East Coast Greenway route in New Jersey. The D&R starts north of Frenchtown, New Jersey and follows the east bank if the Delaware River through Lambertville, which is part of the tourism hub surrounding New Hope, Pennsylvania on the other side of the river. Further downstream, the trail passes Washington Crossing State Park where George Washington and the Continental Army landed on Christmas night 1776 and secured a much-needed victory by capturing 900 surprised Hessian mercenaries in Trenton.

This bridge tender's station, built about 1830, is one of many canal-era structures still remaining on the D&R Trail.

Within the City of Trenton, the D&R Trail angles northeast parallel to US Highway 1 before returning to the canal towpath. The D&R Canal, which began construction in 1830, linked Trenton and New Brunswick. Like other canals, the D&R was gradually replaced by railroads, which were much less susceptible to weather. But fortunately, this trail retains many historic structures from the canal era including the remnants of locks, cobblestone spillways, stone-arch culverts, and 19th century bridges complete with bridge tender's stations.

Between Trenton and New Brunswick, cyclists have the option of peeling off the D&R Trail and cycling into Princeton where they can explore the

Princeton Historic District on miles of car-free paths throughout the campus. Princeton University was chartered in 1746 and now preserves the largest concentration of National Register landmarks in the State of New Jersey. Nassau Hall, built in 1756, saw British troops surrender to George Washington after the 1777 Battle of Princeton and briefly served as the U.S. capitol in 1783. Architectural icons and curiosities appear around every corner here, like the Ionic Greek temple design of Whig Hall and the Richardsonian Romanesque flavor of Richardson Auditorium.

A 2019 study estimated that the completion of the 175 miles of multi-use trails planned for the Delaware Watershed segment of the East Coast Greenway will cost $239 million. In return, these trails will add an estimated $1.77 billion of value to properties within one-quarter mile of the network, save over $45 million in healthcare costs annually, generate $840 million per year in tourism benefits, and produce almost $40 million of ecosystem services including carbon sequestration, water supply/quality, flood mitigation, air quality and wildlife habitat (Econsult 2019). In other words, the benefits of completing a network of trails within this densely-populated region more than justify the investment.

CHAPTER 35

New Mexico: Gearing Up for Bicycles

New Mexico is not yet known as a bicycling paradise. But Albuquerque and Santa Fe are experiencing notable activity on their multiuse trails. And New Mexico itself recently adopted a statewide bicycle network plan that aims to improve health and the environment as well as generate economic benefits by boosting tourism, promoting development and offering mobility options that are much easier on family budgets than owning and operating a car.

In its current Bicycle Friendly State Report Card, the League of American Bicyclists congratulated New Mexico on adopting its 2018 Prioritized Statewide Bicycle Network Plan and the Rio Grande Trail Master Plan (League of American Bicyclists 2020). The statewide plan establishes a hierarchy of bicycle infrastructure with Tier 1 routes having the highest level of regional benefits as bikeways and warranting the highest level of bicycle infrastructure (New Mexico 2018).

In 2017, New Mexico began work on a master plan to create a 500-mile long, cross-state recreational trail for hiking, biking and horseback riding along the Rio Grande River as it flows from Colorado south to El Paso, Texas. The Rio Grande Trail will eventually connect four national wildlife refuges, six national monuments, one national heritage area and six state parks while passing through ten counties and more than 22 cities and towns (New Mexico 2017). The northernmost portion of the trail will meander through the Northern Rio Grande National Heritage Area which includes Santa Fe, Rio Arriba and Taos counties (Northern Rio Grande NHA 2020).

Cyclists can currently ride portions of this cross-state trail in places like Albuquerque, where the 16-mile Paseo del Bosque Multiuse Trail links Rio Grande Valley State Park, the Rio Grande Nature Center, the Albuquerque BioPark and the National Hispanic Cultural Center (Albuquerque 2020). Other bikeways and bike lanes intersect with Paseo del Bosque, leading to the 27,000-student University of New Mexico, the Maxell Museum of Anthropology, and Petroglyph National Monument, where more than 25,000 images were carved into volcanic rock hundreds of years ago (NPS 2019). The city is also working on a 50-mile activity loop that will ultimately connect downtown Albuquerque with Old Town, the museum district and Balloon Fiesta Park, where over 500 hot air balloons ascend during the nine-day International Balloon Fiesta every October.

Santa Fe has also seen the advantages of investing in bicycling. In order to boost ecotourism and economic development, Santa Fe County's Open Space and Trails Program has preserved 24 properties and trails including the nationally recognized Santa Fe Rail Trail which carries cyclists 18 miles south of Santa Fe on the right of way once used by the Atchison, Topeka & Santa Fe Railroad. The county is also cooperating with the City of Santa Fe on development of the Santa Fe River Greenway, a paved multiuse trail starting in downtown Santa Fe and meandering beside this river for 18 miles (Santa Fe County 2020). From Santa Fe, cyclists can use one of New Mexico's Tier 1 bike routes to reach the Wells Petroglyph Preserves on Black Mesa, the Taos Pueblo, and Chimayo sanctuary, the destination of 300,000 Catholic pilgrims every year.

New Mexico is promoting bicycle tourism within the Northern Rio Grande National Heritage Area.

A 2012 report estimated that bicycling contributed over $300 million annually to the New Mexico economy in equipment purchases and travel related expenses (Atencio 2012). Since the time of that estimate, Albuquerque has committed to adding another 300 miles of bikeways and 159 miles of trails to a network that already has 620 miles of on- and off-road bicycle infrastructure (Albuquerque 2015). Similarly, the 2019 Santa Fe Metropolitan Planning Organization Bicycle Master Plan aims to almost double the region's bikeways and trails by 2024 and elevate the City of Santa Fe from a Silver level to a Gold level Bicycle Friendly Community (Santa Fe MPL 2019). Recognizing the economic as well as health, mobility, environmental and recreational benefits, New Mexico is clearly gearing up for bicycles.

CHAPTER 36

Philadelphia, Pennsylvania: At Liberty to Bicycle

Visitors have historically been drawn to Philadelphia by attractions like the Liberty Bell, Independence Hall, the Franklin Institute, and the Philadelphia Museum of Art. The international significance of Philadelphia's legacy was recognized in 2015 when it became UNESCO's first World Heritage City in the United States. Recently, the City of Brotherly Love has started to add 800 miles of other reasons to visit and live here with ambitious plans to build an interconnected multi-use trail system that serves every city neighborhood and extends into the surrounding countryside. Several studies confirm that these trails are good for the economy as well as property values, health, mobility, and overall quality of life.

In the 1800s, docks, rail yards, slaughterhouses, and dumps lined the banks of the Schuylkill River as it meandered through Philadelphia and merged with the Delaware River. By the late 1900s, freeways and rail lines remained after other uses had largely abandoned the waterfront. Transformation began in 1992 when the city cleaned up the area and built a paved trail. Over the next ten years, the Schuylkill River Development Corporation, the city, and partners spent $86 million improving the greenway and its adjacent neighborhoods, winning several awards in the process. Arguably their crowning achievement came in 2014 with the opening of the Schuylkill Banks Boardwalk, the 15-foot-wide concrete pathway that spans a segment of the river where the banks were too narrow to accommodate the trail (Schuylkill Banks 2021).

North of the Schuylkill Banks Boardwalk, the Schuylkill River Trail passes the Philadelphia Museum of Art with the monumental staircase made famous by *Rocky*, the 1976 boxing film in which Sylvester Stallone trains for his title bout by running the stairs. Bike lanes on the Benjamin Franklin Parkway invite an easy spin to other cultural landmarks including the Rodin Museum, the Franklin Institute, and the Barnes Foundation Museum, home to a world-class collection of modern art by such masters as Renoir, Cezanne, Matisse, Picasso, Van Gogh, and Modigliani.

The Schuylkill Banks Boardwalk spans a segment of the river where the shore is too narrow to accommodate the trail.

The Schuylkill River Trail separates the Philadelphia Museum of Art from the Fairmont Water Works, a National Historic Landmark dating from 1815 that now serves as an environmental education center. Upstream, the trail passes the ornate Victorian architecture of the 100-plus year-old rowing clubs on Boathouse Row, the epicenter of regattas on a stretch of the river becalmed by the Fairmont Dam. Further north, cyclists encounter the 1887 Turtle Rock Lighthouse, built in 1887 as a navigational aide for rowers as well as ships carrying coal to Philadelphia from upstate Pennsylvania.

The Schuylkill River Trail passes Turtle Rock Lighthouse, built in 1887 to guide ships carrying coal from upstate Pennsylvania.

Further north, the Schuylkill River Trail links Philadelphia with landmarks from the American Revolution and Industrial Revolution within the Schuylkill River Greenways National Heritage Area, which encompasses parts of five Pennsylvania counties. Planned to ultimately reach 130 gap-free miles, the southernmost trail segment currently extends for 30 miles from southwestern Philadelphia to Valley Forge National Historic Park which preserves the site where George Washington and the Continental Army were encamped through the winter of 1777-1778.

North of Valley Forge, the 20-mile Perkiomen Trail branches east past the John James Audubon Center at Mill Grove where the young naturalist/artist developed the skills that ultimately led to his monumental work: *Birds of America*. Although the Perkiomen Trail primarily serves local residents, it still generates over $2 million per year at trailside restaurants plus sales of beverages and soft goods (Knoch and Tomes 2008).

Heading west, the Schuylkill River Trail reaches the City of Reading, home of the Reading Railroad which was long ago absorbed by Conrail but still runs on Monopoly game boards. After several yet-to-be-closed gaps, the trail ends at Pottsville near the headwaters of the Schuylkill River. In 2009, users of the Schuylkill River Trail were predominantly day trippers but nevertheless spent over $7 million on equipment and soft goods annually (Tomes and Knoch 2009).

In a 2006 poll, 77 percent of residents and business owners expressed support for maintaining and restoring open space along waterways within the City of Philadelphia. A 2010 study confirmed that a completed 50-mile waterfront greenway in the city would generate hard-to-quantify benefits for eco-mobility, storm-water management, wildlife habitat, air quality, and carbon sequestration plus an added ability to attract and retain employers and employees. This study also estimated that a fully-connected greenway would generate $50 million per year in tourist expenditures, add 400 jobs with total earnings of $15 million, and generate $4 million in state and local taxes. In addition, the study calculated an annual recreational value of $28 million to Philadelphia residents who use the greenways, $20 million per year of health care cost savings, and $260 million in increased property value for homes within a quarter mile of the waterfront (Econsult 2010).

Philadelphia has become the hub of many planned trail networks. The Schuylkill River Trail incorporates a section of the East Coast Greenway, the corridor envisioned to extend for 3,000 miles from Florida to Maine. The Schuylkill River Trail also forms a part of the September 11th National Memorial Trail connecting the Pentagon Memorial in Washington DC with the Flight 93 Memorial near Johnstown, Pennsylvania.

Greater Philadelphia aims to extend and link its many trails to make an 800-mile network through nine counties in Pennsylvania and New Jersey known as the Circuit Trails. In addition to the economic benefits from the trails mentioned above, the network includes others like the 165-mile Delaware and Lehigh Trail estimated to have generated an economic impact in 2012 of $19 million (Tomes 2012).

The Circuit Coalition, which includes more than 40 partner organizations, recognizes that trails improve health, mobility, property values, and quality of life as well as business. The Circuit Trails are fortunate to have financial support from many sources, including the William Penn Foundation, as well as political leadership, as illustrated by this 2015 statement from Michael Nutter, the former mayor of Philadelphia: "Of the top ten big cities of America, Philadelphia has the highest percentage of bicycle commuters per capita… Bicycling is a fundamental aspect of this city's mobility, economic development, public health, and environmental sustainability" (ULI 2016, p39).

CHAPTER 37

Pittsburgh, Pennsylvania: From Steel City to Cycle Town

Pittsburgh was once the quintessential industrial city, belching smoke from coal-fired furnaces that produced over half of the nation's total output of steel. Bicycle trails have now replaced the steel plants that lined Pittsburgh's rivers in the past. Today, this evolution seems too logical not to be inevitable. But it took a decade or two for dedicated advocates and visionary public officials to prove that trails are essential to building cities where people want to live and where businesses want to grow.

Before the 1870s, residents enjoyed swimming and boating along the banks of the three rivers that define Pittsburgh. For the next century, these shorelines were taken over by one of the largest steel-making and manufacturing complexes in the world. As heavy industry began to leave, Pittsburgh launched a revival of its blighted riverfronts starting with the 1970 construction of Three Rivers Stadium, once the home of Pittsburgh's major-league baseball and football teams. In 1976, the Pittsburgh History & Landmarks Foundation began demonstrating the wisdom of adaptive-reuse by transforming a former railroad terminal into Station Square, now a successful mixed-use commercial center. Other brownfields were redeveloped, including the Carnegie Science Center on the banks of the Ohio River. In 1991, Mayor Sophie Masloff authorized the first segment of what would become the Three Rivers Heritage Trail on land formally occupied by the steel plants known as the South Side Works, initiating what was to become the Three Rivers Heritage Trail (Knoch 2015; Van Zandt, 2014).

Today, the Three Rivers Heritage Trail is a 24-mile network formed from eight interconnected segments. The North Shore segment, which stretches for seven miles of the Allegheny and Ohio riverfronts, attracts 177,000 trips per year, the highest usage in the entire trail system. Here, fans can walk or bike to take in Pittsburgh Steelers football games at Heinz Field or Pittsburgh

Pirates baseball games at PNC Park. The trail passes the Warhol, a seven-story, industrial warehouse repurposed as an art museum with the world's largest collection of works by Andy Warhol, who grew up and attended school in Pittsburgh. Across from Heinz Field, the Carnegie Science Center is known for the Buhl Planetarium and Roboworld, the planet's largest permanent collection of robot memorabilia. From here, a bike lane leads to the National Aviary, the nation's largest bird zoo and also an important protector of endangered avian species.

The Southside segment of Pittsburgh's Three Rivers Heritage Trail begins at the bottom of the Duquesne Incline, a cable car that takes riders to bluff tops offering a bird's eye view of the city.

On the south side of the Allegheny River, the downtown segment of the Three Rivers Trail links historic, commercial and cultural centers. At "The Point", where the Allegheny and Monongahela rivers meet to form the Ohio River, the Blockhouse stands as the only surviving structure from Fort Pitt, the military base that was pivotal in the Revolutionary War and formed the nucleus of modern-day Pittsburgh. Heading northeast, the Three Rivers Trail passes beneath the cantilevered floors of the David L. Lawrence Convention Center, the nation's highest-rated LEED Platinum certified convention center. Along the way, trail spurs extend into Pittsburgh's Cultural District, featuring theaters, performance centers and museums.

A five-mile loop connects several popular destinations on opposite sides of the Monongahela River. The Southside segment, which alone experiences over 80,000 trips per year, begins at the Duquesne Incline, a cable car that takes riders to bluff tops offering a bird's eye view of the heart of Pittsburgh. Further east, the trail passes Station Square, formerly the terminal for the Pittsburgh and Lake Erie Railroad, now transformed into a mixed-use commercial center listed in the National Register of Historic Places (Station Square 2020). As another popular rest-stop, the Hofbrauhaus offers an interior modeled after the famous beerhall in Munich as well as an extensive outdoor deck overlooking the trail.

Cyclists can enjoy German dishes and brews on the huge deck of Hofbrauhaus Pittsburgh overlooking the Three Rivers Heritage Trail.

Cyclists can reach the north bank of the Monongahela River on the Hot Metal Bridge, which once was used to speed molten iron in ladle cars between the blast furnaces on the northern bank and the open-hearth steel furnaces on the south bank. Heading west on the Eliza Furnace Trail takes bicyclists back to the heart of Pittsburgh known as the Golden Triangle. In the opposite direction, cyclists approach 456-acre Schenley Park, home to the Phipps Conservatory, and Botanical Gardens, originally built in 1893 and now on the National Register of Historic Places.

Using a bike lane in Schenley Drive, cyclists can pedal north into the campus of Carnegie Mellon University, featuring several landmark buildings including the Carnegie Museum of Natural History, built in 1896 by Andrew Carnegie, the steel baron and philanthropist who bankrolled over 2,500 libraries around the world. Next door, the University of Pittsburgh is home to 33,000 students and the 42-story Cathedral of Learning, the tallest academic building in the Western hemisphere.

The Three Rivers Trail generates economic returns as well as healthful exercise, recreation and eco-mobility. The trail experiences 820,000 trips per year and generated a total economic impact of $8.3 million in 2014 (Knoch 2015). Not surprisingly, regional leaders are doubling down, implementing plans to extend the trail an additional 26 miles up the Allegheny River as part of the envisioned 261-mile Erie to Pittsburgh Trail (Lynch 2019). When the completed Erie to Pittsburgh Trail joins the 150-mile Great Allegheny Passage (GAP), which in turn links to the 185-mile C&O Canal Towpath, Pittsburg will become the hub of a trail system stretching for almost 600 miles from Lake Erie to Washington, DC.

CHAPTER 38

Portland, Oregon: Bicycling and Portland's Green Dividend

Portland and Oregon are well known for leadership in sustainability in general and bicycling in particular. Some people wrongly assume that people here are making sacrifices for the good of the environment. But experts calculate that the savings reaped by reduced car dependency create a stronger local economy as well as cleaner air, better health and greater enjoyment of beautiful natural surroundings.

Not surprisingly, Portland's love affair with bicycles started long ago. The 1903 Olmstead Plan proposed the 40-Mile Loop, a greenway connecting parks and other destinations while encircling much of what is now a metropolitan area with over 2.7 million people. Over the last 100-plus years, Portland has made much of that dream a reality. A big step toward completion came in 1990 when the city acquired most of the right of way for the Springwater Corridor, now a 21.5-mile path inducted in the Rail-Trail Hall of Fame. Connecting with the East Esplanade Trail at the edge of downtown, this trail follows the Willamette River and Johnson Creek through Portland neighborhoods, natural areas and farmland to the City of Gresham, which explains why it attracts 1.2 million users per year (40-Mile Loop Land Trust 2019; Rails-to-Trails Conservancy 2011).

Other completed and planned portions of the 40-Mile Loop pass 33,000-student Mt. Hood Community College, several parks along the shores of the Columbia River and the Portland International Airport before circling the 2,000-acre Smith and Bybee natural area, one of the country's largest urban freshwater wetlands and home to numerous species including bald eagles, beaver and painted turtles. After crossing the Willamette River on the historic St. Johns Bridge, loopers can park their bikes and hike the 30-mile Wildwood Trail that meanders through Forest Park, once a logged-and-abandoned mountainside that today stands as living proof of Portland's commitment to the restoration and preservation of nature (Pruetz 2009).

Returning to downtown, the 40-Mile Loop enters Tom McCall Waterfront Park, created when Portland and Oregon removed Harbor Drive in 1974 and replaced it with a green space that now serves as the city's front lawn. Today this park is home to several festivals including Portland's Rose Festival, the venerable celebration held every June since 1907. From Waterfront Park, bridges cross the Willamette River to the Eastbank Esplanade, effectively creating a 2.5-mile inner loop. One segment of the Esplanade is formed by a 1,200-foot-long floating bike/walkway, the longest one of its kind in the United States (Portland Parks & Recreation 2019). From the Esplanade, bikeways radiate east to several destinations including the Oregon Convention Center and Moda Arena, home court for the Portland Trailblazers and home rink for the Portland Winterhawks.

Portland's car-free Tilikum Crossing Bridge carries only trams, pedestrians and cyclists.

The planned 40-Mile Loop has expanded to more than 140 miles throughout Multnomah County, connecting to more than 30 parks (40-Mile Loop Land Trust 2019). Portland alone has built 365 miles of bikeways, including 85 miles of paths and over 35 miles of infrastructure physically separated from car traffic. In response, between 2000 and 2017, commuting by bicycle here increased by 374 percent. Today over 6 percent of commuting in Portland occurs on bicycles, the highest proportion of any large city in the nation. In recognition of these accomplishments, Portland is the only large US city to receive a bicycle-friendly community rating of 'platinum' from the League of American Bicyclists (League of American Bicyclists 2019; Portland Bureau of Transportation 2019).

The local economy benefits in many ways from its emphasis on bicycling. Portland's Green Dividend refers to the fact that the less people drive, the less they spend on driving and the more money they have to spend on other things. According to a 2007 study, since Portlanders drive 20 percent less than average Americans, they have an extra $1.1 billion in their pockets. Furthermore, reducing expenditures on cars and gas (which primarily leave the state), this $1.1 billion has a better chance of being spent in economic sectors with higher local multiplier effects including restaurants and brewpubs. Of course, transit, walking, and compact development as well as bicycling account for Portland's lower auto-dependency. But together, the green dividend concept suggests that Portland's economy is strong because of, rather than despite, its sustainability successes (Cortright 2007).

Vying for a piece of the Portland Green Dividend, developers here are designing buildings geared predominantly to cyclists, such as a multi-use building with housing above a brewpub on the North Williams Avenue bikeway which features bike storage instead of any dedicated car parking. Businesses are attracted to bikeways because cyclists can easily make multiple stops, particularly when convenient bike parking is available in the form of a bike corral replacing a car parking space that was previously located in front of a store or restaurant (Pruetz 2013). As one measure of the popularity of bicycle-supported business, Portland has installed over 6,000 bike racks in public rights of way, including 158 bike corrals requested by adjacent businesses who understand the rewards of catering to cyclists (Portland Bureau of Transportation 2019).

Even in bicycle-friendly Portland, some business owners resist eliminating on-street parking for bike lanes or bike corrals. However, surveys of customers at Portland bars, convenience stores and restaurants find that cyclists spend less per visit than motorists but tend to visit more often and consequently spend almost 25 percent more per month than their car-driving counterparts (Clifton, Morrissey & Ritter 2012).

Oregon offers more than 525 miles of bicycle trails including the 109-mile-long OC&E Trail and the Row River Trail, part of the Covered Bridges Scenic Bikeway (Rails-to-Trails Conservancy 2019). The state recognizes the economic importance of bicycle-related travel on these off-road trails as well as its robust network of bicycle routes. One study estimated that traveling cyclists spent almost $400 million in Oregon in 2012, supporting 4,630 jobs with a payroll of $102 million and tax receipts of almost $18 million. Within that total, the Portland metro area captured $89 million in spending, accounting for 700 jobs, $18.7 in earnings and $4.1 million in state and local tax revenues (Dean Runyan Associates 2013). Consistent with these statewide findings, the Historic Columbia River State Trail alone was found to attract 730,000 cyclists annually, resulting in over $21 million in spending and 273 jobs (Dean Runyan Associates 2014).

Portland's 1903 Olmstead Plan stressed interconnectedness as essential to building a world class park system. Over the intervening 116 years, Portland gradually assembled a 365-mile network of bikeways, including a regional-scale loop linking residential neighborhoods, civic institutions, schools, jobs and businesses as well as parks. That connectivity goes a long way to explaining why Portland is usually ranked as the top US cycling city and achieves a higher proportion of bicycle commuters than any other large American city. And inspirationally, Portland's Green Dividend proves that cycle-centric lifestyles are good for local economies as well as health and happiness.

CHAPTER 39

Raleigh-Durham, North Carolina: New Roles for Tobacco Legacy

The East Coast Greenway envisions a 3,000-mile, people-powered trail connecting 15 states and 450 communities from Maine to Florida. As of 2017, roughly one third of that total route exists (Abrams 2017). Several cities, towns and counties in the Raleigh-Durham region are turning this dream into a reality by linking segments to the American Tobacco Trail to create over 70 miles of off-road, multiuse pathways. In addition to health, recreation and active transportation benefits, researchers conclude that this network in also good for business.

Over a century ago, the Norfolk Southern Railroad shipped tobacco from Wake, Chatham and Durham counties to the center of Durham and the American Tobacco Company, which at one time controlled roughly 90 percent of all tobacco business in the world (Brightleaf Square 2018). Today, cyclists can pedal the 22-mile American Tobacco Trail, or ATT, to the American Tobacco Historic District in downtown Durham, where the original red brick manufacturing buildings have been repurposed for apartments, shops, offices, restaurants and live entertainment venues. In the shadow of the huge Lucky Strike smokestack, the firm's old power plant has been transformed into the Full Frame Theater, now home to the Full Frame Film Festival and the Duke University Center for Documentary Studies.

Bike lanes link the historic district to Brightleaf Square, originally a complex of tobacco warehouses now restored for housing, offices, shops and restaurants. Two miles further west, cyclists reach the campus of Duke University, which began life as a school for Methodist and Quaker families in 1832. Today Duke boasts an enrollment of over 15,000 students and is ranked number nine among national universities (U.S. News and World Report 2018). Over 300,000 visitors from around the world stroll the award-winning grounds of the Duke Gardens in the heart of the university campus

(Duke Gardens 2018).

Fans of both baseball and bicycling can pedal to the home stadium of the Durham Bulls directly across from the ATT's northern trailhead. Beer lovers may prefer to watch the games from a deck overlooking the ballfield at Tobacco Road Sports Café which features Brightleaf IPA and other specialties of Tobacco Road Brewing. For something completely different, the 2,700-seat Durham Performing Arts Center presents plays, concerts and other live entertainment just a few steps from the stadium. Similar events are offered at the Carolina Theater, a beautifully restored Beaux Arts building dating from 1926.

Bike lanes link the American Tobacco Trail with Brightleaf Square, former tobacco warehouses now restored for housing, offices, shops and restaurants.

Before reaching the southern end of the 22-mile ATT, cyclists can use an on-road route to reach the Town of Cary's White Oak Greenway which connects with the Black Creek Greenway, both segments of the East Coast Greenway. These paths link several parks and include a public art trail called Arts Alfresco. Here, artist Brad Spencer has created wonderful excuses to pause a while to contemplate fanciful sculptures fashioned from native North Carolina brick material. At Lake Crabtree County Park, the Black Creek Greenway ends but another multiuse trail continues into William B. Umstead State Park, 5,599 acres of relatively undisturbed nature best enjoyed on foot, by bike, or on horseback.

Studies verify that the greenways here are good for business. On the

American Tobacco Trail alone, roughly 480,000 annual bike and pedestrian trips were estimated to generate $5.6 million in sales revenue. This level of business output supports 78 jobs and creates $2.2 million in labor income. In addition, trip expenditures contribute $219,700 in local and state taxes (North Carolina Department of Transportation 2018).

According to another study, bicyclists pedal over 11 million miles and pedestrians walk more than 7 million miles every year on the 70 miles of trails that form the spine of the East Coast Greenway in the Raleigh-Durham region. This level of use generates over $87 million in economic benefits annually and supports 800 temporary and permanent jobs. This study also found that the health, recreation and active transportation benefits add $164 million to regional property value (East Coast Greenway Alliance 2017).

The trail system in the Triangle region reportedly constitutes the most fully realized metropolitan segment of the planned 3,000-mile East Coast Greenway (Abrams 2017). The economic studies cited above demonstrate that it makes economic sense for Raleigh-Durham to be bullish about bicycles.

CHAPTER 40

Razorback Regional Greenway, Northwest Arkansas: On Track to Becoming a World-Class Bicycling Destination

Arkansas may not be the first place you would expect to find a bike trail linking five cities within a 132-mile regional network. But the Razorback Regional Greenway officially opened in Northwest Arkansas in 2015 and it is already demonstrating that investments in bicycle infrastructure pay off in terms of wealth as well as health and happiness. As you would expect, the jurisdictions are responding to this success by making further trail expansions.

The Razorback Regional Greenway is a 37-mile bikeway spine linking the cities of Bentonville, Rogers, Lowell, Springdale and Fayetteville. According to a prominent bicycle infrastructure planning firm: "The project serves as a national model for active transportation, green infrastructure, healthy living, sustainable economic development, and public-private partnerships" (Alta Planning + Design 2017 P14). The partnership included the Walton Family Foundation and the U.S. Department of Transportation with assistance from the Northwest Arkansas Regional Planning Commission and local governments (Alta Planning + Design 2017).

Although considered as a single trail, the Razorback Greenway is actually a chain of 19 linked trails, beginning at Bella Vista Lake near the northern city limits of Bentonville (Rail-to-Trails Conservancy 2020). Bentonville is home to six segments of the Razorback Greenway, eight additional intra-city trails plus several miles of planned trails (Bentonville 2020). Not surprisingly, Bentonville has been recognized as a Bicycle Friendly Community by the League of American Bicyclists. As an indication of the success of the

Razorback Greenway, the League has also given its Bronze-level ranking to Springdale and its Silver-level ranking to Fayetteville as well as the two-county Northwest Arkansas region (League of American Bicyclists 2020).

In Bentonville, the Razorback Greenway passes through the Crystal Bridges complex, which includes an art museum, performance center, and sculpture garden enclosed within nature-inspired architecture designed by Moshe Safdie. The grounds are also home to the Bachman House, an example of Frank Lloyd Wright's Usonian design which he developed as a model for affordable American housing. In addition to art and architecture, visitors can explore nature on eight trails within Crystal Bridges including a hiking trail leading to Crystal Springs, the natural spring that gave this complex its name (Crystal Bridges Museum of American Art 2020).

The next 7.4 miles of the Razorback Greenway cruise through the City of Rogers, a city that already has 27 other trails and plans to complete a 60-mile network connecting parks, schools, commercial centers and neighborhoods with one another as well as the regional trail system (Rogers 2020).

After a short stretch through the City of Lowell, the Razorback travels for nine miles through Springdale, passing the Shiloh Historical District listed in the National Register and the Shiloh Museum of Ozark History, which celebrates the pioneer past of the region in general and Springdale in particular, which was originally named Shiloh (Shiloh Museum of Ozark History 2020). From the Razorback Greenway, a connecting trail leads to the Jones Center, a multi-purpose fitness/recreation center featuring ice skating, swimming and a bike park designed to train riders for the growing popularity of mountain biking in the region (Jones Center 2020). Nearby, the 10,000-seat Rodeo of the Ozarks has been doing all things cowboy and cowgirl since 1944 (Rodeo of the Ozarks 2020).

In Fayetteville, the Razorback Greenway is part of a 40-mile system of paved, shared-use trails. A six-mile segment encircles Lake Fayetteville, a 458-acre, in-city park for boating and fishing. This loop also serves the Botanical Garden of the Ozarks, a 44-acre greenspace that attracts 80,000 visitors a year with 12 separate gardens and the only native butterfly house in the region (Botanical Garden of the Ozarks 2020).

Further south in Fayetteville, the Greenway intersects with Dickson Street, a lively entertainment district featuring performance venues like the Walton Arts Center and George's Majestic Lounge which claims to be the longest running club and live music stage in Arkansas. Turning west, the Razorback intersects with the bike network of the University of Arkansas, famous for championship teams and for the four-mile long Senior Walk inscribed with the names of more than 170,000 graduates of the university, and counting (University of Arkansas 2020).

Cyclists are responding to the expansion of bike trails in Northwest Arkansas. In the two years following completion of the Greenback Greenway in 2015, annual bicycle counts rose by 24 percent. In terms of cyclists per 1,000 population, Northwest Arkansas ranked between Portland, Oregon and San Francisco, California in 2017 (Walton Family Foundation 2017).

Another study proves that investments in trails here are paying off. Bicycling in general contributes $137 million per year in health and economic benefits to Northwest Arkansas. Of this amount, health benefits represent $86 million, and the other $51 million are business benefits. Of that $51 million, $21 million is generated by resident spending on bicycles, bicycling equipment, and events while $27 million annually comes from the spending of out-of-state bicycle tourists at local businesses throughout the region. The study also documents that entrepreneurs want to locate their establishments near the Razorback, primarily to attract customers but also to improve visibility and facilitate access for employees as well as customers. In addition, the study found that homes within a quarter mile of the Razorback Greenway sell for $15,000 more on average than comparable homes two miles from the trail (BBC Research & Consulting 2018).

The Razorback Trail was officially completed in 2015 but the expansion of Northwest Arkansas trails continues. The Regional Bicycle and Pedestrian Master Plan proposes trail interconnections between and within 32 jurisdictions in Benton and Washington counties with the aim of making Northwest Arkansas a "…world-class bicycle and pedestrian destination" (NWA Regional Planning Commission 2015, ES1). These communities are accepting that challenge. For example, the City of Bella Vista, located between Bentonville and the Arkansas – Missouri border, announced in 2018 that it was doubling the length of its natural-surface, multi-use trails, creating a 100-mile network with help from the Walton Family Foundation (Bella Vista 2018). As shown by the 2017 studies mentioned above, the Razorback and other trails in the region are promoting health, economic vitality, eco-mobility and, ultimately, public demand for more trails. Just another good example of the virtuous cycle.

CHAPTER 41

South Haven - Kalamazoo, Michigan: Adding Trails to the Tourism Mix

Bicycles are good for business in Michigan. A 2014 study prepared for the Michigan Department of Transportation found that bicycling here annually adds $224 million to the economy: $175 million in retail spending, $38 million on bicycle events and tourism plus $11 million on bike related manufacturing. In addition, this study estimated that bicycling saved $256 million in health care costs and $187 million in avoided costs of work absenteeism, or a total annual economic impact of $667 million (BBC Research & Consulting 2014a).

Case studies also estimated the annual economic benefits to five individual Michigan cities in 2014. In Ann Arbor, home to the 46,000-student University of Michigan, bicycling annually generates $25.4 million to the economy, with roughly half coming from spending on bicycling-related items, tourism and events. A total annual benefit of $20.7 million is contributed by bicycling in two Detroit neighborhoods with a total population of roughly 163,000: Southwest Detroit and the area surrounding the 9-mile Conner Creek Greenway which connects Eight Mile with the Detroit River. The case study of Grand Rapids, the second-largest city in Michigan, estimated that bicycling there annually adds a total of $39 million to the economy including $12.6 million from spending on bicycling related items, tourism and events. The case study of Holland, a city of 33,000 people on the eastern shore of Lake Michigan, estimated that bicycling annually generates $6.4 million, with roughly one third of this total coming from bicycling expenditures, manufacturing, tourism and events. Finally, the case study for Traverse City, a city of 15,000 people, on Grand Traverse Bay near the northern end of Michigan's Lower Peninsula, estimated that bicycling annually contributes a total annual economic impact of $5.5 million, with almost half produced by household spending on bicycling, tourism and events (BBC Research & Consulting 2014b - f).

At the Kalamazoo end of the trail, the Henderson Castle welcomes cyclists.

Kalamazoo is similarly boosting its bicycling benefits by closing gaps in an already-extensive network in southwestern Michigan (Wedel 2017). The 34-mile Kal-Haven State Trail begins just east of South Haven, a city of beaches, boats, bars, and the Michigan Maritime Museum, featuring a historic tall ship that served in the War of 1812. Only a mile from the trailhead, cyclists cross the Black River on a covered bridge and then pass through five classic trail towns before entering the western outskirts of Kalamazoo, population 75,000. Here, restaurants, microbreweries and inns welcome cyclists including the Henderson Castle, a 25-room, Queen Anne mansion built in 1895 that now offers guest rooms, dining, and its own wine label (Henderson Castle 2019).

After refueling at any of several craft brewpubs in downtown Kalamazoo, cyclists can travel north on the Kalamazoo River Valley Trail as it meanders out of the city and through the 1,100-acre Kalamazoo Nature Center. Going east on the Kalamazoo River Valley Trail currently involves negotiating a gap at Galesburg.

But eventually cyclists reach the City of Battle Creek, which earned a silver rating as a bicycle-friendly community from the League of American Bicyclists. Battle Creek is also famous as the birthplace of the Seventh-day

Adventist Church, an important stop on the Underground Railroad, the home of African-American abolitionist Sojourner Truth, and the city where Dr. John Harvey Kellogg invented and popularized breakfast cereals.

The Kal-Haven Trail crosses Black River on a covered bridge.

Looking to extend the trail system to the south, Kalamazoo is also working to improve connections to Portage, a city of 46,000 people with a 60-mile system of bike trails and lanes plus a bike-friendly community rating of bronze from the League of American Bicyclists. By continuing to extend and link trails, Kalamazoo, South Haven, Battle Creek and other communities in southwestern Michigan should one day complete a 200-mile trail network and further expand the many benefits of cycling (Wedel 2017).

CHAPTER 42

Sacramento, California: The Great California Delta Trail Promises Great Results

In 2019, the Sacramento-San Joaquin Delta became one of 55 National Heritage Areas in the US. Destinations within this National Heritage Area will eventually be linked via the planned Great California Delta Trail, stretching 80 miles between the San Francisco Bay Trail and existing trails in Yolo and Sacramento counties. Although it is being planned as of 2019, the trail already incorporates the Sacramento River Parkway in the City of Sacramento. This city is also home to a large stretch of existing bike trails within the American River Parkway, a 1,500-acre open space that already attracts over eight million visitors a year and generates substantial visitor spending. Based on the success of these existing trails, the Great Delta Trail promises to generate hefty benefits for local economies as well as expand opportunities for recreation, historic/cultural discovery, health, and human-powered transportation alternatives.

The National Park Service provides planning and limited financial assistance to local governments, private property owners and citizens within a National Heritage Area. But the locals ultimately decide how best to preserve and showcase the history, culture, and landscape of these regions (National Park Service 2019).

Together with San Francisco Bay, the California Delta is the largest estuary on the west coast of the Americas and the National Heritage Area designation aims to protect the water, wildlife and recreational opportunities of its vast network of sloughs, marshes and river channels. In addition, the delta is historically significant as the main route to the California Gold Rush, as one of the nation's largest reclamation projects, for its multi-ethnic traditions, for its agricultural abundance, and for its importance to the state's water resources (Delta Protection Commission 2012).

So far, five trails have been adopted as segments of The Great California

Delta Trail: the Carquinez Loop Trail, the Big Break & Marsh Creek Trail, the Clarksburg Branch Line Trail, the West Sacramento River Walk and the Sacramento River Parkway Trail (Delta Protection Commission 2019).

The Sacramento River Trail passes through Old Sacramento State Historic Park, the business district that sprang into being in the 1850s to serve miners who flocked here during the California Gold Rush. After several severe floods, an ambitious earth-moving project raised the elevation of the entire district beginning in the 1860s, preserving various remnants of the original city underground. Nevertheless, the area fell into decline before finally being revitalized and reborn as a thriving entertainment and tourist district, attracting five million visitors a year (California State Parks 2019; Old Sacramento Waterfront 2019).

Old Sacramento State Historic Park is now a National Historic Landmark and an ideal base camp for cyclists. Here, California Parks and its partners have recreated the Eagle Theater, originally built in 1849 and swept away by a flood shortly thereafter. Nearby, the B.F. Hastings Building (1853) once housed the California Supreme Court and served as the western terminus of the Pony Express, the short-lived service that used horses and riders to speed mail from Sacramento to St. Joseph, Missouri in ten days. Today, the B.F. Hastings Building houses a visitors' center and the Wells Fargo History Museum. Nearby, the Big Four Building (1855) got its name from four merchants who proceeded to found the First Transcontinental Railroad and the Southern Pacific Railroad. Next door, the California Railroad Museum offers train rides as well as 225,000 square feet of railroad memorabilia. There are more than 50 other landmarks in Old Sacramento including the What Cheer House (1853) which began life as a hotel and is now home to G. Willikers Toy Emporium and other upscale retailers. Another highlight is the Delta King, a riverboat launched in 1927 that carried passengers between Sacramento and San Francisco until a highway connecting those two cities was completed in 1940. The Delta King has since been converted into a hotel and restaurant with a permanent home just off the trail (California State Parks 2019; Old Sacramento Waterfront 2019).

A mile north of Old Sacramento, the Sacramento River Trail reaches the confluence of the Sacramento and American rivers, then merges with the Two River Trail, which follows the south bank of the American River through the campus of California State University at Sacramento with an enrollment of over 30,000 students. By turning south on the Sacramento Bikeway North, cyclists soon reach the bike lane network of downtown Sacramento, which can be used to reach Sutter's Fort State Historic Park, Governor's Mansion State Historic Park, the California Capitol Building and a concentration of public and private offices.

Alternatively, cyclists can use the Sacramento Bikeway North to cross to the north side of the American River on a car-free bridge and pedal east for

32 miles on the Jedediah Smith Memorial Trail, which is also known as the American River Bike Trail. Along the way, this trail passes through the City of Folsom, made famous by Folsom State Prison and Johnny Cash. The state still uses this 1880 facility. However, the public is welcome to visit a small prison museum which is located on the prison grounds but, fortunately, outside the prison's formidable stone walls. In addition to exhibits about inmates, escapes and executions, the museum celebrates the connection to Johnny Cash who made an album from two concerts here in 1968 which included the legendary recording of Folsom Prison Blues. As a further connection, the Johnny Cash Trail now links the American River Trail with Folsom Lake, the Folsom Historic District and Folsom Prison itself (Johnny Cash Trail 2019).

Bike lanes and a path next to Interstate 80 connect the Sacramento River Trail in Old Sacramento with the City of Davis. After 15 miles, cyclists are in Davis, the first city to receive a Platinum level rating as a bicycle friendly community by the League of American Bicyclists and home to the University of California at Davis, which itself receives a Platinum rating as a bicycle-friendly campus (League of American Bicyclists 2019). In an effort to achieve the higher rating of Diamond level, the city's 2014 bicycle action plan, entitled *Beyond Platinum*, sets a goal of becoming a world class bicycling city where most people of all ages and abilities choose cycling as their primary mode of making everyday trips. This plan recognizes that bicycles are particularly good for businesses in Davis. As in other cities, cyclists here make more trips per month to downtown businesses than customers who arrive by car. But a 2014 study found that these cyclists also spend more per trip and consequently more total money per month than their car-bound counterparts (Davis 2014).

In 2012, the American River Parkway alone attracted 8 million visitors and generated an estimated $376 million from all sources including annual visitor spending for recreation-related activities. To capitalize on this success, the city plans to complete the Two Rivers Trail on the south side of the American River and close current gaps in the trail system on the east side of the Sacramento River, creating a continuous 25-mile, river-adjacent trail through the City of Sacramento (Sacramento Department of Parks and Recreation 2012). This project is not inexpensive. It involves the acquisition of rights from 200 privately-owned properties. But Sacramento recognizes that this investment will pay off as an economic development tool. As stated in the current update of the Sacramento River Parkway Plan, in addition to enhancing recreation, habitat, flood control, health, natural resources and cultural assets, this project will: "Contribute significant direct and indirect economic benefits to the City" (Sacramento Department of Public Works 2019).

CHAPTER 43

San Francisco Bay Region, California: The Bay Trail Is Getting Around

A 500-mile bicycle trail through the nine counties that surround San Francisco Bay is an ambitious undertaking. Although much of this planned loop already exists, multi-million-dollar gaps remain to be closed. But once it is completed, trips on the San Francisco Bay Trail are projected to double and the returns are estimated to be well worth the investment in terms of additional jobs, income and tax revenues as well as recreation, healthful exercise, environmental education and planet-friendly transportation.

The Ferry Building marks the start of the planned 500-mile San Francisco Bay Trail. Opened in 1898, the Ferry Building survived two significant earthquakes and has been seen or used by more people than any other city landmark. Until the 1930s, the Ferry Building was the main portal to the city, accommodating up to 50,000 passengers per day. When construction of the Golden Gate Bridge and Bay Bridge offered alternatives to water transport around the bay, ferry passenger volumes dropped. Over the following decades, the Ferry Building fell victim to insensitive remodeling and the indignity of being cut off from the rest of the city by the Embarcadero Freeway. But, after the 1989 Loma Prieta earthquake, San Francisco removed the freeway and restored the Ferry Building's connections to the city's transit, pedestrian and bicycle network. In 2003, the Ferry Building was lovingly restored and is now home to restaurants, offices and a thriving farmers market while still serving as the terminal for a reemerging water transportation system (Noe Hill 2019; Ferry Building Marketplace 2019).

Heading north from the Ferry Building, the Bay Trail passes the boats that travel to and from Alcatraz Island, now a National Park Service historical site where visitors can wander around and imagine its days as a federal penitentiary. Next door, Pier 39 has become San Francisco's most visited attraction by combining stores, restaurants, entertainment venues, an aquarium and hundreds of sea lions. Seafood lovers will be tempted to stop after another 1,000 feet at Fisherman's Wharf, which started in 1900 as a simple dock and is now home to a variety of restaurants, fresh fish markets and a working fleet of fishing boats. Bicycling tourists encounter endless distractions here, including repurposed industrial buildings like the Cannery and a turntable for cable cars, the iconic vehicles invented in San Francisco 150 years ago and now a National Historic Landmark (San Francisco Municipal Transportation Agency 2019.)

The Bay Trail then passes Ghirardelli Square, the former chocolate factory that was transformed into an entertainment venue/retail space in 1964, making it the first successful adaptive-reuse project in the United States (Ghirardelli Square 2019). Steps away, the San Francisco Maritime Historic Park preserves a large collection of floating ships including the *Balclutha,* an 1886 square-rigger (National Park Service 2019a). Next door, Fort Mason, at one time a major embarkation point for millions of troops, is now an award-winning theater and cultural center and part of the massive Golden Gate National Recreation Area, the most visited National Park in the country with over 15 million visitors per year (Fort Mason 2019).

A short jog off the Bay Trail takes cyclists to the Palace of Fine Arts. This fanciful reimagining of a Roman temple is the only surviving building from the 1915 Panama-Pacific International Exhibition hosted by San Francisco to show the world that the city had bounced back from its devastating 1906 earthquake (Palace of Fine Arts 2019).

For the next mile, the Bay Trail traces the northern boundary of the Presidio, a 1,500-acre multi-use park incorporated within the Golden Gate National Recreation Area. The Presidio served as a military post for Spain, Mexico and finally the United States until 1994 when the Army closed this base and it became part of the Golden Gate National Recreation Area. Today, the Presidio is a National Historic Landmark District with many of the buildings rehabilitated and reused for recreation, museums, cultural events and 16 restaurants. Fort Point, at the northern tip of the Presidio offers stunning views of the Golden Gate Bridge as well as a preserved fort built during the California Gold Rush to defend San Francisco Bay (National Park Service 2019b).

From the Presidio, the Bay Trail uses the Golden Gate Bridge to cross into Marin County. Upon completion in 1937, the Golden Gate was the longest suspension bridge in the world. With its sleek, Art Deco design, the bridge is widely considered as one of the most graceful structures on the planet and serves as the internationally recognized symbol of San Francisco and the State of California (Golden Gate National Parks Conservancy 2019).

The portion of the Bay Trail that follows the coast of Marin County offers mile after mile of scenic cycling. The trail passes through Sausalito, known for bootlegging during Prohibition and shipbuilding in World War II. The abandoned shipyards here have been replaced by houseboats, marinas and upscale establishments aimed at wealthy residents and tourists.

Further north, the Bay Trail passes Corte Madera Marsh State Marine Park, the San Francisco Bay National Estuarine Research Reserve and China Camp State Park, which protects the remnants of a former Chinese fishing village, one of many such villages established after demand for Chinese laborers declined following the gold rush and completion of the transcontinental railroad in the 1880s (California State Parks 2015).

Cyclists can tour Franklin D. Roosevelt's presidential yacht USS Potomac, now docked at Oakland's Jack London Square on the Bay Trail.

Further north, the trail passes through the City of Novato where some cyclists may want to detour to Olompali State Historic Park, home to many inhabitants over time including people of the Coast Miwoc culture, Mexican generals, American ranchers, and the Grateful Dead rock band (California State Parks 2011).

In Sonoma County, the Bay Trail explores the San Pablo Bay National Wildlife Refuge, home to more than 13,000 acres of mudflats and pickleweed that provide habitat for migratory waterfowl as well as resident species. In Napa County, a spur of the Bay Trail circles the City of Napa and proceeds south through the City of Vallejo in Solano County before crossing the Carquinez Strait, the point where San Francisco Bay meets the delta formed by the confluence of the Sacramento and San Joaquin rivers.

In Contra Costa County, the Bay Trail passes several coastal cities and wanders through the Point Pinole Regional Shoreline, 2,315 acres of primarily marshes, woodlands and restored sites once used to manufacture gunpowder and dynamite. The Bay Trail then passes the Rosie the Riveter National Historical Park, housed in buildings once used by the Kaiser Shipyards in Richmond, California to build 747 ships during World War II including the *SS Red Oak Victory*, the last ship to be built at this factory and now open to the public. The visitors center here celebrates the six million women who entered the workforce during World War II, often taking positions in war industry jobs while ten million men joined the military (National Park Service 2017).

In Alameda County, the Bay Trail extends from Berkeley to Emeryville, often within 1,854-acre McLaughlin Eastshore State Park, named for Sylvia McLaughlin, a co-founder of Save the Bay. In Oakland, the Bay Trail passes through Jack London Square, a working waterfront as well as a business and entertainment district named after the popular author who spent much of his youth here. London drew inspiration for some of his characters from his time at Heinold's First and Last Chance Saloon, built in 1883 with wood from a dismantled whaling ship (Jack London Square 2019).

As it loops around the southern lobe of San Francisco Bay, the Bay Trail passes by and through several important natural areas including Oyster Bay Regional Shoreline, Hayward Regional Shoreline, Eden Landing Ecological Reserve, Coyote Hills Regional Park, Don Edwards National Wildlife Refuge, Stevens Creek Shoreline Nature Study Area, Palo Alto Baylands Nature Preserve, Ravenswood Preserve, Bair Island Ecological Reserve, Redwood Shore Ecological Reserve, Coyote Point Recreation Area, and Candlestick Point State Recreation Area. Many of these public greenspaces were created by dismantling former commercial salt flats and restoring the natural water flows needed to attract migratory birds and resident species.

Throughout this circumnavigation of San Francisco Bay, the Trail is often still a plan rather than a reality. But back in the City of San Francisco, an uninterrupted off-road path starts at Oracle Park, home of the San Francisco Giants, and parallels Embarcadero Drive past several parks and under the Bay Bridge to return to the starting point at the Ferry Building. Throughout the city, cyclists have many options to exit the Bay Trail on an extensive network of bike lanes and paths, which partly explains why San Francisco is ranked as a Gold level bike-friendly community (League of American Bicyclists 2019).

A 2005 study calculated that closing the gaps in the Bay Trail would cost almost $188 million. However, the popularity of the trail prompted the authors to estimate that trail usage would almost double from 38 million to 71 million per year. The study noted that the trail generates traditional benefits like non-polluting, muscle-powered mobility, healthful exercise and access to shorelines and open space, particularly for underserved populations. In addition, this study found that the trail lets people enjoy the marshes and other open spaces being restored after centuries of abuse and neglect. In terms of economic development, the trail supports the region's significant tourism sector, particularly in areas where it links major regional destinations like the Ferry Building, Fisherman's Wharf and Pier 39. The trail also adds to the livability of San Francisco, helping to attract and retain high quality workers. The 2005 study acknowledges that expenditures directly attributable are low on a per trip basis. But because of the high volume of individual trips, the study projects that trail users will ultimately spend almost $190 million per year at businesses near the trail (Association of Bay Area Governments 2005).

CHAPTER 44

Smyrna, Georgia – Alabama State Line: Silver Comet Trail Keeps Growing

The Silver Comet Trail currently begins in the northern Atlanta suburb of Smyrna and heads 61 miles west to the Georgia state line. At that point, the Silver Comet becomes the Chief Ladiga Trail which travels for another 33 miles before reaching its western trailhead in Anniston, Alabama. Used by roughly two million people annually, the Silver Comet is clearly a recreational, health and active transportation success. But a 2013 study estimated that the trail was also annually contributing almost $120 million to the economy and recommended doubling the Silver Comet's mileage with spurs to several other communities and greenways including Atlanta's Belt Line Trail. Many of these dreams are becoming reality.

The benefits and potential of the Silver Comet Trail were calculated in a combined economic impact analysis and planning study prepared in 2013 for the Northwest Georgia Regional Planning Commission. This study reported that every dollar invested in trails generates at least three dollars of return in tourism and related activities including lodging, equipment rentals and food/beverage purchases. The report suggested that this might be a conservative estimate considering that rates of return were much higher from some trails, including 900 percent in North Carolina's Outer Banks and 1,180 percent in Kansas City (Alta 2013).

As of 2013, 1.9 million users walked, jogged, biked or roller skated on the Silver Comet Trail, which got its name from the train that once sped passengers between New York City and Birmingham, Alabama. Based on extensive surveys, the Alta study estimated that these trail users directly spent $57 million per year on food, clothing, lodging and other trip-related items. This direct spending generated an additional $61 million of indirect spending, creating a total impact of almost $120 million within the State of Georgia, while supporting roughly 1,300 jobs and producing $37 million in earnings.

In 2013, this direct and indirect spending combined generated roughly $3.5 million in income tax, sales tax and business tax revenues (Alta 2013).

A popular rest stop on the Silver Comet spur to Powder Springs.

Many users of the Silver Comet come from communities that are not adjacent to the trail including 23 counties in eight different states, with some arriving from as far as the State of Washington at the opposite corner of the United States. Trail users come from other countries too, as documented by the visitor log maintained by Ramona Ruark, the manager of the Cedartown Welcome Center, which is housed in a replica rail station on the Silver Comet Trail.

Of those who responded to the 2013 survey, over one fifth stayed overnight when visiting the trail. These bicycle tourists spend roughly $20 million annually on their visits to the Silver Comet (Alta 2013). In the trail town of Dallas, Georgia, Jackie Crum, owner of the Ragsdale Inn, estimated that more than half of her guests are Silver Comet Trail riders. "Tourism is wonderful for the local economy," she explained in 2014. "It generates income without the infrastructure needs and tax burdens of residential development."

Several studies have documented the increased value of real estate associated with proximity to bicycle trails. For example, a nine percent premium was identified for properties near a trail in Brown County, Wisconsin and adjacency to a greenway was found to add $5,000 to the sales price of homes in Apex, North Carolina. The Alta study assumed a property value increase ranging from 4 to 7 percent for homes within one quarter mile of the Silver Comet. Using the low end of this range, a 4 percent value increase to homes within one quarter mile of the Silver Comet Trail produced a total value increase of $180 million and additional property tax revenues of over $2 million per year for the jurisdictions and school districts adjacent to the trail. The 2013 study even estimated that vacant land near the trail could attract new development with a value of up to $41 million, which would annually produce an extra $500,000 in property tax revenue (Alta 2013).

The Silver Comet Trail offers lots of rural scenery between trail towns.

The Alta report included recommendations for more than doubling the length of the Silver Comet Trail by adding spurs to commercial centers near the trail as well as longer extensions to various Georgia cities including Marietta, Rome and Atlanta. The price tag for expanding the Silver Comet network from 61 to 127 miles was estimated at $59 million. But the report also demonstrated that the economic returns would more than offset these costs (Alta 2013).

In keeping with these recommendations, Cobb County and many of its incorporated cities are investing in trails, including spurs that capitalize on the success of the Silver Comet. Given Cobb County's location just north of Atlanta, it is not surprising that trailheads here experience the highest user counts on the Silver Comet. In 2013, 434,000 riders were estimated to pass through the trailhead in Smyrna, a Cobb County city of 51,000 people just 10 miles northwest of downtown Atlanta. Similarly, the trailhead in the unincorporated Cobb County community of Mableton sees an estimated 350,000 users annually (Atla 2019), which is one reason why Comet Trail Cycles, a bike sales, service and rental shop, thrives at this location.

As of 2018, Cobb County offered 84 miles of existing multi-use greenway trails and side paths, of which 50 miles had been constructed within the prior 10 year period. In its 2018 Greenways and Trails Master Plan, Cobb County proposed construction of another 207 miles of trails including several trails that would link with and effectively extend the Silver Comet (Cobb County 2018).

A high priority for Cobb County and Northwestern Georgia involves connecting the Silver Comet with the Atlanta Beltline, the evolving 22-mile loop around downtown Atlanta which is revitalizing the neighborhoods and parks that it connects by transforming the way city dwellers live, shop, exercise and enjoy themselves. In 2013, a citizen's organization called Connect the Comet formed to advocate linking the Silver Comet Trail to the Beltline with a 6.5-mile connection that would ultimately create 105 miles of continuous bicycling (Strategic Vision Plan 2017). That dream came closer to reality in 2019 when Cox Enterprises of Atlanta donated $6 million toward the construction of this connector (Lutz 2019). The success of both the Atlanta Belt Line and the Silver Comet creates the self-reinforcing upward spiral that produces this level of enthusiasm and generosity. Once again, the virtuous cycle appears to be at work in Georgia.

CHAPTER 45

St. Louis — Sedalia - Kansas City, Missouri: The Katy Trail Is Just the Beginning

Katy Trail State Park, stretching 240 miles from Clinton, Missouri to the Saint Louis suburbs, opened its first segment in 1990 and today is considered the nation's longest continuous, individual rail trail. In 2007, the Rails-to-Trails Conservancy added the Katy to its Rail Trail Hall of Fame. This honor recognized the Katy Trail's scenic beauty, often threading a narrow path between limestone bluffs and the Missouri River, and its historical significance, following the route of the Lewis and Clark expedition. But it is also now an acknowledged redevelopment engine, attracting wineries, brew pubs, restaurants, lodging and other new businesses as it links 40 communities across the state, often giving struggling former rail towns a badly needed dose of economic vitality (RTC 2007).

Before the arrival of the Katy Trail, the economy of the City of Rocheport consisted of a few antique shops (RTC 2007). Today, this 240-person community offers seven bed-and-breakfast inns, four restaurants, one food store, one canoe/kayak outfitter, one bike shop and an upscale winery.

About 50 miles west, the City of Sedalia is also transforming itself from an era in which 90 percent of the local economy was the responsibility of now-departed railroads and their related depots, repair shops, schools, and stockyards. Today, visitors can follow the Heritage Trail through Sedalia's Downtown Historic District, with 120 landmarks in the National Register of Historic Places. For more than 35 years, this district has provided a fitting setting for the Scott Joplin Ragtime Festival, a 5-day celebration of ragtime music and the era when Joplin played nightly here at the Maple Leaf Club. Two miles west, the Katy Trail passes the Missouri State Fairgrounds, home to another 66 structures in the National Register of Historic Places and considered one of the five remaining historic state fairgrounds in the US. At the fairground entrance, a larger-than-life monument recreates the days when cowboys used the Historic Sedalia Trail to drive longhorn cattle from Texas to Sedalia for rail shipment east (Sedalia 2018).

By taking a spur across the Missouri River, cyclists arrive in Jefferson City, where they can explore various landmarks including sculptures depicting key figures from the Lewis and Clark expedition. The Missouri State Capitol is stuffed with historical artifacts and features the 1936 room-sized mural painted by Thomas Hart Benton depicting all eras of Missouri's history.

The Missouri State Capitol is home to the 1936 room-sized mural painted by Thomas Hart Benton depicting all eras of Missouri's history, including this rendering of Mark Twain's Huck Finn.

At least 21 wineries can be reached on the Katy Trail including five wineries in the City of Hermann alone. To avoid accusations of favoritism, Hermann features the Black Shire Distillery and the Tin Mill Brewery, housed in a 100-year-old landmark grain mill. Hermann becomes particularly lively during its month-long Octoberfest celebration, attracting more than 7,000 thirsty visitors every year.

A 2012 economic impact study estimated that the Katy Trail annually attracted 400,000 visitors, creating a catalyst for tourism development in the form of wineries, restaurants, shops and lodging of all kinds. Visitor spending contributed $8.2 million to local communities and generated a total impact of $18.5 million, supporting 367 jobs with a payroll of $5 million. Roughly two-thirds of trail users lived more than 30 miles from the trail and more than one quarter stayed overnight near the trail. Almost 90 percent of the respondents to the survey conducted for this study reported that the Katy Trail was the main reason for their visit (Synergy/PRI/JPA 2012).

Although the Katy Trail now ends in St. Charles County, connections to St. Louis are evolving as part of a planned 600-mile "River Ring" network joining 45 individual greenways within bicycling distance of 90 percent of the region's population. This ambitious project became more realistic in 2000, when the voters of the City of St. Louis, St. Louis County and St. Charles County, Missouri overwhelmingly approved a one-tenth of one cent sales tax that generates $10 million per year. Perhaps that dedicated source of funding freed the Green Rivers Greenway District to dream big, with a system planned to ultimately connect corridors along and between the Mississippi, Missouri and Merrimac rivers (Great Rivers Greenway 2019).

This monument at the Missouri State Fairgrounds commemorates cattle drives on the Historic Sedalia Trail between Texas and Sedalia.

A total of 125 miles of the Great Rivers Greenway exist today, with several segments converging on Forest Park, the crown jewel of the St. Louis City Parks System. Forest Park was the site of the 1904 World's Fair, immortalized in the 1944 film *Meet Me in St. Louis*. The St. Louis Art Museum is the only surviving building from the fair but the city has since added four other major institutions including the Saint Louis Science Center, the Missouri Historical Museum, and the St. Louis Zoo.

When its gaps are closed, the 17-mile Centennial Trail will link Forest Park with the Katy Trail by way of Washington University and the Delmar

Loop, home of the historic Loop Trolley and the City's walk of fame which memorializes famous people associated with St. Louis including Ulysses S. Grant, T.S. Elliot, and Maya Angelou.

The Chocteau Trail will ultimately connect Forest Park with Gateway Arch National Park. Although the exact route is being planned as of Summer 2019, this trail seems likely to access St Louis University and use an existing linear park that features City Garden, an open space combining splash pools, playgrounds and a child-friendly sculpture garden.

From Gateway Arch National Park, cyclists can already travel north on the Mississippi Greenway to the Chain of Rocks Bridge, which is now a car-free part of the Route 66 Bikeway, allowing cyclists to access trails on the east side of the Mississippi River in Illinois (NPS 2019). Ultimately, this greenway will extend south from downtown St. Louis, creating a 32-mile riverfront trail linking the confluence of the Mississippi and Missouri rivers with the Gateway Arch, River City Casino, Jefferson Barracks Park, Cliff Cave Park, and the Merrimac Greenway.

As of Summer 2019, Missouri is deliberating acceptance of a 144-mile stretch of rail right of way once used by the Rock Island Line. If this proceeds, the Rock Island Trail will ultimately begin in Kansas City at the western edge of Missouri and extend east to join the Katy Trail near the eastern edge of the state. Presumably, the decision of whether or not to green light a complete Rock Island Trail will rest, at least in part, on expectations of economic benefit for the 26 small towns linked by this now-abandoned rail right of way. Given the Show-Me State's legendary preference for hard evidence, the results of the 2012 study of the Katy Trail should provide a solid argument for going forward with completion of this ambitious 450-mile state-wide trail loop (BikeRockIsland.com 2019).

CHAPTER 46

Tallahassee – St. Marks, Florida: Capitalizing on Bicycling

Tallahassee is home to three college campuses and numerous offices surrounding the Florida state capitol. Those who study, work, and live here are fortunate that they can start pedaling south on a well-maintained rail trail and end up 25 miles away overlooking the Gulf of Mexico. In addition to healthful, non-polluting recreation and alternative transportation, the city and other trail-adjacent communities are benefiting from the economic impacts generated by the Tallahassee-St. Marks Historic Railroad State Trail.

The right of way for this trail was cleared in the 1830s by the Tallahassee Rail Road, which initially used mules to haul cotton from plantations to wharfs on the St. Marks River where it would be loaded on ships for its journey to textile mills in the northeastern United States and England. After changing hands many times, the rail corridor was abandoned in 1983 and purchased by the Florida Department of Transportation as the state's first recreational trail. Today, the Tallahassee – St. Marks Historic Railroad State Trail is a paved multi-use trail designated as a National Recreation Trail. It also forms a segment of the Florida National Scenic Trail (Florida State Parks 2018a; RTC 2018).

The northern end of the trail begins near Florida A&M University, Florida State University and Tallahassee Community College, giving a combined total of over 90,000 students easy access to the recreational and non-motorized transportation benefits of the Tallahassee – St. Marks trail. Heading east from these three schools, bicyclists on a spur called the Capital Cascades Trail cross an artfully-designed pedestrian bridge and arrive in Cascades Park, where a network of walkways lead to the Cascades Park Amphitheater and other recreational attractions. The city partnered with Leon County to remediate land here that was contaminated by coal tar produced by the manufactured gas plant that once occupied this site (Merchant 2008). The former power generation building has now been restored and repurposed as the upscale Edison Restaurant which overlooks the amphitheater and the park's postmodern waterfall.

From Cascades Park, bicyclists can pedal from the heart of Tallahassee to the City of St. Marks, 25 miles to the south. Although tiny, (population 272), St. Marks is home to San Marcos de Apalache State Historic Park, the site of various forts held by Spanish, English, and Confederate as well as American forces (Florida State Parks 2018b). But likely those who have bicycled all the way from Tallahassee to St. Marks will first want to visit the Riverside Café, where the weary can relax on a deck cantilevered over the St. Marks River and sip a beer while watching the boats heading to and from the Gulf of Mexico.

Cyclists can get a fleeting glimpse of manatees at Wakulla Springs State Park.

Those who want to extend their rides can take Lighthouse Road through the St. Marks National Wildlife Refuge featuring 68,000 acres of coastal marshes, tidal creeks and the estuaries of seven rivers that meander to the Gulf of Mexico. The refuge is a Globally Important Bird Area and riders here are likely to spot eagles, migratory waterfowl and many different species of shore birds as well as alligators. But regardless of whether or not the wildlife cooperates, those who pedal to the end of the road are always rewarded with a view of the picturesque St. Marks Lighthouse, built in 1842 and listed in the National Register of Historic Places (U.S. Fish & Wildlife Service 2018).

Some cyclists opt for a side jaunt from the trail to Wakulla Springs State Park, where they can take a guided boat trip to hopefully glimpse manatees, the marine mammals that are protected here. These creatures are elusive and sighting them is not easy despite the fact that they can weigh 1,500 pounds and live in crystal clear water that is only ten feet deep. In addition to manatee, the naturalists onboard point out alligators, numerous bird species, and the jungle-like settings used as locations for several movies including several early Tarzan flicks and the original *Creature from the Black Lagoon*.

The Tallahassee – St. Marks Trail has been so successful that the Capital Region Transportation Planning Agency (CRTPA) is planning a greatly-expanded system of trails radiating from Capital Cascades Park to Ochlockonee River State Park and other destinations within Leon, Wakulla and, eventually, three other counties. This plan, known as the Capital City to the Sea Trails, will link with two existing trails, the Trout Pond Trail, and the Ochlockonee Bay Trail, in what could become a 120-mile network. In support of this ambitious project, CRTPA emphasizes that multi-purpose trails are good for business and employment as well as health, alternative transportation and, of course, enjoyment (Capital Region Transportation Planning Agency 2013).

In fiscal year 2015-16, the Florida State Park System estimated that the 148,000 people using the Tallahassee – St. Marks trail produced a total direct economic impact of $13,065,398, generating $890,913 in state sales tax and supporting 209 jobs (Florida Department of Environmental Protection 2016).

The popularity of this trail is understandable considering that it is long, shaded, paved and links a city of 380,000 people with a relatively pristine section of Florida's Gulf Coast. Implementation of the Capital City to Sea Trails plan will greatly expand the options for cyclists and consequently multiply these benefits.

CHAPTER 47

Tucson, Arizona: Connecting the Dots

Arizona has loads of sunshine, great scenery and an evolving network of bicycle trails. As a result, the Grand Canyon State is seeing enviable returns from its investment in bicycle infrastructure. As a prime example, Pima County has recently teamed with Tucson and neighboring cities to complete a 131-mile loop that is already attracting 750,000 visitors a year. For every dollar spent on building the Loop, Pima County receives $9.40 in benefits (Pima County 2014).

In a 2013 study, the state Department of Transportation observed that Arizona's spectacular scenery and warm weather create competitive advantages for bicycle tourism. Furthermore, the climate is particularly suitable for sports, like cycling, that require year-around activity to maintain conditioning. Not surprisingly, Arizona hosts roughly 250 cycling events annually, attracting about 39,000 in-state and 14,000 out-of-state participants. These formal cycling events combined with manufacturing, wholesaling and retailing of bikes are estimated to support over 700 jobs, $88 million in spending and $31 million in labor income for Arizona (Arizona Department of Transportation 2013).

Focusing on the Tucson Region, The Loop began life in 1983 when devastating floods prompted Pima County to stabilize the banks of the Rillito, Pantano and Santa Cruz rivers, an effort that led to the creation of the River Parks system. Visionaries saw the potential for a trail network between and through these parks that ultimately became today's 131-mile Loop. (Pima County 2014).

The five distinct sections of the Loop link a total of 41 parks connected to bike lanes leading to many other attractions including the Reid Park Zoo, the Tucson Botanical Gardens, downtown Tucson, and the Pima Air and Space Museum featuring over 350 aircraft (Pima County 2014). Trail connections are also underway to San Xavier Mission, originally established in 1692 and today the site of a 'new' mission listed on the National Register of Historic Places dating from the late 18th century (National Park Service 2019).

Catalina State Park, located near the end of the Canada Del Oro portion of The Loop, protects 5,500 acres of the Sonoran Desert including over 150 bird species and almost 5,000 saguaro cactuses. Bicycle trails and lanes that link with The Loop extend to other large parks including Saguaro National Park, Tucson Mountain Park, the Arizona-Sonora Desert Museum and Colossal Cave Mountain Park, home to stone structures built by the Civilian Conservation Corps in the 1930s and now on the National Register of Historic Places.

Birders flock to The Loop for a glimpse of road runners and numerous other species.

The Loop is also becoming a 131-mile-long public art gallery, with 60 art pieces installed along the trail as of 2019. The selections include traditional pieces like *Boy and Girl on Horse* in Brandi Fenton Park and *Family Ride*, a life-size sculpture of pioneers riding a buckboard at Steam Pump Ranch. But whimsical artworks also delight cyclists here, including a series depicting bicycle-riding bats (Pima County 2019).

A 2013 cost-benefit analysis estimated that for every dollar of investment, The Loop generates $9.40 of economic return. Based on studies that quantify the link between property value and proximity to bike trails, this study estimated that The Loop adds $300 million in tax base, thereby generating more than $3 million per year in extra property tax revenue. This report also notes that bicycling accounts for a portion of the $2.4 billion spent annually on tourism in Pima County and Tucson, which is ranked as a gold level bicycle-friendly community by the League of American Bicyclists. In addition to bicycle tourism, The Loop attracts Audubon Society field trips and other birders who flock to the trail for sightings of species ranging from migratory waterfowl to resident roadrunners. When combining jobs, outdoor recreation, regional sales tax, home values, property tax revenue, and averted health care costs, this study estimated the total annual return from The Loop at $940 million (Pima County 2013).

In a 2017 report entitled *The Loop Means Business*, Pima County presented specific examples of The Loop's economic development capabilities. At its current location on The Loop, the Rillito Farmers Market attracts about 100,000 visitors a year. Building on the natural affinity between bike trails and craft beer, the owners of a brew house called the Hop Shop estimate that 15 percent of their business is related to the Loop (Pima County 2017). Countless other stories illustrate how Greater Tucson profits from a bikeway network that enjoyably connects people with jobs, schools, parks, and businesses.

CHAPTER 48

Utah: Seeing the Beauty of Bicycle Tourism

Bicycle paths are good for our parks and the communities that serve them. By getting people out of their cars, multiuse trails promote healthful exercise and improve fun factors by reducing the congestion, noise, air pollution and environmental degradation caused by motor vehicles. As recognized by the National Park Service, bicycle/pedestrian paths are also good for businesses and employment within and near our national parks, including those in Utah.

A 2017 study found that bicycle tourists annually contribute over $61.17 million to the Utah economy in the form of direct spending on transportation, food, lodging, shopping, entertainment and other expenditures. When multipliers are applied, the statewide annual total economic impact doubles to $121.9 million in spending, supporting 1,499 jobs with $46.73 million of employment income. The ability to prosper from cyclist spending is easy to see in Washington County, Utah, home to Zion National Park (Feer & Peers 2017). There are 7,273 tourism jobs in Washington County, making tourism the leading private sector employment group here (St. George 2017).

In its quest to return Zion National Park to nature, the National Park Service now prohibits unauthorized private motorized vehicles from using Zion Canyon Scenic Drive, the route to Zion's greatest rock hits including Court of the Patriarchs, the Grotto, Weeping Rock, the Temple of Sinawava, the Riverside Walk, and the Narrows. However, bicycles are free to share Zion Canyon Scenic Drive with the park's shuttle buses, making cycling the most planet-friendly and independent way of exploring this spectacular park.

The park service has also built the multiuse Pa'rus Trail connecting the park entrance with Zion Canyon Scenic Drive. This paved path crosses the Virgin River repeatedly and offers a relaxing way to reach the Zion Museum and the Zion Nature Center as well as enjoy views of some of Zion's iconic red-rock escarpments and mountain peaks, including the Watchman, with an elevation of over 6,500 feet.

Bike trails are also popular in and around Bryce Canyon National Park, 70 miles northeast of Zion. Cyclists can reach Bryce Canyon on the 17-mile Red Canyon Trail, a paved multi-use path that winds past red, pink and orange rock cliffs and free-standing towers accented with ponderosa pine. Bryce Canyon itself offers a network of bicycling trails that connect many popular park destinations including Bryce Canyon Lodge, Sunrise Point, Sunset Point and Inspiration Point. These shared-use paths often access trailheads where cyclists can park their bikes and wander for hours or days through the hoodoos and other fantastical formations that attract 2.6 million visitors a year to this park.

The multiuse Pa'rus Trail in Zion National Park illustrates the Park Service's active-transportation initiative.

In eastern Utah, Grand County, home to Arches National Park and the City of Moab, is a well-known mountain biking mecca. But multi-use trails here are also gaining in popularity. The Moab Canyon Pathway now links Lions Park with the entrance to Arches National Park by way of a restored railway bridge over the Colorado River. From the bridge, connecting trails extend south to the lodging and restaurants of Moab as well as east, offering stunning views of the massive red rock cliffs forming the northern bank of the Colorado River. Combining mountain bikers and road bikers with car-bound tourists, visitors to Arches and Bureau of Land Management areas in

Grand County annually generate more than $177 million in local output, supporting 2,447 jobs and a total labor income of $117.5 million (St. George 2017).

Bike trails link many popular destinations in Bryce Canyon National Park, including Inspiration Point.

In its guidebook on active transportation, the National Park Service identifies six benefits offered by infrastructure geared to pedestrians and bicyclists rather than cars. Multiuse trails promote resource protection by limiting the damage caused by cars on air quality, wildlife and other natural resources. Trails allow visitors to experience nature without the noise and other concerns caused by motor vehicles. These paths provide access to the disabled and people who do not own or drive cars. Active transportation offers healthful opportunities for recreation and exercise while reducing the automobile congestion that diminishes enjoyment for park visitors. And, importantly, the National Park Service recognizes "...Economic and Social Benefits: Promoting economic growth by attracting visitors who will then support local businesses (e,g,, bike shops, sports stores, restaurants), providing jobs and contributing to the quality of life for surrounding communities" (National Park Service 2018, IN-3).

CHAPTER 49

Vancouver, British Columbia: Copenhagenizing in Canada

Vancouver, British Colombia, and Montreal, Quebec, are the only two cities in North America to make it onto the Top 20 list of bicycle-friendly cities according to the Copenhagenize Index, the self-described 'most comprehensive and holistic ranking of bicycle-friendly cities on planet earth' (Copenhagenize 2019). A trip to this city, only 30 miles north of the US – Canada border, confirms that Vancouver emulates Utrecht, Amsterdam, and, of course, Copenhagen, at the top of that list.

Bike trails and lanes pleasantly connect many of Vancouver's key destinations and entice cyclists to travel into the surrounding countryside on various routes including The Great Trail, the evolving cross-country path planned to eventually link Victoria, British Columbia with Halifax, Nova Scotia. In the process, the Province of British Columbia is gaining health, recreation, environmental and cultural benefits as well as economic rewards.

Over a million passengers are expected to arrive by cruise ships in 2019 at Canada Place at Vancouver's waterfront (Port of Vancouver 2019). Next door, the stunning LEED-Platinum Vancouver Convention Centre annually attracts over 100,000 out-of-town delegates (Vancouver Convention Centre 2018). Below the Convention Centre, Seawall Adventure Centre rents bikes allowing visitors to explore Vancouver on two wheels using more than 279 miles of bike lanes and trails (Metro Vancouver Convention and Visitors Bureau 2019a).

On a trail along the seawall below the Convention Centre, many cyclists gawk at the gigantic cruise ships moored at Canada Place and watch the seaplanes taking off and landing on the calm waters of Vancouver Harbor. Heading west past the yachts in the marinas lining Coal Harbour Seawalk, bicyclists are treated to a six-mile loop around the perimeter of 988-acre Stanley Park. Here, the nine totem poles at Brockton Point are British Columbia's most visited attraction. Other favorite stops on the Stanley Park

Loop include several beaches, Brockton Point Lighthouse and Siwash Rock, a famous spire of basalt topped by a solitary tree.

Heading southwest from Canada Place, cyclists can use protected bike lanes to reach the trails that meander beneath the high-rise towers lining the north shore of False Creek. Heading west, protected lanes bridge False Creek, leading to attractions on English Bay including the Vancouver Maritime Museum and several beaches. Heading east on the south bank of False Creek, Island Park Walk is an enjoyable way to reach Granville Island, home to theaters, restaurants, brewpubs, art galleries, and a 7-day-a-week, indoor public market that largely explains why Granville Island annually draws over ten million visitors (Metro Vancouver Convention and Visitors Bureau 2019b).

Cyclists can use Vancouver's extensive bike network to reach the totem poles in Stanley Park, British Columbia's most visited attraction.

After two more miles on the scenic south shore of False Creek, cyclists reach Olympic Village, the ultra-sustainable neighborhood built when Vancouver hosted the 2010 Winter Olympics. Featuring habitat restoration, energy efficient construction, and a renewable energy heating system, the Olympic Village won LEED Platinum status and was lauded as the greenest neighborhood on earth in 2010 (CTV News 2010). Today, the Olympic Village is a thriving, mixed use complex that serves as a popular rest stop for cyclists seeking a coffee shop, restaurant, or brewpub.

Anchoring the east end of False Creek, a geodesic sphere originally built for Vancouver's 1986 World's Fair houses the well-attended TELUS World of Science. When completing the False Creek loop, cyclists pass BC Place, a soccer/football stadium and Roger's Arena, home of the Vancouver Canucks NHL hockey team. Alternatively, bikers can head north through Vancouver's Chinatown and finish riding in Gastown, a well-preserved historic district that is also home to art galleries, shops, and trendy restaurants.

The trails in Stanley Park, English Bay, False Creek, and many others in Vancouver and neighboring communities are segments of The Great Trail, the planned network that will eventually encompass almost 15,000 miles of bicycle trails across Canada connecting over 15,000 communities (The Great Trail 2019). A 2004 study estimated that The Great Trail will ultimately contribute a total of $2.4 billion annually to the economy of the Canadian Province of Ontario (Price Waterhouse Coopers 2004). Presumably, British Columbia will also experience significant benefits as this cross-country trail nears completion.

Cycle path beneath the Vancouver Convention Centre passes Canada Place.

British Columbia's Ministry of Forests, Lands and Natural Resource Operations manages 11,600 kilometers within 800 trails used by all-terrain vehicles, snowmobiles, hikers, and skiers as well as cyclists on provincial Crown land. A 2011 study explored how these trails provide recreational, educational, environmental and cultural benefits as well as spending, employment, and tax revenue impacts. Specifically, in 2009-2010, an estimated 6.3 million people used these trails including 114,000 visiting from outside of the province. These trail users spent almost $137 million, supporting 1,567 jobs, and generating $5 million in federal tax, $5.4 million in provincial tax, and $1.5 million in municipal tax (Meyers Norris Penny 2011).

Bicycling is the fastest growing mode of transportation in Vancouver (Vancouver 2019a). The city aims to build on this momentum by completing 23 new bike routes and upgrading 15 existing routes by 2022. Sooner or later, all of these routes will meet AAA standards, meaning bicycling infrastructure designed for All Ages & Abilities (Vancouver 2019b). Vancouver's 2040 Transportation Plan recognizes that cycling is good for business by including shopping areas in the list of important destinations that should be conveniently accessed by way of a coherent bicycling network. The plan does not state any aim to compete with the world's best cycling cities, but implementation of this plan would put Vancouver in good position to climb the Copenhagenize Index (Vancouver 2019c).

CHAPTER 50

Vermont: Bikes Help Green the Green Mountain State

Vermont's roads treat bicyclists to spectacular scenery, particularly in fall for muscle-powered leaf peeping. The Green Mountain State has also been expanding its eco-mobility network, which today includes over 300 miles in 37 multi-use trails with some classics like the Island Line Trail, the West River Trail, and the Cross Vermont Trail which will someday stretch across the entire state from Lake Champlain to the Connecticut River. The economic spinoffs can be seen in the cafes, brewpubs, bike shops, and B&Bs that have sprouted along these trails.

The Island Line Rail Trail, now in the Rail-Trail Hall of Fame, takes cyclists from Downtown Burlington onto a causeway jutting into Lake Champlain. With a short ferry trip across a gap in the causeway, cyclists reach the quiet roads of South Hero Island to explore miniature stone castles and Snow Farm Vineyard, which offers a summer calendar of concerts as well as wine tastings.

At the southern end of the West River Trail, Brattleboro, a town of 12,000 people and two bike shops, hugs the banks of the Connecticut River near the site of a fort built in 1724. The Vermont Asylum for the Insane, founded here in 1824, has been retooled as Retreat Farm, a community resource for sustainable agriculture with miles of trails including several to the stone tower built by the patients in 1887 as a form of therapy. The West River Trail follows the route of the 36-mile rail line that once sped passengers from Londonderry, Vermont, to Brattleboro, where Whetstone Brook powered a saw mill, paper mill, textile mill, and the Estey Organ Company, once the nation's largest manufacturer of melodeons. Upstream from where these mills once churned, Whetstone Brook is still spanned by the Creamery Covered Bridge built in 1879.

Today in Brattleboro's downtown, stores selling hardware and shoes mix with 19th century buildings repurposed as restaurants, boutiques, studios, and art galleries. On the first Friday of each summer month, Brattleboro holds its Gallery Walk featuring art exhibits, bands, dancing, and an open-air market with a pop-up beer garden.

The 1879 Creamery Covered Bridge still spans Whetstone Brook in Brattleboro, Vermont.

In 2009, bicycle- and pedestrian-related tourism, events, infrastructure, programs, and businesses generated almost $83 million in Vermont, supporting over 1,400 employees, producing a payroll of more than $41 million, and contributing $2.4 million in taxes and fees to the State of Vermont. In addition, a 2009 study estimated that bike and walking infrastructure added $350 million to real estate value and saved $85 million in public and private transportation costs (Vermont 2012).

In March 2021, the Vermont Transportation Agency committed to improving the state's multiuse trail network as part of a new Bicycle and Pedestrian Strategic Plan that promotes eco-mobility for people of all ages and abilities (Vermont 2021). In keeping with that goal, the Cross Vermont Trail Association continues to complete an 87-mile trail linking the Island Line Trail in Burlington with Wells River on the eastern edge of the state by way of the historic village of Waterbury and the state capital of Montpelier. To the west, the Cross Vermont Trail will link with 1,100 miles of trails and routes in New York and Quebec as well as Vermont. At the other end of the state, cyclists can cross the Connecticut River and keep peddling east into New Hampshire, which has also discovered that cycling is good for business.

CHAPTER 51

Washington State: Going Long on Trails

The League of American Bicyclists ranks Washington as the most bicycle friendly state in the nation (League of American Bicyclists 2019). It has over 1,240 miles of off-road trails, many of which are connected (or close to being connected), creating a long-distance bicycling paradise (Rails-to-Trails Conservancy 2019). The Palouse to Cascades State Park Trail alone forms one of the longest single links in the Great American Rail Trail, a planned 3,700-mile bikeway network connecting Seattle, Washington with Washington, DC. In response to its impressive projects and programs, bicycling is making a major contribution to Washington's economy.

When its current gaps are closed, the Palouse to Cascades Trail will stretch for 224 miles from the Idaho-Washington state line to Olallie State Park on the outskirts of Seattle. A 5-mile extension east into Idaho would connect the Palouse to Cascades Trail with the spectacular 72-mile Trail of the Coeur d'Alenes Rail Trail. Alternatively, cyclists can head to and from Spokane by way of the 130-mile Columbia Plateau Trail, the 9-mile Fish Lake Trail, and on-road connections.

From the site of the 1974 Expo in downtown Spokane, cyclists have the option of riding west on the 37-mile Spokane River Centennial State Park Trail to explore Riverside State Park or east though Gonzaga University and along the Spokane River ultimately linking with the 24-mile North Idaho Centennial Trail traveling east to Coeur d'Alene, Idaho and the shores of Lake Coeur d'Alene. Washington State Parks estimates that the Spokane River Centennial State Park Trail alone contributes $30 million to the regional economy (Stark 2014).

In Eastern Washington, the Palouse to Cascades Trail traverses dry, bleak terrain menacingly referred to as "channeled scablands". But the scenery gets greener as the trail passes the college town of Ellensburg and begins to follow the Yakima River up the eastern slope of the Cascade Mountain Range. After the long climb to the summit, cyclists are rewarded with a cool ride through the 2.3-mile-long Snoqualmie Tunnel followed by an 18-mile, downhill thrill ride to the trailhead at Rattlesnake Lake.

In 2019, the western half of the Palouse to Cascades Trail became part of the Mountains to Sound Greenway National Heritage Area (NHA), a 1.5-million-acre designation stretching from Ellensburg to Seattle. This NHA includes the Upper Basin of the Yakima River as well as the Snoqualmie River Valley and the Alpine Lakes Wilderness. The Mountains to Sound Greenway joins 53 other NHAs created to protect historic, cultural, and natural resources such as the Blue Ridge NHA (Mountains to Sound Greenway NHA 2019).

At the end of the Palouse to Cascade Trail, the route of the Great American Rail Trail continues west beginning with the 31-mile Snoqualmie Valley Trail, which travels through a mix of dairy farms, forests, and the Three Forks Natural Area, one of many greenspaces protected by King County, a jurisdiction that excels in open space preservation (Pruetz 2012). Here a short side trip takes riders to the stunning Snoqualmie Falls with an impressive 268-foot drop.

The monorail station at Seattle Center, site of the 1962 World's Fair.

Three trails take cyclists another 12 miles downhill through Preston to Issaquah, a city that reflects US industrial history, beginning as a mining and timber town before welcoming modern firms including Microsoft. Following the shores of Lake Sammamish and the Sammamish River, two more connected trails take cyclists to the burgeoning Woodinville wine country. Along with 119 other tasting rooms here, cyclists can visit the elegant Chateau Ste. Michelle winery, the oldest winery in the State of Washington. Just south of the Sammamish River Trail, guests at the upscale Willows Lodge can borrow a bike to cycle to as many wineries as they want.

The Elliot Bay Trail passes Seattle's Olympic Sculpture Park.

In the City of Bothell, the Sammamish River Trail connects with the 18-mile Burke-Gilman Trail. This Rail-Trail Hall of Famer rounds the top of Lake Washington, enters the City of Seattle and passes through the University of Washington campus with a total enrollment of 46,000 students. On a clear day, cyclists can glimpse distant Mount Rainier from Rainier Vista, a preserved landscaping feature from the 1909 Alaska-Yukon-Pacific Exposition world's fair. Further west, the trail passes Gas Works Park, which is designed to showcase the rusted towers of a former coal gasification plant. Built in 1978, the Burke-Gilman Trail was an early inspiration for the rail trail movement. It also demonstrated bicycle trails as an economic development tool. As early as 1987, the trail attracted three quarters of a million users per year and properties near the trail were enjoying a six percent boost in sales prices (Seattle 1987).

Navigating south, the route of the Great American Rail Trail enters the Elliot Bay Trail, a waterfront path that offers spectacular views of the islands in Puget Sound backed by the mountains of the Olympic Peninsula.

Monumental art pieces accent this trail and invite cyclists to venture into Olympic Sculpture Park for a closer look at works by several famous artists including Jaume Plensa, Alexander Calder, and Mark di Suvero. Once they are on top of the bluff, cyclists can pedal a few more blocks to Seattle Center, home to a stadium, museum, theater, and a monorail that shuttles travelers to and from downtown Seattle. Of course, the star attraction here is the Space Needle, originally built for the 1962 World's Fair and now Seattle's signature landmark.

The Elliott Bay Trail merges with the Seattle Waterfront Pathway where cyclists can continue on the Great American Rail-Trail by taking a ferry to Bainbridge Island and eventually riding the Olympic Discovery Trail, a trail that will ultimately span 130 miles of the Olympic Peninsula once various gaps are closed. A completed section currently follows the peninsula's northern shoreline to Port Angeles, a major gateway to Olympic National Park. The 30-mile Spruce Railroad Trail, another completed section of the Olympic Discovery Trail, follows the shoreline of Lake Crescent and the green rainforest of Olympic National Park.

A 2015 study calculated that bicycling contributes over $3.1 billion per year to the Washington state economy of which $113,494,490 represents equipment purchases and the remaining $3 billion comes from trip related expenditures (Earth Economics 2015). Cycling advocates emphasize the fact that 96 percent of the $3.1 billion total is generated by spending within local economies on shopping, lodging and eating, supporting their mantra that bicyclists are "wallets on wheels" (Trask 2015). As proof that it pays to go long on trails, much of this economic development success is likely due to Washington's ongoing efforts to link individual trails into region-wide greenways that attract bicycle tourism.

CHAPTER 52

Yellowstone-Grand Teton Loop Bicycle Pathway, Wyoming-Idaho-Montana: Thinking Big Out West

The Town of Jackson, Wyoming, and Jackson Hole, the surrounding valley, have a burgeoning multi-use trail network that entices outdoor sports enthusiasts to come here for more than just the world-class skiing. Work is underway to expand the current trail network over Teton Pass and up the eastern edge of Idaho into Montana. Even more ambitiously, advocates envision enlarging that crescent into a 272-mile loop through five counties, three states, and two national parks. An economic study of this Yellowstone – Grand Teton Loop Bicycle Pathway confirms that thinking big would be well worth the effort in terms of economic impact as well as offering a healthful and planet-friendly way of enjoying some of the most magnificent scenery on earth.

In 1996, Jackson Hole welcomed its first paved pathway, a four-mile trail along Flat Creek linking adjacent neighborhoods with the high school. Today, 56 miles of pathways cluster within the Town of Jackson and radiate into Teton County and beyond. One off-road trail parallels a highway heading south, allowing a car-free route to the trailhead of Game Creek Trail which in turn connects with Cache Creek Trail. Another path links the Town of Jackson with Teton Village and the Jackson Hole Mountain Resort, benefiting bike rental businesses at both ends. Heading north, another trail passes the National Elk Refuge and links with the pathway system within Grand Tetons National Park, which offers more miles of off-road walkways and cycleways than any other US national park (Friends of Pathways 2021; Jackson Hole Mountain Resort 2021).

Within Grand Teton National Park, one path leads to Antelope Flat Road, which passes Mormon Row Historic District and the mountain-backed

Moulton Barn that has come to symbolize Jackson Hole. Another path reaches the community of Moose, home to a national register historic district where visitors can cross the Snake River on a replica of the current-powered ferry originally operated by a homesteader starting in 1894. Nearby, local ranchers in 1925 built the Chapel of the Transfiguration, a church built of logs with a window behind the altar that frames a cluster of Grand Teton peaks known as the Cathedral Group. Heading north, the path leads to Jenny Lake, where cyclists can hike, go kayaking, or just take endless snapshots of picture-perfect mountains reflected in the water.

One of the trails in the Jackson Hole Pathway System gives cyclists a car-free way to enjoy Grand Teton National Park.

Wyoming Pathways and its partners are implementing a regional trail system planned to extend the existing trails to Colter Bay within Grand Teton National Park, connect several trails over Teton Pass, continue up the west side of Idaho, and end at the City of West Yellowstone in Montana. Towns, cities, and counties along this crescent-shaped route recognize the mobility, recreation, and community-development benefits to be generated by connecting existing, isolated pathway segments into a continuous 180-mile Greater Yellowstone Trail through these iconic western landscapes.

As Tom Cluff, Fremont County Planning and Building Administrator, puts it: "The Greater Yellowstone Trail will reconnect our small towns in a way reminiscent of the bygone railroad era. If we cooperate as one region in promoting the trail experience, we all stand to benefit from its tourism potential" (Wyoming Pathways 2021, p88).

Cyclists have a good chance of seeing wildlife like this coyote in Grand Teton National Park.

Some segments of the Greater Yellowstone Trail will employ existing trails while others will require pathway development using acquired land and abandoned railroad rights of way. In Eastern Idaho, the loop can use a 34-mile railroad right-of-way that starts near West Yellowstone, follows Warm River through Caribou-Targhee National Forest, and eventually ends near the City of Warm River, population three, which claims the title of Smallest City in Idaho. After a short gap, the existing 30-mile Ashton-Tetonia Trail offers scenic views of the less-frequently-seen western face of the Grand Teton Mountains plus a ride over three historic train trestles including a 670-foot-long 1911 bridge that carries cyclists roughly 120 feet above Conant Creek (Idaho 2021). Further south, the Victor to Driggs Trail passes by the Spud Drive-in Theater featuring a giant potato at its entrance.

Thinking even bigger, some advocates envision a 262-mile Yellowstone-Grand Teton Loop Bicycle Pathway that would make the crescent of the Greater Yellowstone Trail into a complete circle by going through both Grand Teton and Yellowstone national parks as well as five counties in three states. A 2015 study concluded that the Loop would support 1,451 jobs within the five-county region and add $131 million every year to the regional gross domestic product. The study also estimated that the loop would produce $48 million in labor income plus $74 million in value added and that visitor spending would generate 97 percent of this impact (Jenson and Scoresby 2015).

A bison poses near the bicycle loop in Yellowstone National Park.

At 180 or 262 miles, completing either of these trail networks will be no small task. But there will likewise be huge rewards for car-free mobility, recreation, health and, of course, tourism-based economic development. It just proves that big thinking is still alive and well in the West.

REFERENCES

**References: Chapter 1
– The Virtuous Cycle - Economic Benefits of Bicycling**

Alta. 2013. Silver Comet Trail: Economic Impact Analysis and Planning Study. Accessed 11-5-19 at http://www.bwnwga.org/wp-content/uploads/Silver_Comet_Combined.pdf.

Angelou Economics. The Trail: Economic Impact Analysis 2016. Accessed 2-6-20 at https://www.thetrailfoundation.org/wp-content/uploads/2016/11/ttf-economic-impact-analysis-2016.pdf.

Atencio, E. 2012. Trails for the People and Economy of Santa Fe. Accessed 2-9-20 at https://sfct.org/wp-content/uploads/2012/07/Trails-for-the-People-and-Economy-of-Santa-Fe.pdf.

Atlanta Beltline. 2018a. The Atlanta BeltLine: Where Atlanta Comes Together. Accessed on July 13, 2018 from https://beltline.org/about/the-atlanta-beltline-project/atlanta-beltline-overview/.

BBC Research & Consulting. 2014. Community and Economic Benefits of Bicycling in Michigan. Accessed 8-27-19 at https://www.michigan.gov/documents/mdot/MDOT_CommAndEconBenefitsOfBicyclingInMI_465392_7.pdf.

BBC Research & Consulting. 2016. Economic and Health Benefits of Bicycling and Walking. Denver: Colorado Office of Economic Development and International Trade.

BBC Research & Consulting. 2018. Economic and Health Benefits of Bicycling in Northwest Arkansas. Accessed 3-10-20 at https://www.waltonfamilyfoundation.org/learning/economic-and-health-benefits-of-bicycling-in-northwest-arkansas.

Bokhari, Sheharyar. 2016. How Much is a Point of Walkscore Worth? Accessed 5-30-20 at https://www.redfin.com/blog/how-much-is-a-point-of-walk-score-worth/.

Celis-Morales, Carlos, et. al 2017. Association between Active Commuting and Incident Cardio-Vascular Disease, Cancer and Mortality: Prospective Cohort Study. Accessed 6-1-20 at https://www.bmj.com/content/bmj/357/bmj.j1456.full.pdf.

Centers for Disease Control. 2019. Physical Activity Guidelines for Americans. Accessed 5-29-20 at https://www.cdc.gov/physicalactivity/downloads/trends-in-the-prevalence-of-physical-activity-508.pdf.

Centers for Disease Control. 2020. Physical Activity – Why It Matters. Accessed 5-29-20 at https://www.cdc.gov/physicalactivity/about-physical-activity/why-it-matters.html.

Clifton, J., Morrisey, S. & Ritter, C. 2012. Business Cycles: Catering to the Bicycling Market. Accessed 11-27-19 at http://kellyjclifton.com/Research/EconImpactsofBicycling/TRN_280_CliftonMorrissey&Ritter_pp26-32.pdf.

Cortright, Joe. 2007. Portland's Green Dividend. CEOs for Cities. Accessed 6-12-20 at https://forwardcities.org/wp-content/uploads/2018/04/Portland-Green-Dividend-Report.pdf.

Cortright, Joe. 2009. Walking the Walk: How Walkability Raises Home Values in U.S. Cities. Accessed 5-31-20 at https://nacto.org/docs/usdg/walking_the_walk_cortright.pdf.

Davis. 2014. Bicycle Action Plan: Beyond Platinum. Accessed 12-5-19 at http://documents.cityofdavis.org/Media/CityCouncil/Documents/PDF/CDD/Planning/Subdivisions/West-Davis-Active-Adult-Community/Reference-Documents/City_of_Davis_Beyond_Platinum_Bicycle_Action_Plan_2014.pdf.

Dean Runyan Associates. 2013. The Significance of Bicycle-Related Travel in Oregon: Detailed State and Travel Region Estimates, 2012. Accessed 11-26-19 at http://www.deanrunyan.com/doc_library/bicycletravel.pdf.

Earth Economics. 2015. Economic Analysis of Outdoor Recreation im Washington State. Accessed 11-2-19 at https://drive.google.com/file/d/0ByzIUWI76gWVR1Z4SmpIdUZyUWc/view?pref=2&pli=1.

East Coast Greenway Alliance. 2017. *The Impact of Greenways in the Triangle: How the East Coast Greenway Benefits the Health and Economy of North Carolina's Triangle Region.* Accessed on August 19, 2018 from https://www.greenway.org/uploads/attachments/cjgqs3ffg03yyp8qitykwkvz8-triangle-impact-report.pdf.

Feer & Peers. 2017. Economic Impacts of Active Transportation: Utah Active Transportation Benefits Study. Accessed 10-28-19 at https://static1.squarespace.com/static/5b8b54d1f407b40494055e8f/t/5bdc820c4fa51a4d9f77e014/1541177878083/Utah+Active+Transportation+Benefits+Study+-+Final+Report.pdf.

Fleming, K. *et al.* 2013. *The Economic Impact of Des Moines Parks and Recreation Services.* University of Northern Iowa. Cedar Falls, IA.

file:///C:/Users/Richard/Documents/Prosperity%20economic_impacts_de

s_moines_parks.pdf.

Florida Department of Environmental Protection. 2016. State Park System Direct Economic Impact Assessment – Fiscal Year 2015-2016 District 1. Tallahassee: Florida Department of Environmental Protection.

Flusche, Darren. 2012. Bicycling Means Business: The Economic Benefits of Bicycle Infrastructure. League of American Bicyclists. Accessed 6-12-20 at https://bikeleague.org/sites/default/files/Bicycling_and_the_Economy-Econ_Impact_Studies_web.pdf.

Garrett-Peltier, Heidi. 2011. Pedestrian and Bicycle Infrastructure: A National Study of Employment Impacts. Political Economy Research Institute: University of Massachusetts, Amherst. Accessed 6-13-20 at file:///C:/Users/Richard/Downloads/PERI_ABikes_October2011%20(1).pdf.

Gotschi, Thomas. 2011. Costs and Benefits of Bicycling Investments in Portland, Oregon. Journal of Physical Activity and Health. Accessed 5-30-20 at https://www.portlandmercury.com/images/blogimages/2011/03/03/1299202929-portland_bike_cost_study.pdf.

Grabow, M., Hahn, M., Whited, M. 2010. Valuing Bicycling's Economic and Health Impacts in Wisconsin. The Nelson Institute for Environmental Studies. University of Wisconsin – Madison. Accessed 8-20-19 at file:///C:/Users/Richard/Documents/Prosperity%20WI%20Econ%20Grabow%202010.pdf.

Grabow, Maggie et al. 2012. Air Quality and Exercise-Related Health Benefits from Reduced Car Travel in the Midwestern United States. Accessed g-7-20 at https://ehp.niehs.nih.gov/doi/10.1289/ehp.1103440.

Hammons, Hagen Thames. 2015. *Assessing the Economic and Livability Value of Multi-Use Trails: A Case Study into the Tammany Trace Rail Trail in St. Tammany Parish, Louisiana.* Master of Community and Regional Planning thesis. University of Oregon Department of Planning, Public Policy and Management. Accessed on July 5, 2018 from https://scholarsbank.uoregon.edu/xmlui/handle/1794/18963.

International Resource Panel. 2017. *The Weight of Cities: Resource Requirements of Future Urbanization.* Accessed 6-11-20 at https://www.resourcepanel.org/reports/weight-cities.

Karadeniz, Duygu. 2008. The Impact of the Little Miami Scenic Trail on Single Family Residential Property Values. Accessed 6-1-20 at https://www.americantrails.org/files/pdf/LittleMiamiPropValue.pdf.

Kelly, T. 2010. Status of Summer Trail Use (2007-09) on Five Paved State Bicycle Trails and Trends Since the 1990s. Minnesota Department of Natural Resources. Accessed 8-19-19 at http://files.dnr.state.mn.us/aboutdnr/reports/trails/trailuse.pdf.

Knoch, C. 2015. Three Rivers Heritage Trail 2014 User Survey and Economic Impact Analysis. Accessed 2-14-20 at https://www.railstotrails.org/resourcehandler.ashx?name=three-rivers-heritage-trail-2014-user-survey-and-economic-impact-analysis&id=5646&fileName=Three-Rivers-Heritage-Trail-Users-SurveyLORES.pdf.

Knoch, C. 2017. Heritage Rail Trail County Park 2017 User Survey and Economic Impact Analysis. Accessed 3-3-20 at https://drive.google.com/file/d/1yWX2yona3hLmSP0ST87SQJ7cClb1519j/view.

Komanoff, Charles and Cara Roelofs. 1993. The Environmental Benefits of Bicycling and Walking. U.S. Department of Transportation. Federal Highway Administration. Accessed 6-10-20 at https://www.americantrails.org/files/pdf/BikePedBen.pdf.

Lankford, J. *et al.* 2011. *Economic and health Benefits of Bicycling in Iowa.* Sustainable Tourism and Environmental Program, University of Northern Iowa. Cedar Falls, IA. Accessed 8-18-19 at https://headwaterseconomics.org/wp-content/uploads/Trail_Study_74-economic-health-benefits-cycling-iowa.pdf.

Lee, Allison and Alan March. 2007. Bike Parking in Shopping Strips. Accessed 6-13-20 at http://colabradio.mit.edu/wp-content/uploads/2010/12/Value_of_Bike_Parking_Alison_Lee.pdf.

Litman, Todd. 2020. Evaluating Active Transport Benefits and Costs: Guide to Valuing Walking and Cycling Improvement and Encouragement Programs. Victoria Transport Policy Institute. Accessed 5-29-20 at https://www.vtpi.org/nmt-tdm.pdf.

Magnini, V. and Uysal, M. 2015. The Economic Significance of West Virginia's State Parks and Forests. Accessed 3-9-20 at https://wvstateparks.com/EconomicResearch2015.pdf.

Maxwell. Tonya. 2014. Study confirms Swamp Rabbit Trail is a boon to businesses. Greenville Online. Accessed on August 7, 2018 from https://www.greenvilleonline.com/story/news/local/2014/12/03/official-swamp-rabbit-trail-greenville-travelers-rest-good-businesses-according-recreation-district-study/19837599/.

Miami Valley Regional Planning Commission. 2017. Miami Valley Trail User Report. Accessed 9-18-19 at

https://www.mvrpc.org/sites/default/files/trail_user_survey_report_2017.pdf.

Mulley, Corrine et.al. 2013. Valuing active travel: Including the health benefits of sustainable transportation in transportation appraisal frameworks. Research in Transportation Business & Management. Accessed 6-2-20 at https://www.sciencedirect.com/science/article/abs/pii/S2210539513000023?via%3Dihub.

National Association of Realtors. 2017. Millenials and Silent Generation Drive Desire for Walkable Communities, Say Realtors. Accessed 5-30-20 at https://www.nar.realtor/newsroom/millennials-and-silent-generation-drive-desire-for-walkable-communities-say-realtors.

North Carolina Department of Transportation. 2018. *Evaluating the Economic Impact of Shared Use Paths in North Carolina: Final Report.* Raleigh: North Carolina Department of Transportation - Division of Bicycle & Pedestrian Transportation.

Oishi, Shigehiro, Minkyung Koo and Nicholas Buttrick. 2018. The socioecological psychology of upward social mobility. *American Psychologist.* Accessed 6-11-20 at https://psycnet.apa.org/record/2018-63708-001.

Pima County. 2013. The Loop: Economic, Environmental, Community and Health Impact Study. Accessed 11-11-19 at

file:///C:/Users/Richard/Documents/Prosperity%20Tucson%20Econ%20Study%20of%20Loop.pdf.

Rabl, Ari and Audrey de Nazelle. 2012. Benefits of shift from car to active transport. *Transport Policy.* Accessed 6-6-20 at https://www.locchiodiromolo.it/blog/wp-content/uploads/2012/02/science.pdf.

Sinnett, Danielle et al. 2013. Making the Case for Investment in the Walking Environment: A review of the evidence. Accessed 6-1-20 at https://uwe-repository.worktribe.com/output/971643.

SQW. 2007. Valuing the benefits of cycling: A report to Cycling England. Accessed 6-21-20 at https://webarchive.nationalarchives.gov.uk/20110407101006/http://www.dft.gov.uk/cyclingengland/site/wp-content/uploads/2008/08/valuing-the-benefits-of-cycling-full.pdf.

Stark, L. 2014. Washington's Centennial Trail State Park – Trail of the Month: February 2014. Accessed 11-2-19 at https://www.railstotrails.org/trailblog/2014/february/01/washingtons-centennial-trail-state-park/.

Synergy/PRI/JPA. 2012. Katy Trail Economic Impact Report: Visotors and MGM2 Economic Impact Analysis. Accessed on 8-17-19 at

https://mostateparks.com/sites/mostateparks/files/Katy_Trail_Economic_Impact_Report_Final.pdf.

The Progress Fund. 2009. The Great Allegheny Passage Economic Impact Study (2997-2008). Accessed 2-21-20 at

file:///C:/Users/Richard/Downloads/GAPeconomicImpactStudy200809%20(1).pdf

Trail Facts. 2005. NCR Trail User Survey and Economic Impact Analysis. Accessed on 3-3-20 at https://www.railstotrails.org/resourcehandler.ashx?id=4792.

Velo Quebec, 2003. Cyclists spend over $95 million CAD (($64 million USD) annually along the Route verte. Accessed 1-18-20 at http://www.velo.qc.ca/en/pressroom/20030508171603/Cyclists-spend-over-$95-million-CAD-$64.6-million-USD-annually-along-the-Route-verte.

Velo Quebec. 2016. Bicycling in Quebec: 2015. Accessed 1-18-20 at http://www.velo.qc.ca/files/file/expertise/VQ_Cycling2015.pdf

Venegas, E. 2009. Economic Impact of Recreational Trail Use in Different Regions of Minnesota. University of Minnesota Tourism Center, Accessed 8-19-19 at https://conservancy.umn.edu/bitstream/handle/11299/168117/economic%20impact%20of%20recreational%20trails%202009.pdf?sequence=1&isAllowed=y.

Walk Score. 2020. Bike Score. Accessed 5-31-20 at https://www.walkscore.com/bike-score-methodology.shtml.

References: Chapter 2
– Abington - Damascus - Whitetop, Virginia: Saved by the Creeper

Barter Theatre. 2013. About. Accessed on July 30, 2018 from https://bartertheatre.com/about/history.

Bowker, J.M., Bergstrom, J., Gill, J. 2007. Estimating the economic value and impacts of recreational trails: a case study of the Virginia Creeper Rail Trail. *Tourism Economics*. 13(2): 241-260.

Economic Development Studio [Stephen Cox, Jonathan Hedrick, Chelsea Jeffries, Swetha Kumar, Sarah Lyon-Hill, William Powell, Katherine Shackelford, Sheila Westfall, Melissa Zilke]. 2011. Building Connectivity Through Recreation Trails: A Closer Look at New River Trail State Park and the Virginia Creeper Trail. Blacksburg: Economic Development Studio - Virginia Tech.

Gill, Joshua. 2004. *The Virginia Creeper Trail: An Analysis of Net Economic Benefits and Economic Impacts of Trips*. Thesis – Master of Science Degree. Athens: University of Georgia.

National Park Service. 2018. Abington Historic District. Accessed on July 31, 2018 from https://www.nps.gov/nr/travel/vamainstreet/abingdon.htm.

Stark, Laura. 2013. Virginia Creeper National Recreation Trail. *American Trails*. Accessed on July 30, 2018 from https://www.railstotrails.org/trailblog/2013/may/01/virginia-creeper-national-recreation-trail/.

Traillink. 2018. Virginia Creeper National Recreation Trail. Accessed on January 6, 2018 at https://www.traillink.com/trail/virginia-creeper-national-recreation-trail/.

References: Chapter 3
– Austin, Texas: Closing Gaps - Opening Opportunities

Angelou Economics. The Trail: Economic Impact Analysis 2016. Accessed 2-6-20 at https://www.thetrailfoundation.org/wp-content/uploads/2016/11/ttf-economic-impact-analysis-2016.pdf.

Austin. 2014. 2014 Austin Bicycle Plan. Accessed 2-6-20 at https://austintexas.gov/sites/default/files/files/2014_Austin_Bicycle_Master_Plan__Reduced_Size_.pdf.

Austin. 2020a. Trail Directory. Accessed 2-7-20 at http://www.austintexas.gov/page/trail-directory.

Austin. 2020b. Nature Preserves and Nature Based Programs. Accessed 2-7-20 at https://austintexas.gov/naturepreserves.

Austin. 2020c. Ann and Roy Butler Hike and Bike Trail and Boardwalk at Lady Bird Lake. Accessed 2-7-20 at http://www.austintexas.gov/department/ann-and-roy-butler-hike-and-bike-trail.

League of American Bicyclists. 2020. Bicycle-Friendly Communities. Accessed 2-6-20 at https://bikeleague.org/sites/default/files/bfareportcards/BFC_Fall_2015_ReportCard_Austin_TX.pdf.

References: Chapter 4
– Atlanta, Georgia: The Beltline: Economic Development Engine

Atlanta Beltline. 2018a. The Atlanta BeltLine: Where Atlanta Comes Together. Accessed on July 13, 2018 from https://beltline.org/about/the-atlanta-beltline-project/atlanta-beltline-overview/.

Atlanta BeltLine. 2018b. Project History. Accessed on July 15, 2018 from https://beltline.org/progress/progress/project-history/.

Fernbank 2018. Fernbank Museum of Natural History. Accessed on July 15, 2018 from http://www.fernbankmuseum.org/explore/permanent-features/.

Jimmy Carter Library. 2018. Museum. Accessed on July 15, 2018 from https://www.jimmycarterlibrary.gov/museum.

National Park Service. 2016. Martin Luther King, Jr. National Historic Park. Accessed on July 14, 2018 from https://www.nps.gov/malu/index.htm.

Piedmont Park Conservancy. 2018. History. Accessed on July 14, 2018 from https://www.piedmontpark.org/park-history/.

The Carter Center. 2018. About. Accessed on July 15, 2018 from https://www.cartercenter.org/.

Urban Land Institute. 2016. *Active Transportation and Real Estate: The Next Frontier.* Washington, DC: The Urban Land Institute.

References: Chapter 5:
– Blackstone River Trail, Massachusetts and Rhode Island: Birthplace of the American Industrial Revolution

Leonard, H. 2014. Leonard 2014 Bike Path Study. Rhode Island Bicycle Coalition.

Mass Humanities. 2021. Congress Designates Blackstone River Valley National Heritage Corridor. Accessed 10-10-21 at https://www.massmoments.org/moment-details/congress-designates-blackstone-river-valley-national-heritage-corridor.html.

McBurney, C. 2021. Slater Mill Now Part of a National Park. Accessed 10-10-21 at http://smallstatebighistory.com/slater-mill-now-part-of-a-national-park/#:~:text=In%20December%202014%2C%20Slater%20Mill,both%20northern%20Rhode%20Island%20and.

Mitchell, L. 2021. Chocolateville's Sweet Legacy. Rhode Tour. Accessed 10-10-21 at https://rhodetour.org/items/show/32.

St. Ann. 2021. St. Ann Arts and Cultural Center. Accessed 10-10-21 at http://www.stannartsandculturalcenter.org/.

Traillink. 2021. Blackstone River Greenway. Accessed 10-9-21 at https://www.traillink.com/trail/blackstone-river-greenway/.

References: Chapter 6
– Boise, Idaho: Gathering at the River

Berg, Sven. 2018. Boise bike riders want a Greenbelt-to-North-End route.

This is ACHD's answer. *Idaho Statesman.* November 15, 2018. Accessed on February 22, 2019 from https://www.idahostatesman.com/news/local/community/boise/article221718505.html.

Boise State University. 2014. The Boise River Greenbelt: Polishing a Community Gem. May 2014. Boise: Urban Research: College of Social Sciences & Public Affairs at Boise State University.

Boise Parks & Recreation Department. 2019. Boise Whitewater Park. Accessed on February 23, 2019 at https://www.boisewhitewaterpark.com/new-page.

Idaho. 2014. Idaho Statewide Bicycle and Pedestrian Study. Boise: Idaho Transportation Department.

Idaho Department of Fish and Game. 2019a. Boise River: Tributary of Snake River. Accessed on February 23, 2019 from https://idfg.idaho.gov/ifwis/fishingplanner/water/1170217438155.

Idaho Department of Fish and Game. 2019b. Idaho Birding Trail. Southwest: Boise River. Accessed on February 23, 2019 from https://idfg.idaho.gov/ifwis/ibt/site.aspx?id=89.

JUMP. 2019. Accessed on Febraury 23, 2019 from http://jumpboise.org/.

Vos, Japp. 2014. Results of 2013 Greenbelt User Survey. Boise: Department of Community and Regional Planning. Boise State University.

**References: Chapter 7
– Charlotte, North Carolina: Bicycling and the Redevelopment Playbook**

Charlotte. 2018. The Cross Charlotte Trail (XCLT). Accessed on August 17, 2018 from http://charlottenc.gov/charlottefuture/CIP/Pages/CrossCharlotteTrail.aspx.

Goodwin, Alan. 2017. Charlotte Rail Trail: A Place for Experimentation. Slide show accessed on August 7, 2018 from http://railvolution.org/wp-content/uploads/2017/10/Alan-Goodwin-CharlotteRailTrail.pdf.

North Carolina Department of Transportation. 2018. *Evaluating the Economic Impact of Shared Use Paths in North Carolina: Final Report.* Raleigh: North Carolina Department of Transportation - Division of Bicycle & Pedestrian Transportation.

**References: Chapter 8
– Chattanooga, Tennessee: The Trail to Revitalization**

Chattanooga Theatre Center. 2018. History. Accessed on July 29, 2018 from http://theatrecentre.com/about/history/.

Eichenthal, David and Windeknecht, Tracy. 2008. *A Restoring Prosperity Case Study: Chattanooga, Tennessee.* Washington, D.C.: Brookings.

Landscape Architecture Foundation. 2018. Renaissance Park. Accessed on July 28, 2018 from https://landscapeperformance.org/case-study-briefs/renaissance-park.

National Geographic. 2018. Walnut Street Bridge, Chattanooga, Tenn. Accessed on July 21, 2018 from https://www.tennesseerivervalleygeotourism.org/content/walnut-street-bridge-chattanooga-tenn/tenfa23eb4dac27e55b3.

Trust for Public Land. 1999. The Economic Benefits of Parks and Open Space: How Land Conservation Helps Communities Grow Smart and Protect the Bottom Line. Accessed on July 27, 2018 at https://www.tpl.org/sites/default/files/cloud.tpl.org/pubs/benfits_EconBenef_Parks_OpenSpaceL.pdf.

**References: Chapter 9
– Chicago, Illinois: Building on a Green Legacy**

Chicago Park District. 2018. Mayor Emanuel Outlines the Future if Chicago as a Two Waterfront City in the D+Secong Building on Burham Address. Accessed 8-27-19 at https://www.chicagoparkdistrict.com/about-us/news/mayor-emanuel-outlines-future-chicago-two-waterfront-city-second-building-burnham.

Chicago Park District. 2019. Lakefront Trail. Accessed on 8-27-19 at https://www.chicagoparkdistrict.com/index.php/parks-facilities/lakefront-trail.

Friends of the Lakefront Trail. 2013. Public Engagement Report. Accessed 8-26-19 at http://activetrans.org/sites/files/Public%20Engagement%20Report.pdf.

Trails for Illinois. 2013. Making Trails Count: Illinois Prairie Path. http://www.ipp.org/wp-content/uploads/IPP-Trail-Survey-2013.pdf.

Trails for Illinois. 2012. Making Trails Count in Illinois. Accessed 8-27-19 at https://www.recpro.org/assets/Library/Trails/making_trails_count_illinois.pdf.

**References: Chapter 10
– Cockeysville, Maryland – York, Pennsylvania: Torrey C. Brown Rail Trail – Heritage Rail Trail County Park: Cycling through History**

Knoch, C. 2017. Heritage Rail Trail County Park 2017 User Survey and Economic Impact Analysis. Accessed 3-3-20 at https://drive.google.com/file/d/1yWX2yona3hLmSP0ST87SQJ7cClb1519j/view.

Maryland. 2020. Gunpowder Falls State Park. Accessed 3-4-20 at https://dnr.maryland.gov/publiclands/Pages/central/gunpowder.aspx.

Stark, L. 2015. Pennsylvania's Heritage Rail Trail County Park and Maryland's Torrey C. Brown Rail Trail. Accessed 3-3-20 at https://www.railstotrails.org/trailblog/2015/september/18/pennsylvania-s-heritage-rail-trail-county-park-and-maryland-s-torrey-c-brown-rail-trail/.

Trail Facts. 2005. NCR Trail User Survey and Economic Impact Analysis. Accessed on 3-3-20 at https://www.railstotrails.org/resourcehandler.ashx?id=4792.

York County History Center. 2020. Museums. Accessed 3-5-20 at https://www.yorkhistorycenter.org/york-pa-museums.

**References: Chapter 11
– Colorado: High on Bicycling**

BBC Research & Consulting. 2016. Economic and Health Benefits of Bicycling and

Walking. Denver: Colorado Office of Economic Development and International Trade.

Colorado the Beautiful. 2019. The Colorado 16. Accessed 10-31-19 at https://cdnr.us/#/cothebeautiful.

Denver. 2019. Denver Moves: Pedestrian & Trails. Accessed 10-30-19 at https://www.denvergov.org/content/dam/denvergov/Portals/Denveright/documents/pedestrians-trails/Denver-Moves-Pedestrians-Trails-2019.pdf.

Georgia Institute of Technology. 2009. Red Fields to Green Fields: Parks Redefine & Transform. Accessed 10-29-19 at http://rftgf.org/PP/pdf-presentations/CityStudies/DenverR2G.pdf.

Hickenlooper, J. 2016. Gov. Hickenlooper announces 16 highest priority trail projects. Accessed 10-31-19 at https://cdnr.us/content/docs/16PriorityTrails.pdf.

League of American Bicyclists. 2019. Bicycle Friendly America: Award Database. Accessed 10-30-19 at

https://bikeleague.org/bfa/awards?gclid=EAIaIQobChMIi9a7j7PE5QIVIONkCh2z0gOWEAAYASAAEgIsiPD_BwE#community.

Urie, H. 2012. Survey finds Boulder's bike industry supports $52 million in sales. *Boulder Daily Camera*. Accessed 10-30-19 at

https://www.dailycamera.com/2012/01/25/survey-finds-boulders-bike-industry-supports-52-million-in-sales-hundreds-of-jobs/.

References: Chapter 12
– Covington - Mandeville - Slidell, Louisiana: Tammany Trace Builds Community

Hammons, Hagen Thames. 2015. *Assessing the Economic and Livability Value of Multi-Use Trails: A Case Study into the Tammany Trace Rail Trail in St. Tammany Parish, Louisiana.* Master of Community and Regional Planning thesis. University of Oregon Department of Planning, Public Policy and Management. Accessed on July 5, 2018 from https://scholarsbank.uoregon.edu/xmlui/handle/1794/18963.

Stark, Laura. 2017. Louisiana's Tammany Trace: Trail of the Month: August 2017. Rails to Trails Conservancy. Accessed on July 5, 2018 from https://www.railstotrails.org/trailblog/2017/august/16/louisiana-s-tammany-trace/.

References: Chapter 13
– Dayton - Cincinnati, Ohio: Little Miami Scenic Trail Generates Big Results

Loveland Castle. 2019. Loveland Castle. Accessed 9-19-19 at

http://www.lovelandcastle.com/.

Miami Valley Regional Planning Commission. 2017. Miami Valley Trail User Report. Accessed 9-18-19 at https://www.mvrpc.org/sites/default/files/trail_user_survey_report_2017.pdf.

Miami Valley Trails. 2019. Miami Valley Trails. Accessed 9-18-19 at https://www.miamivalleytrails.org/.

Rails-to-Trails Conservancy. 2019. Great American Rail Trail. Accessed 9-18-19 at http://www.railstotrails.org/greatamericanrailtrail/route/washington/.

Re-Cycle. 2019. Huffy History (Dayton, Ohio). Accessed 9-19-19 at http://re-cycle.com/History/Huffy.aspx.

References Chapter 14
– Delaware & Lehigh Trail: A Trail of Two Revolutions

Econsult. 2019. Investing in Our Future: Quantifying the Impact of Completing the East Coast Greenway in the Delaware River Watershed. Accessed 9-22-21 at https://econsultsolutions.com/wp-content/uploads/2019/04/ECG-in-the-Delaware-Valley-Report-3.7.pdf.

Stark, L. 2018. Pennsylvania's D&L Trail. Accessed 9-221 at Pennsylvania's D&L Trail (railstotrails.org).

Tomes, P. 2012. *D&L Trail 2012 User Survey and Economic Impact Analysis*. Rails-to-Trails Conservancy.

TrippUmbach. 2013. The Economic Impact of National Heritage Areas. Accessed 9-24-21 at https://www.nps.gov/subjects/heritageareas/upload/The-Economic-Impact-of-National-Heritage-Areas_Final-Report-pdf-2.pdf.

References: 15
– Des Moines, Iowa: It Pays to Make Connections

Iowa DOT 2018. Iowa Bicycle and Pedestrian Long Range Plan. Accessed 8-18-19 at https://iowadot.gov/iowainmotion/files/BikePedPlanDraft.pdf.

Fleming, K. *et al.* 2013. *The Economic Impact of Des Moines Parks and Recreation Services*. University of Northern Iowa. Cedar Falls, IA.

file:///C:/Users/Richard/Documents/Prosperity%20economic_impacts_des_moines_parks.pdf.

Lankford, J. et al. 2011. *Economic and health Benefits of Bicycling in Iowa*. Sustainable Tourism and Environmental Program, University of Northern Iowa. Cedar Falls, IA. Accessed 8-18-19 at https://headwaterseconomics.org/wp-content/uploads/Trail_Study_74-economic-health-benefits-cycling-iowa.pdf.

References: Chapter 16
– East Bay Bicycle Path, Rhode Island: A Car-Free Way to Get In and Out of Town

Blithewold. 2021. Accessed 10-11-21 at https://www.blithewold.org/.

Coggeshall. 2021. Coggeshall Farm Museum. Accessed 10-11-21 at https://www.coggeshallfarm.org/.

Herreshoff. 2021. Herreshoff Marine Museum. Accessed 10-11-12 at https://herreshoff.org/.

Leonard, H. 2014. Leonard 2014 Bike Path Study. Rhode Island Bicycle Coalition.

Rails-to-Trails Conservancy. 2021. East Bay Bike Path - Rhode Island. Accessed 10-11-21 at https://www.traillink.com/trail/east-bay-bike-path/.

References: Chapter 17
– Erie Canal Trail, New York: Transformational Then and Now

Parks & Trails New York. No Date. Bicyclists Bring Business: A Guide for Attracting Bicyclists to New York's Canal Communities. Accessed 9-28-21 at https://www.ptny.org/application/files/8514/3387/5238/Bicyclists_bring_business.pdf.

Scipione, P. 2014. The Economic Impact of the Erie Canalway Trail: An Assessment and User Profile of New Yorkd's Longest Multi-Use Trail. Accessed 9-28-21 at https://headwaterseconomics.org/wp-content/uploads/Trail_Study_109-NY-Econ-Impact-Erie-Canalway.pdf.

References: Chapter 18
– Farmington Canal Heritage Trail, Connecticut:
   A Key Link in Two Long-Distance-Trail Chains

Bushnell Park Foundation. 2021. Arch Tours and History. Accessed 10-13-21 at http://www.bushnellpark.org/attractions/soldiers-sailors-memorial-arch.

East Coast Greenway Alliance. 2021. Connecticut – Current Progress. Accessed 10-13-21 at https://www.greenway.org/states/connecticut.

Farmington Historical Society. 2021. The Amistad Captives. Accessed 10-12-21 at https://fhs-ct.org/1841/03/31/the-amistad-captives/.

Mark Twain House. 2021. Mark Twain House and Museum. Accessed 10-13-21 at https://marktwainhouse.org/.

Rails to Trails Conservancy. 2012. Farmington Canal Heritage Trail, Connecticut. Accessed 10-13-21 at https://www.railstotrails.org/trailblog/2012/april/01/farmington-canal-heritage-trail-connecticut/.

Rails-to-Trails Conservancy. 2020. New England Rail-Trail Spine Network. Accessed 10-14-21 at https://www.railstotrails.org/resource-library/resources/new-england-rail-trail-spine-network-map/.

Simsbury Historical Society. 2021. Simsbury Historical Society. Accessed 10-13-21 at https://simsburyhistory.org/.

Traillink. 2021. Farmington Canal Heritage Trail - Connecticut. Accessed 10-12-21 at https://www.traillink.com/trail/farmington-canal-heritage-trail/.

**References: Chapter 19
– Great Allegheny Passage/C&O Canal Trails: Trails and Towns Are Good for Each Other**

Allegany County. 2020. General Washington's Headquarters. Accessed 2-23-20 at https://www.mdmountainside.com/george-washingtons-headquarters.

Allegheny Trail Alliance. 2020. The GAP Trail. Accessed 2-22-20 at https://gaptrail.org/.

Fallingwater. 2020. Fallingwater. Accessed 2-22-20 at https://fallingwater.org/what-is-fallingwater/.

Glambrone, A. 2018. Map: What a regional bike trail network could look like in the D.C. area. Accessed 2024-20 at https://dc.curbed.com/2018/8/13/17683388/dc-region-bike-trails-network-cycling-map.

Herr, D. 2017. Analysis of 2016 Trail Usage Patterns along the Great Allegheny Passage. Accessed 2-21-20 at https://gaptrail.org/system/resources/W1siZiIsIjIwMTcvMDcvMjQvMjEvM DgvMDUvODkwLzIwMTZfR3JIYXRfQWxsZWdoZW55X1Bhc3NhZ2VfVH JhaWxfQ291bnRfRmluYWxfUmVwb3J0XzJfLnBkZiJdXQ/2016%20Great %20Allegheny%20Passage%20Trail%20Count%20Final%20Report%20 %282%29.pdf.

Lynch, J. 2019. Riverfront Resurgence: Pittsburgh's Three Rivers Heritage Trail. Accessed 2-20-20 at http://magazine.railstotrails.org/resources/magflipbooks/2019_winter/files /assets/common/downloads/publication.pdf.

National Park Service. 2020a. Chesapeake & Ohio Canal National Historic Park. Accessed 2-21-20 at https://www.nps.gov/choh/index.htm.

National Park Service. 2019. Williamsport Launch Boat Program. Accessed 2-24-20 at https://www.nps.gov/choh/planyourvisit/williamsport-launch-boat-program.htm.

National Park Service. 2020b. Downtown Cumberland Historic District. Accessed

2-23-20 at https://www.nps.gov/nr/travel/cumberland/dwn.htm.

Rivers of Steel. 2020. Attractions. Accessed 2-22-20 at https://riversofsteel.com/attractions/.

RTC (Rails-to-Trails Conservancy). 2020. Great Allegheny Passage. Accessed 2-22-20 at https://www.traillink.com/trail/great-allegheny-passage/.

The Progress Fund. 2009. The Great Allegheny Passage Economic Impact Study (2997-2008). Accessed 2-21-20 at

file:///C:/Users/Richard/Downloads/GAPeconomicImpactStudy200809%20(1).pdf

The Progress Fund. 2015. Trail User Survey and Business User Survey. Great Allegheny Passage. Accessed 2-21-20 at

https://gaptrail.org/system/resources/W1siZiIsIjIwMTYvMDkvMTMvMjAvMjgvMzEvNDExLzIwMTVfR0FQX1JlcG9ydC5wZGYiXV0/2015-GAP-Report.pdf.

The Progress Fund. 2017. The Trail Town Guide. Accessed 2-22-20 at https://www.trailtowns.org/wp-content/uploads/2017/10/TrailTownGuide.2.pdf.

Trail Town Program. 2015. Ohiopyle. Accessed 2-22-20 at https://www.trailtowns.org/Great-Allegheny-Passage.

References: Chapter 20
– Caldwell - Cass, West Virginia: Greenbrier River Trail: Boom Towns, Ghost Towns, and Bike Towns

Lynch, J. 2012. Greenbrier River Trail West Virginia: Trail of the Month – June 2012. Accessed 3-9-20 at https://www.railstotrails.org/trailblog/2012/june/01/greenbrier-river-trail-west-virginia/.

Magnini, V. and Uysal, M. 2015. The Economic Significance of West Virginia's State Parks and Forests. Accessed 3-9-20 at https://wvstateparks.com/EconomicResearch2015.pdf.

Rails-to-Trails Conservancy. 2020. Greenbrier River Trail. Accessed 3-9-20 at https://www.traillink.com/trail/greenbrier-river-trail/.

Schultz, D. 2014. Traveling 219: Old Watoga Town. Accessed 3-9-20 at http://www.traveling219.com/blog/old-watoga-town/.

West Virginia State Parks. 2020. Cass Scenic Railroad State Park. Accessed 3-9-20 at https://wvstateparks.com/park/cass-scenic-railroad-state-park/.

References: 21
– Greenville, South Carolina: The Swamp Rabbit
  Inspires More Trail Reproduction

Greenville. 2018a. Downtown Reborn. Accessed on August 1, 2018 from https://grvlsc.maps.arcgis.com/apps/Cascade/index.html?appid=d08f31d4489d475c8115ac7ccbacb25b.

Greenville. 2018b. War Memorials. Access on August 4, 2018 from https://www.greenvillesc.gov/299/War-Memorials.

Maxwell. Tonya. 2014. Study confirms Swamp Rabbit Trail is a boon to businesses. Greenville Online. Accessed on August 7, 2018 from https://www.greenvilleonline.com/story/news/local/2014/12/03/official-swamp-rabbit-trail-greenville-travelers-rest-good-businesses-according-recreation-district-study/19837599/.

Reed, Julian. 2014. *Greenville Health System Swamp Rabbit Trail: Year Three Findings.* Greenville: Furman University.

Stark, Laura. 2016. South Carolina's Greenville Health System Swamp Rabbit Trail. Accessed on August 3, 2018 from https://www.railstotrails.org/trailblog/2016/february/14/south-carolina-s-greenville-health-system-swamp-rabbit-trail/.

Traillink. 2018. Greenville Health System Swamp Rabbit Trail Itinerary. Accessed on July 3, 2018 from https://www.traillink.com/trail-itinerary/greenville-health-system-swamp-rabbit-trail/.

References: Chapter 22
– Gulf Coast, Alabama: Snow Birds Flock Here

Alabama Gulf Coast Recovery Council. 2018. About. Accessed on July 10, 2018 at https://www.restorealabama.org/.

Alabama State Parks. 2016. *Alabama's Gulf State Park Master Plan.* Accessed on July 9, 2018 at http://mygulfstatepark.com/wp-content/uploads/2016/10/160823_GSP_MasterPlan_Final_lowres.pdf.

Alabama Department of Transportation. 2017. *Alabama Statewide Bicycle and Pedestrian Plan.* Montgomery: Alabama Department of Transportation.

Orange Beach Alabama Community Website. 2018. Alabama Gulf Coast Recovery Council selects projects for draft plans; eight projects in Orange Beach. Accessed on July 10, 2018 at https://obawebsite.com/alabama-gulf-coast-recovery-council-selects-projects-for-draft-plans-8-projects-in-orange-beach.

References: Chapter 23:
– Harmony - Preston - Lanesboro - Houston, Minnesota:
  Linking Art and Crafts

Commonweal Theater. Accessed 8-19-19 at https://www.commonwealtheatre.org/.

Kelly, T. 2010. Status of Summer Trail Use (2007-09) on Five Paved State Bicycle Trails and Trends Since the 1990s. Minnesota Department of Natural Resources. Accessed 8-19-19 at http://files.dnr.state.mn.us/aboutdnr/reports/trails/trailuse.pdf.

Lanesboro Arts. Accessed on 8-19-19 at https://lanesboroarts.org/

Minnesota 2019. A-Z listing of Minnesota State Trails. Accessed 8-19-19 at https://www.dnr.state.mn.us/state_trails/list.html.

Park & Trails Council of Minnesota 2017. State of the Trails. Accessed on 8-19-19 at https://www.parksandtrails.org/wp-content/uploads/2015/09/State-of-the-Trails-Report.pdf.

Venegas, E. 2009. Economic Impact of Recreational Trail Use in Different Regions of Minnesota. University of Minnesota Tourism Center, Accessed 8-19-19 at https://conservancy.umn.edu/bitstream/handle/11299/168117/economic%20impact%20of%20recreational%20trails%202009.pdf?sequence=1&isAllowed=y.

References: Chapter 24
– Hattiesburg - Prentiss, Mississippi: Adding Spokes to Hub City

Bunch, Beth. 2018. Longleaf Trace: Latest .85-mile extension will carry popular trail from Depot to Chain Park. Hub City Spokes. Posted March 8, 2018. Accessed on July 8, 2018 at https://hubcityspokes.com/news-hattiesburg/longleaf-trace.

Exploring by Bicycle. 2017. The economic impact of Mississippi's Longleaf Trace. Exploring by bicycle. Posted March 23, 2017. Accessed on July 8, 2018 at https://exploringbybike.wordpress.com/2017/03/23/the-economic-impact-of-mississippis-longleaf-trace/.

Historic Hattiesburg Downtown Association. 2018. History of Downtown Hattiesburg. Accessed on July 7, 2018 from

https://downtownhattiesburg.com/our-organization/history/.

McNeill, George. 2005. Longleaf Trace a fitness and economic boon in South Mississippi. Mississippi Business Journal. Posted January 31, 2005. Accessed on July 8, 2018 at http://msbusiness.com/2005/01/longleaf-trace-a-fitness-and-economic-boon-in-south-mississippi/.

Moore, James. 2011. Bike Trails Boosts Business in Mississippi. Quoted in News from the League. League of American Bicyclists. Accessed on July 8, 2018 at https://bikeleague.org/content/bike-trail-boosts-business-mississippi.

Mussiett, Mon. 2015. Longleaf Trace to extend two miles into Hattiesburg. WDAM-TV News. July 14, 2015. Accessed on July 8, 2018 at http://www.wdam.com/story/29548604/longleaf-trace-to-extend-2-miles-into-hattiesburg.

Pearl and Leaf Rivers Rails to Trails Recreational District. Undated a.

Call for Projects – NTEC – Community Benefits. Accessed on July 8, 2018 at http://www.longleaftrace.org/Awards/Combenefit/communitiesbenefit.htm.

Pearl and Leaf Rails to Trails Recreational District. Undated b. How's Business Along the Trace? Accessed on July 8, 2018 at http://www.longleaftrace.org/EcoDev/NewDev.html.

Saenger. 2018. History of the Movie Palace. Access on July 7, 2018 from http://www.hattiesburgsaenger.com/index.cfm/history.

References: Chapter 25
– Indianapolis - Carmel, Indiana: Slowing Down Pays Off

Flusche, D. 2012. Bicycling Means Business: The Economic Benefits of Bicycle Infrastructure. League of American Bicyclists. Accessed 8-31-19 at https://bikeleague.org/sites/default/files/Bicycling_and_the_Economy-Econ_Impact_Studies_web.pdf.

Indiana University Public Policy Institute. 2015. Assessment of the Impact of the Indianapolis Cultural Trail: A Legacy of Gene and Marilyn Glick. Accessed 9-17-19 at http://indyculturaltrail.org.s3.amazonaws.com/wp-content/uploads/2015/07/15-C02-CulturalTrail-Assessment.pdf.

Rails-to-Trails Conservancy. 2009. Trail of the Month: March 2009. Accessed 8-31-19 at http://www.railstotrails.org/trailblog/2009/march/01/indianas-monon-trail/.

Rails-to-Trails Conservancy. 2019. Indianapolis Cultural Trail. Accessed 9-17.19 at https://www.traillink.com/trail/indianapolis-cultural-trail/.

References: Chapter 26
– La Crosse - Madison - Milwaukee, Wisconsin: The Route of the Badger

Grabow, M., Hahn, M., Whited, M. 2010. Valuing Bicycling's Economic and Health Impacts in Wisconsin. The Nelson Institute for Environmental Studies. University of Wisconsin – Madison. Accessed 8-20-19 at file:///C:/Users/Richard/Documents/Prosperity%20WI%20Econ%20Grabow%202010.pdf.

Kapp, A. 2016. Meet the Badger: 500-mile network takes hold in Southeastern Wisconsin. Rails-to-Trails Conservancy. Accessed 8-20-19 at https://www.railstotrails.org/trailblog/2016/march/03/meet-the-badger-500-mile-trail-network-takes-hold-in-southeast-wisconsin/.

Kazmierski, B. et.al. 2009. Trails and their gateway communities: A case study of recreational use compatibility and economic impacts. Accessed 8-20-19 at https://cdn.shopify.com/s/files/1/0145/8808/4272/files/G3880.pdf.

Lewis, C. 2016. Trails in southeastern Wisconsin make for biking bliss. Milwaukee Journal-Sentinel. Accessed 8-25-19 at

https://www.jsonline.com/story/travel/wisconsin/day-out/2016/07/15/day-out-trails-in-southeastern-wisconsin-make-for-biking-bliss/87171910/.

Milwaukee. 2019. Riverwalk History. Milwaukee Department of Community Development. Accessed 8-25-19 at https://city.milwaukee.gov/RiverWalk/RiverWalk-History.htm#.XWKGRHdFzIU.

Wisconsin Bike Fed. 2019. Economic Impact. Accessed 8-20-19 at https://wisconsinbikefed.org/advocacy/economic-impact/.

Wisconsin DNR 2019. Wisconsin State Park System Bicycle Trails. Accessed 8-20-19 at https://dnr.wi.gov/topic/parks/activities/bike.html#touring.

Wisconsin DOT. 1998. Wisconsin Bicycle Transportation Plan 2020. Accessed 8-20-19 at

https://wisconsindot.gov/Documents/projects/multimodal/bike/2020-plan.pdf.

References: Chapter 27
– Lackawanna River Heritage Trail, Pennsylvania:
   From Electric City to Coal Country

Jones *et.al.* 2015. *Lackawanna Valley National Heritage Area. Evaluation Findings.* Prepared for U.S. National Park Service. Accessed 9-27-21 at https://www.nps.gov/subjects/heritageareas/upload/Lackawanna-v2016.pdf.

Lackawanna Heritage Valley. 2017. 2016 Trail User Survey and Economic Impact Analysis. Accessed 9-27-21 at https://lhva.org/Publications.php.

References: Chapter 28
– Louisville, Kentucky: Getting Everyone in The Loop

Ahn, A. 2018. Kentucky's Louisville Loop. Accessed 9-20-19 at http://www.railstotrails.org/trailblog/2018/february/12/kentuckys-louisville-loop/.

Olmstead Parks Conservancy. 2019. Our Parks. Accessed 9-20-19 at https://www.olmstedparks.org/our-parks/.

The Cultural Landscape Foundation. 2019. Louisville Parks and Parkways System. Accessed 9-20-19 at

https://tclf.org/landscapes/louisville-parks-and-parkways-system.

Rails-to-Trails. 2019. Louisville Loop. Accessed 9-21-19 at http://www.railstotrails.org/policy/trailstransform/louisville/.

The Parklands of Floyds Fork. 2018. The Parklands Releases 2017 Annual Report. Accessed 9-20-19 at https://www.theparklands.org/News/The-Parklands-Releases-2017-Annual-Report.

The Parklands of Floyds Fork. 2019 year in Review. Accessed 9-20-19 at https://www.theparklands.org/res/uploads/media//2018-Annual-Report-FINAL-digital_1.pdf.

**References: Chapter 29
– Maine: Seeing the Light**

Andrews, J. 2018. The Economic Impacts of the Eastern Trail in Southern Maine. Accessed on 10-1-21 at https://www.easterntrail.org/documents/ETEconomicImpactStudy2018.pdf

Eastern Trail Alliance. 2021. Over the River Campaign. Accessed 10-3-21 at https://www.easterntrail.org/over-the-river/.

Wilber Smith. 2001. Bicycle Tourism in Maine: Economic Impacts and Marketing. Accessed 10-1-21 at https://headwaterseconomics.org/wp-content/uploads/Trail_Study_80-bicycle-tourism-maine.pdf.

**References: Chapter 30
– Minneapolis, Minnesota: Learning from the Grand Rounds**

Cleveland. 1888. From "The Aesthetic Development of the United Cities of St. Paul and Minneapolis" (Minneapolis: AC Bausman), as quoted in Daniel J. Nadenicek (1993), "Nature in the City: Horace Cleveland's Aesthetic," *Landscape and Urban Planning* 26:5-15.

Koutsky, L. 2016. The History of Lake Harriet Park's Architecture. Southwest Journal. Accessed 11-24-19 at https://www.southwestjournal.com/focus/neighborhood-spotlight/2016/06/the-history-of-lake-harriets-park-architecture/.

League of American Bicyclists. 2019. Award Database. Accessed 11-25-19 at https://bikeleague.org/bfa/awards.

Minneapolis. 2011. Minneapolis Bicycle Master Plan. Accessed 12-25-19 at http://www.minneapolismn.gov/www/groups/public/@publicworks/documents/webcontent/convert_275983.pdf.

Minneapolis Parks & Recreation Board. 2019. Parks and Destinations. Accessed 11-23-19 at https://www.minneapolisparks.org/.

Pruetz, R. 2012. *Lasting Value: Open Space Planning and Preservation Successes*. Chicago: American Planning Association.

Rails-to-Trails Conservancy. 2019. Trail: Minnesota. Accessed 11-25-19 at https://www.traillink.com/trailsearch/?state=MN.

Stark, L. 2015. Minnesota's Midtown Greenway: Trail of the Month. Accessed 11-251-9 at https://www.railstotrails.org/trailblog/2015/october/16/minnesotas-midtown-greenway/.

Urban Land Institute. 2016. Active Transportation and Real Estate: The Next Frontier. Accessed 11-25-19 at http://uli.org/wp-content/uploads/ULI-Documents/Active-Transportation-and-Real-Estate-The-Next-Frontier.pdf.

Venegas, E. Economic Impact of Recreational Trail Use in Different Regions of Minnesota. Access 11-25-19 at https://headwaterseconomics.org/wp-content/uploads/Trail_Study_4-trail-use-in-minnesota.pdf.

References: Chapter 31
– Minuteman Commuter Bikeway, Greater Boston, Massachusetts: Declaring Independence from the Automobile

Boston. 2013. Boston Bike Network Plan. Accessed on 10-8-21 at

https://www.cityofboston.gov/images_documents/Boston%20Bike%20Network%20Plan%2C%20Fall%202013_FINAL_tcm3-40525.pdf.

East Coast Greenway. 2021. East Coast Greenway – Massachusetts. Accessed 10-8-21 at https://www.greenway.org/states/massachusetts.

MassTrails. 2021. Impacts of Shared Use Paths: A Study of the Economic, Health, Transportation, Environmental, Safety, and Accessibility Impacts of Four Shared Use Paths in Massachusetts. Accessed 10-5-21 at https://www.mass.gov/doc/masstrails-shared-use-path-impacts-study/download#:~:text=The%20shared%20use%20paths%20contributed,%243%2C600%20on%20a%20weekend%20day.

Rails-to-Trails Conservancy. 2021. Massachusetts Rail-Trail Stats. Accessed 10-7-21 at https://www.railstotrails.org/our-work/united-states/massachusetts/#state.

References: Chapter 32
– Montreal - Quebec, Quebec, Canada: *Route verte* - Green in Many Ways

Copenhagenize. 2020. Copenhagenize Index 2019. Accessed 1-18-20 at https://copenhagenizeindex.eu/the-index.

The Great Trail. 2020. Map. Accessed 1-18-20 at https://thegreattrail.ca/explore-the-map/.

Velo Quebec, 2003. Cyclists spend over $95 million CAD (($64 million USD) annually along the Route verte. Accessed 1-18-20 at http://www.velo.qc.ca/en/pressroom/20030508171603/Cyclists-Spend-over-$95-million-CAD-$64.6-million-USD-annually-along-the-Route-verte.

Velo Quebec. 2010. Cycling in Quebec. 6th Edition. Montreal: Velo Quebec.

Velo Quebec. 2016. Bicycling in Quebec: 2015. Accessed 1-18-20 at http://www.velo.qc.ca/files/file/expertise/VQ_Cycling2015.pdf.

Velo Quebec. 2017. La Route verte: A provincial treasure. Accessed 1-15-20 at http://www.velo.qc.ca/en/50years/The-Route-verte-A-provincial-treasure.

References: Chapter 33
– New Hampshire: Bridging the Old and the New

Alta. 2020. New Hampshire DOT Statewide Pedestrian & Bicycle Transportation Plan and Economic Impact Study. Accessed 9-30-21 at

https://www.nh.gov/dot/programs/bikeped/advisory-committee/documents/200110_NHDOT_TechMemo4-EconomicImpactAnalysis.pdf.

East Coast Greenway. 2019. Greenway poised for record New Hampshire growth following rail corridor acquisition. Accessed 10-1-21 at https://www.greenway.org/stories/greenway-poised-for-record-new-hampshire-growth-following-rail-corridor-acquisition.

Penna, C. 2002. New England Greenway Symposium Presentation. Accessed 10-1-21 at https://www.umass.edu/greenway/news/newsletter-Vol4/NE/RTC.html#:~:text=Interestingly%2C%20New%20Hampshire%20alone%20has,New%20England%20totaling%201%2C023%20miles.

Rails-to-Trails Conservancy. New Hampshire Rail Trail Stats. Accessed 9-30-21 at https://www.railstotrails.org/our-work/united-states/new-hampshire/#state.

References: Chapter 34
– New Jersey: Cultivating the Garden State

Econsult. 2019. Investing in Our Future: Quantifying the Impact of Completing the East Coast Greenway in the Delaware River Watershed. Accessed 9-22-21 at https://econsultsolutions.com/wp-content/uploads/2019/04/ECG-in-the-Delaware-Valley-Report-3.7.pdf.

Traillink. 2021. New Jersey. Accessed 9-22-21 at https://www.traillink.com/trailsearch/?mmloc=NJ.

Brown, C. *et. al.* 2011. The Economic Impacts of Active Transportation in New Jersey. Accessed 9-22-21 at http://recon.rutgers.edu/wp-content/uploads/2014/03/Economic-Impacts-of-Active-Transportation-in-NJ.pdf.

Resources: Chapter 35
– New Mexico: Gearing Up for Bicycles

Albuquerque. 2015. Bikeways & Trails Facilities Plan. Accessed 2-11-20 at http://documents.cabq.gov/planning/adopted-longrange-plans/BTFP/Final/BTFP%20FINAL_Jun25.pdf.

Albuquerque. 2020. Paseo del Bosque Trail. Accessed 2-11-20 at https://www.cabq.gov/parksandrecreation/open-space/lands/paseo-del-bosque-trail.

Atencio, E. 2012. Trails for the People and Economy of Santa Fe. Accessed 2-9-20 at https://sfct.org/wp-content/uploads/2012/07/Trails-for-the-People-and-Economy-of-Santa-Fe.pdf.

League of American Bicyclists. 2020. Bicycle Friendly State Report Card: New Mexico. Accessed 2-9-20 at https://bikeleague.org/sites/default/files/BFS%20Report%20Card_2019_NewMexico.pdf.

National Park Service. 2019. Petroglyph National Monument. Accessed 2-11-20 at https://www.nps.gov/petr/learn/historyculture/what.htm.

Northern Rio Grande NHA. 2020. Northern Rio Grande National Heritage Area. Accessed 2-10-20 at https://riograndenha.org/index.html.

New Mexico. 2017. Rio Grande Trail Master Plan. Accessed 2-10-20 at http://www.riograndetrailnm.com/.

New Mexico. 2018. New Mexico Prioritized Statewide Bicycle Network Plan. Accessed 2-9-20 at

https://dot.state.nm.us/content/dam/nmdot/BPE/NM_Bike_Plan.pdf.

Santa Fe County. 2020. Santa Fe County Open Space, Trails & Parks Program. Accessed 2-11-20 at https://www.santafecountynm.gov/open_space_and_trails_program/properties.

Santa Fe Metropolitan Planning Organization. 2019. Santa Fe Metropolitan Planning Organization Bicycle Master Plan. Accessed 2-11-20 at https://santafempo.org/plans/bicycle-master-plan/.

References: Chapter 36
– Philadelphia, Pennsylvania: At Liberty to Bicycle

Econsult. 2010. The Potential Economic, Environmental, Health, and Quality of Life Benefits of a Fully Connected Waterfront Greenway in Philadelphia. Accessed 9-19-21 at https://whyy.org/wp-content/uploads/planphilly/assets_6/fully-connected-waterfront-greenway-in-philadelphia-potential-economic-environmental-health-and-quality-of-life-benefits-final-report-2010-09-21.original.pdf.

Knoch, C. and P. Tomes. 2008. *Perkiomen Trail 2008 User Survey and Economic Impact Analysis*. Rails-to-Trails Conservancy.

Schuylkill Banks. 2021. A Brief History of Lower Schuylkill. Retrieved 9-21-21 at https://www.schuylkillbanks.org/.

Tomes, P. and C. Knoch. 2009. *Schuylkill River Trail 2009 User Survey and Economic Analysis*. Rails-to-Trails Conservancy.

Tomes, P. 2012. D&L *Trail 2012 User Survey and Economic Impact Analysis*. Rails-to-Trails Conservancy.

ULI (Urban Land Institute). 2016. *Active Transportation and Real Estate: The Next Frontier*. Accessed 9-20-21 at http://uli.org/wp-content/uploads/ULI-Documents/Active-Transportation-and-Real-Estate-The-Next-Frontier.pdf.

References: Chapter 37
– Pittsburgh, Pennsylvania: From Steel City to Cycle Town

Knoch, C. 2015. Three Rivers Heritage Trail 2014 User Survey and Economic Impact Analysis. Accessed 2-14-20 at https://www.railstotrails.org/resourcehandler.ashx?name=three-rivers-heritage-trail-2014-user-survey-and-economic-impact-analysis&id=5646&fileName=Three-Rivers-Heritage-Trail-Users-SurveyLORES.pdf.

Lynch, J. 2019. Riverfront Resurgence: Pittsburgh's Three Rivers Heritage Trail. Accessed 2-20-20 at http://magazine.railstotrails.org/resources/magflipbooks/2019_winter/files/assets/common/downloads/publication.pdf.

Station Square. 2020. History. Accessed 2-20-20 at https://www.stationsquare.com/history/.

Van Zandt, L. 2014. Station Square: PHLF's Greatest Saves. Accessed 2-21-20 at https://phlf.org/2015/07/30/station-square-phlf-greatest-saves/.

References: Chapter 38
– Portland, Oregon: Bicycling and Portland's Green Dividend

40-Mile Loop Land Trust. 2019. History of the Loop. Accessed 11-27-19 at https://40mileloop.org/wordpress/?page_id=6.

Clifton, J., Morrisey, S. & Ritter, C. 2012. Business Cycles: Catering to the Bicycling Market. Accessed 11-27-19 at http://kellyjclifton.com/Research/EconImpactsofBicycling/TRN_280_CliftonMorrissey&Ritter_pp26-32.pdf.

Cortright, J. 2007. Portland's Green Dividend Accessed 11-27-19 at http://cityobservatory.org/portlands-green-dividend/.

Dean Runyan Associates. 2013. The Significance of Bicycle-Related Travel in Oregon: Detailed State and Travel Region Estimates, 2012. Accessed 11-26-19 at http://www.deanrunyan.com/doc_library/bicycletravel.pdf.

Dean Runyan Associates. 2014. Columbia River Gorge Bicycle Recreation: Economic Impact Forecast for the Communities Along the Historic Columbia River Highway. Accessed 11-27-19 at https://headwaterseconomics.org/trail/67-columbia-river-gorge-bicycle-rec/.

League of American Bicyclists. 2019. Portland Oregon Report Card. Accessed 11-26-19 at https://bikeleague.org/sites/default/files/BFC_Fall_2017_ReportCard_Portland_OR.pdf.

Portland Bureau of Transportation. 2019. Bicycles in Portland Fact Sheet. Accessed 11-26-19 at https://www.portlandoregon.gov/transportation/article/407660.

Portland Parks & Recreation. 2019. Eastbank Esplanade. Accessed 11-27-19 at https://www.portlandoregon.gov/parks/finder/index.cfm?PropertyID=105&action=ViewPark.

Pruetz, R. 2009. *Green Legacy: Communities Worth Leaving to Future Generations.* Hermosa Beach, California: Arje Press.

Pruetz, R. 2013. Prosperity Comes in Cycles. Planning. Accessed on 11-27-19 at https://www.planning.org/planning/2013/nov/prosperitycomesincycles.htm.

Rails-to-Trails Conservancy. 2011. Oregon's Springwater Corridor. Accessed 11-26-19 at https://www.railstotrails.org/trailblog/2011/september/01/oregons-springwater-corridor/.

Rails-to-Trails Conservancy. 2019. Trail Search: Oregon. Accessed 11-27-19 at https://www.traillink.com/trailsearch/?state=OR.

**References: Chapter 39
– Raleigh-Durham, North Carolina: New Roles for Tobacco Legacy**

Abrams, Amanda. 2017. Boosters Argue that the Proposed East Coast Greenway Could Revitalize Forgotten North Carolina Towns. Indy Week. Accessed on August 19, 2018 from https://www.indyweek.com/indyweek/boosters-argue-that-the-proposed-east-coast-greenway-could-revitalize-forgotten-north-carolina-towns/Content?oid=8359505.

Brightleaf Square. 2018. History. Accessed on August 19, 2018 from https://historicbrightleaf.com/history/.

Duke Gardens. 2018. About. Accessed on August 19, 2018 from http://gardens.duke.edu/about.

East Coast Greenway Alliance. 2017. *The Impact of Greenways in the Triangle: How the East Coast Greenway Benefits the Health and Economy of North Carolina's Triangle Region.* Accessed on August 19, 2018 from https://www.greenway.org/uploads/attachments/cjgqs3ffg03yyp8qitykwkvz8-triangle-impact-report.pdf.

North Carolina Department of Transportation. 2018. *Evaluating the Economic Impact of Shared Use Paths in North Carolina: Final Report.* Raleigh: North Carolina Department of Transportation - Division of Bicycle & Pedestrian Transportation.

U.S. News and World Report. Education. Accessed on August 19, 2018 from https://www.usnews.com/best-colleges/duke-university-2920.

References: Chapter 40
– Bentonville-Fayetteville, Arkansas: On the Path to Becoming a World-Class Bicycling Destination

Alta Planning + Design. 2017. Trail Program Implementation: A Peer + Aspirational Review. Accessed 3-10-20 at https://www.waltonfamilyfoundation.org/learning/trail-program-implementation-a-peer-aspirational-review.

BBC Research & Consulting. 2018. Economic and Health Benefits of Bicycling in Northwest Arkansas. Accessed 3-10-20 at https://www.waltonfamilyfoundation.org/learning/economic-and-health-benefits-of-bicycling-in-northwest-arkansas.

Bella Vista. 2018. New 50-mile Trail System Announced for Bella Vista. Accessed 3-21-20 at https://www.bellavistaar.gov/news_detail_T12_R69.php.

Bentonville. 2020. Paved Trails and Road Rides. Accessed 3-11-20 at https://www.visitbentonville.com/bike/trail-maps/paved/.

Botanical Garden of the Ozarks. 2020. Accessed 3-10-20 at https://www.bgozarks.org/

Crystal Bridges Museum of American Art. Accessed 3-11-20 at https://crystalbridges.org/.

Fayetteville. 2020. Paved Shared-Use Trails. Accessed 3-10-20 at http://www.fayetteville-ar.gov/3486/Paved-Shared-Use-Trails.

Jones Center. 2020. Accessed 3-11-20 at https://www.thejonescenter.net/.

League of American Bicyclists. 2020. Bicycle Friendly Communities. Accessed 3-11-20 at https://bikeleague.org/bfa/awards.

Northwest Arkansas Regional Planning Commission. 2015. Walk Bike Northwest Arkansas: Regional Bicycling and Pedestrian Plan – Executive Summary. Accessed

3-11-20 at http://www.nwabikepedplan.com/final-plan-and-documents.html.

Rodeo of the Ozarks. 2020. About. Accessed 3-11-20 at http://www.rodeooftheozarks.org/about-us.

Rogers. 2020. Our Trails. Accessed 3-11-20 at http://rogersar.gov/211/Our-Trails.

Rails to Trails Conservancy. 2020. Razorback Regional Greenway. Accessed 3-10-22 at https://www.traillink.com/trail/razorback-regional-greenway/.

Shiloh Museum of Ozark History. 2020. Accessed 3-11-20 at https://shilohmuseum.org/.

Walton Family Foundation. 2017. Northwest Arkansas Trail Usage Monitoring Report. Accessed 3-10-20 at

https://www.waltonfamilyfoundation.org/learning/northwest-arkansas-trail-usage-monitoring-report.

University of Arkansas. 2020. Senior Walk. Accessed 3-10-20 at https://registrar.uark.edu/graduation/senior-walk.php.

References: Chapter 41
– South Haven - Kalamazoo, Michigan

BBC Research & Consulting. 2014a. Community and Economic Benefits of Bicycling in Michigan. Accessed 8-27-19 at https://www.michigan.gov/documents/mdot/MDOT_CommAndEconBenefitsOfBicyclingInMI_465392_7.pdf.

BBC Research & Consulting. 2014b. Economic and Health Benefits of Bicycling in Ann Arbor. Accessed on 8-28-19 at https://www.michigan.gov/documents/mdot/MDOT_AnnArborCaseStudy_465391_7.pdf.

BBC Research & Consulting. 2014c. Southwest Detroit and Connor Creek Greenway Case Study - Community and Economic Benefits of Bicycling. Accessed on 8-28-19 at

https://www.michigan.gov/documents/mdot/MDOT_DetroitCaseStudy_465393_7.pdf.

BBC Research & Consulting. 2014d. Grand Rapids Case Study – Community and Economic Benefits of Bicycling. Accessed on 8-28-19 at https://www.michigan.gov/documents/mdot/MDOT_GrandRapidsCaseStudy_465394_7.pdf.

BBC Research & Consulting. 2014e. Holland Case Study – Community and Economic Benefits of Bicycling. Accessed on 8-28-19 at https://www.michigan.gov/documents/mdot/MDOT_HollandCaseStudy_4

65395_7.pdf.

BBC Research & Consulting. 2014f. Traverse City Case Study – Community and Economic Benefits of Bicycling. Accessed on 8-28-19 at https://www.michigan.gov/documents/mdot/MDOT_TraverseCityCaseStudy_465402_7.pdf.

Henderson Castle. 2019. About. Accessed on 8-28-19 at https://www.hendersoncastle.com/.

Wedel, M. 2017. Long promised trail connections are starting to link up. Accessed on 8-27-19 at https://www.secondwavemedia.com/southwest-michigan/features/Long-promised-trail-connections-are-starting-to-link-up-1005.aspx.

Resources: Chapter 42
– Sacramento, California:
The Great California Delta Trail Promises Great Results

California State Parks. 2019. Old Sacramento State Historic Park. Accessed 12-5-19 at http://www.parks.ca.gov/?page_id=497.

Davis. 2014. Bicycle Action Plan: Beyond Platinum. Accessed 12-5-19 at http://documents.cityofdavis.org/Media/CityCouncil/Documents/PDF/CDD/Planning/Subdivisions/West-Davis-Active-Adult-Community/Reference-Documents/City_of_Davis_Beyond_Platinum_Bicycle_Action_Plan_2014.pdf.

Delta Protection Commission. 2012. Feasibility Study for a Sacramento-San Joaquin Delta National Heritage Area. Accessed 12-2-19 at http://delta.ca.gov/wp-content/uploads/2016/10/Delta_NHA_Study.pdf.

Delta Protection Commission. 2019. Great California Delta Trail. Accessed 12-2-19 at http://delta.ca.gov/recreation/delta_trail/.

Johnny Cash Trail. 2019. About the Johnny Cash Trail. Accessed 12-5-19 at https://folsomcasharttrail.com/the-trail/about.

League of American Bicyclists. 2019. Data Base. Accessed 12-5-19 at https://www.bikeleague.org/bfa/awards.

National Park Service. National Heritage Areas FAQs. Accessed on 12-2-19 at https://www.nps.gov/articles/national-heritage-areas-faqs.htm.

Old Sacramento Waterfront. History. Accessed 12-4-19 at https://www.oldsacramento.com/history.

Sacramento Department of Parks and Recreation. 2012. American & Sacramento River Parkway Plans. Accessed on 11-29-19 at http://www.cityofsacramento.org/-/media/Corporate/Files/Public-

Works/Projects/Sac-River-Pkwy/2012-American-and-Sacramento-River-Parkway-Plans.pdf?la=en.

Sacramento Department of Public Works. 2019. Sacramento River Parkway. Accessed 11-30-19 at https://www.cityofsacramento.org/Public-Works/Engineering-Services/Projects/Current-Projects/Sacramento-River-Parkway.

Resources: Chapter 43
– San Francisco Bay Region, California: The Bay Trail Is Getting Around

Association of Bay Area Governments. 2005. The San Francisco Bay Trail Project: Gap Analysis Study. Accessed 12-11-19 at https://baytrail.org/wp-content/uploads/2015/11/Final-Gap-Analysis-Study-2005-09-15-reduced.pdf.

California State Parks. 2011. Olompali State Historic Park. Accessed 12-10-19 at http://www.parks.ca.gov/pages/465/files/OlompaliWebBrochure2011.pdf.

California State Parks. 2015. China Camp State Park. Accessed 12-10-19 at http://www.parks.ca.gov/pages/466/files/ChinaCampSPWebLayout2015.pdf.

Ferry Building Marketplace. 2019. History. Accessed 12-8-19 at https://www.ferrybuildingmarketplace.com/about/.

Fort Mason. 2019. About. Accessed 12-20-19 at https://fortmason.org/about/.

Ghirardelli Square. 2019. History of Ghirardelli Square. Accessed 12-10-19 at https://www.ghirardellisq.com/history.

Golden Gate National Parks Conservancy. 2019. About. Accessed 12-10-19 at https://www.parksconservancy.org/parks/golden-gate-bridge?gclid=EAIaIQobChMIusus1Nmr5gIVhchkCh3RIwJrEAAYASAAEgK4XvD_BwE.

Jack London Square. 2019. History. Accessed 12-10-19 at https://jacklondonsquare.com/About-us/.

League of American Bicyclists. 2019. San Francisco. Accessed 12-11-19 at https://www.bikeleague.org/sites/default/files/bfareportcards/BFC_Fall_2016_ReportCard_San_Francisco_CA.pdf.

National Park Service. 2017. Rosie the Riveter National Historical Park: History & Culture. Accessed 12-10-19 at https://www.nps.gov/rori/learn/historyculture/index.htm.

National Park Service. 2019a. San Francisco Maritime National Historic Park. Accessed 12-10-19 at https://www.nps.gov/safr/index.htm.

National Park Service. 2019b. Fort Point: History and Culture. Accessed 12-10-19 at https://www.nps.gov/fopo/learn/historyculture/index.htm.

Noe Hill. 2019. San Francisco Ferry Building. Accessed 12-8-19 at https://noehill.com/sf/landmarks/sf090.asp.

Palace of Fine Arts. 2019. History. Accessed 12-10-19 at https://palaceoffinearts.com/info/.

Presidio. 2019. Visitor Guide. Accessed 12-10-19 at https://www.presidio.gov/visit-internal/Shared%20Documents/Presidio-Visitor-Guide-English.pdf.

San Francisco Municipal Transportation Agency. 2019. Cable Cars. Accessed 12-10-19 at https://www.sfmta.com/getting-around/muni/cable-cars.

**References: Chapter 44
– Smyrna, Georgia – Alabama State Line: Silver Comet Trail Keeps Growing**

Alta. 2013. Silver Comet Trail: Economic Impact Analysis and Planning Study. Accessed 11-5-19 at http://www.bwnwga.org/wp-content/uploads/Silver_Comet_Combined.pdf.

Alta. 2019. Silver Comet Executive Summary. Accessed 11-5-19 at https://altaplanning.com/wCp-content/uploads/Silver-Comet-Executive-Summary_all072213-2.pdf.

Cobb County. 2018. Cobb County Greenways and Trails Master Plan: Final Draft Plan. Accessed 11-5-19 at https://s3.us-west-2.amazonaws.com/cobbcounty.org.if-us-west-2/prod/2018-09/GTMP_MasterPlan_Document.pdf.

Lutz, M. 2019. Cox gives $6 million to connect Silver Comet to Atlanta. Atlanta Journal Constitution. September 30, 2019. Retrieved 10-4-19 at https://www.ajc.com/news/local-govt--politics/cox-gives-million-connect-silver-comet-atlanta/pKMbgS1tDhORwX182Mt3II/.

Strategic Vision Plan. 2017. 'Connect the Comet' Group Advocates for Silver Comet and ATL Beltline Connectivity. Accessed 11-4-19 at https://www.smyrnavision.com/connect-comet-group-advocates-silver-comet-trail-atl-beltline-connectivity/.

**References: Chapter 45
– St. Louis – Sedalia - Kansas City, Missouri:
The Katy Trail is Just the Beginning**

BikeRockIsland.com. 2019. Accessed on 8-17-19 at https://bikerockisland.com/.

Great Rivers Greenway. 2019. Accessed on August 1, 2019 from https://greatriversgreenway.org/.

Great Rivers Greenway. 2019. https://greatriversgreenway.org/projects/

Trust for Public Land. 2016. Connecting and Strengthening Communities: The

Economic Benefits of Great Rivers Greenway. Accessed 1 August 2019 from file:///C:/Users/Richard/Documents/Prosperity%20St%20Louis%20Great%20Rivers%20Geenway%20Econ%20Study%20TPL%20GRG%20report_final_low-res.pdf.

NPS (National Park Service) 2019. Chain of Rocks Bridge. Accessed 8-17-19 at https://www.nps.gov/nr/travel/route66/chain_of_rocks_bridge_illinois_missouri.html.

RTC (Rails-to-Trails Conservancy). 2007. Missouri's Katy Trail State Park. Accessed on 8-17-19 at http://www.railstotrails.org/trailblog/2007/september/01/missouris-katy-trail-state-park/.

Sedalia Convention & Visitors Bureau. 2018. Sedalia Missouri Visitors Guide. Accessed on 8-17-19 at https://www.visitsedaliamo.com/wp-content/uploads/2018/01/2018-Sedalia-Vistors-Guide.pdf.

Synergy/PRI/JPA. 2012. Katy Trail Economic Impact Report: Visotors and MGM2 Economic Impact Analysis. Accessed on 8-17-19 at

https://mostateparks.com/sites/mostateparks/files/Katy_Trail_Economic_Impact_Report_Final.pdf.

References: Chapter 46
– Tallahassee – St. Marks, Florida: Capitalizing on Bicycling

Capital Region Transportation Planning Agency. Capital City to the Sea Trails. Newsletter: April 2013. Accessed on July 12, 2018 from https://cc2st.files.wordpress.com/2013/06/newsletter1_final_revised_flat.pdf.

Florida Department of Environmental Protection. 2016. State Park System Direct Economic Impact Assessment – Fiscal Year 2015-2016 District 1. Tallahassee: Florida Department of Environmental Protection.

Florida State Parks. 2018a. Welcome to Tallahassee-St. Marks Historic Railroad State Trail. Accessed on July 12, 2018 from https://www.floridastateparks.org/trail/Tallahassee-St-Marks.

Florida State Parks. 2018b. Welcome to San Marcos de Apalache Historic State Park. Accessed on July 12, 2018 from

https://www.floridastateparks.org/park/San-Marcos.

Merchant, Brian. 2008. EPA's 1st "Excellence in Site Reuse" Award Goes to Tallahassee's Ex-Gas Plant Park. November 15, 2008. Accessed on July 12, 2018 from https://www.treehugger.com/corporate-responsibility/epas-1st-excellence-in-site-reuse-award-goes-to-tallahassees-ex-gas-plant-park.html.

RTC (Rails to Trails Conservancy). 2018. Tallahassee St. Marks Historic Railroad State Trail. Accessed on July 12, 2018 from

https://www.traillink.com/trail-history/tallahassee-st-marks-historic-railroad-state-trail/.

U.S. Fish & Wildlife Service. 2018. St. Marks National Wildlife Refuge. Accessed on July 12, 2018 from https://www.fws.gov/refuge/St_Marks/about.html.

**References: Chapter 47
– Tucson, Arizona: Connecting the Dots**

Arizona Department of Transportation. 2013 An Economic Impact Study of Bicycling in Arizona: Out of State Bicycle Tourists & Exports. Accessed 11-12-19 at https://apps.azdot.gov/files/ADOTLibrary/Multimodal_Planning_Division/Bicycle-Pedestrian/Economic_Impact_Study_of_Bicycling-Executive_Summary-1306.pdf.

National Park Service. 2019. National Historic Landmarks Program: San Xavier Del Bac. Accessed 11-11-19 at

https://web.archive.org/web/20070728053727/http://tps.cr.nps.gov/nhl/detail.cfm?ResourceId=103&ResourceType=Building.

Pima County. 2013. The Loop: Economic, Environmental, Community and Health Impact Study. Accessed 11-11-19 at

file:///C:/Users/Richard/Documents/Prosperity%20Tucson%20Econ%20Study%20of%20Loop.pdf.

Pima County. 2014. The Loop: 2014 Annual Report. The First 100 Miles. Accessed 11-11-19 at
https://webcms.pima.gov/UserFiles/Servers/Server_6/File/Government/The%20Loop/Annual%20Reports/1386%20-%20Loop%20Annual%20Report_web-ready.pdf.

Pima County. 2017. The Loop: 2015-2017 Report - The Loop Means Business. Accessed 11-11-19 at
https://webcms.pima.gov/UserFiles/Servers/Server_6/File/Government/The%20Loop/1703%20MARCH/2764%20-%20Loop%20Report%202015-17%20WEB1.pdf.

Pima County. 2019. Art on The Loop. Accessed 11-11-19 at
https://webcms.pima.gov/UserFiles/Servers/Server_6/File/Government/The%20Loop/Loop%20Art%20Map/8245%20loop%20art%20map%20update%202019%20v4%20WEB%20RTP.pdf.

**References: Chapter 48
– Utah: Seeing the Beauty of Bicycle Tourism**

Feer & Peers. 2017. Economic Impacts of Active Transportation: Utah Active Transportation Benefits Study. Accessed 10-28-19 at https://static1.squarespace.com/static/5b8b54d1f407b40494055e8f/t/5bdc820c4fa51a4d9f77e014/1541177878083/Utah+Active+Transportation+Benefits+Study+-+Final+Report.pdf.

National Park Service. 2018. National Park Service Active Transportation Guidebook. Accessed 10-28-19 at https://www.nps.gov/subjects/transportation/upload/UPDATED_NPS_Guidebook_July2018_Final_UpdateSept2018-High-Res_WEB-2.pdf.

St. George. 2017. Active Transportation Plan. Accessed 10-28-19 at https://www.sgcity.org/pdf/transportationandengineering/general/activetransportationplan/activetransportationplan.pdf.

References: Chapter 49
– Vancouver, British Columbia: Copenhagenizing in Canada

Copenhagenize. 2019. Copenhagenize Index. Accessed 11-17-19 at

https://copenhagenizeindex.eu/.

CTV News, 2010. Olympic Village hailed as world's greenest neighborhood. Accessed 11-17-19 at

https://bc.ctvnews.ca/olympic-village-hailed-world-s-greenest-neighbourhood-1.484437,

Metro Vancouver Convention and Visitors Bureau. 2019a. Bicycle Culture. Accessed 11-17-19 at https://www.tourismvancouver.com/activities/cycling-mountain-biking/bicycle-culture/.

Metro Vancouver Convention and Visitors Bureau. 2019b. Secrets of Granville Island. Accessed 11-17-19 at

https://www.tourismvancouver.com/activities/attractions/secrets-of-granville-island/.

Meyers Norris Penny. 2011. The Social and Economic Impacts of BC Recreation Sites and Trails. Accessed 11-17-19 at

https://www.orcbc.ca/wp-content/uploads/2019/07/RSTBC-Economic-1.pdf.

Port of Vancouver. 2019. News: 2019 expected to bring a record number of cruise passengers to Canada Place. Accessed 11-17-19 at https://www.portvancouver.com/news-and-media/news/2019-expected-to-bring-a-record-number-of-cruise-passengers-to-vancouver/.

Price Waterhouse Coopers. 2004. Economic Impact Anaysis: Trans Canada Trail in Ontario. Accessed 11-17-19 at

https://www.americantrails.org/images/documents/TransCanadaEcon.pdf

The Great Trail. 2019. Accessed 11-17-19 at https://thegreattrail.ca/.

Vancouver 2019a. Protected Bicycle Lanes. Accessed 11-18-19 at https://vancouver.ca/streets-transportation/protected-bicycle-lanes.aspx.

Vancouver. 2019b. 5-year Cycling Network Additions & Upgrades: 2018-2022. Accessed 11-18-19 at https://vancouver.ca/files/cov/5-year-cycling-network-map-additions-and-upgrades-2018-to-2022.pdf.

Vancouver. 2019c. Transportation 2040 Plan. Accessed 11-18-19 at https://vancouver.ca/files/cov/Transportation_2040_Plan_as_adopted_by_Council.pdf.

Vancouver Convention Centre. 2018. Vancouver Gears Up for Busiest Convention Year Ever. Accessed 11-17-19 at https://www.vancouverconventioncentre.com/news/vancouver-gears-up-for-busiest-convention-year-ever.

References: Chapter 50
– Vermont: Bikes Help Green the Green Mountain State

Vermont. 2012. Economic Impact of Bicycling and Walking in Vermont. Accessed 6-4-21 at https://accd.vermont.gov/sites/accdnew/files/documents/VDTM-Research-2012EconomicImpactBikingWalkingFullReport.pdf.

Vermont. 2021. VTrans Bicycle and Pedestrian Strategic Plan. Accessed 6-11-21 https://vtrans.vermont.gov/sites/aot/files/planning/bikeplan/VTrans_BPSP_Report_FINAL_20210310-FullReportAndAppendices.pdf.

References: 51
– Washington State: Going Long on Trails

Earth Economics. 2015. Economic Analysis of Outdoor Recreation im Washington State. Accessed 11-2-19 at https://drive.google.com/file/d/0ByzIUWI76gWVR1Z4SmpIdUZyUWc/view?pref=2&pli=1

League of American Bicyclists. 2019. Bicycle Friendly State Report Card: Washington. Accessed 11-1-19 at https://bikeleague.org/sites/default/files/BFS2017_ReportCard_Washington.pdf.

Mountains to Sound Greenway National Heritage Area. 2019. Accessed 11-1-19 at https://mtsgreenway.org/learn/national-heritage-area/.

Pruetz, R. 2012. *Lasting Value: Open Space Preservation Successes*. Chicago: American Planning Association.

Rails to Trails Conservancy. 2019a. Washington. Accessed on 11-1-19 at https://www.traillink.com/trailsearch/?mmloc=Washington.

Rails to Trails Conservancy. 2019b.The Great American Rail Trail. Accessed on 11-2-19 at https://gis.railstotrails.org/grtamerican/.

Seattle. 1987. Evaluation of the Burke-Gilman Trail's Effect on Property Values and Crime. Accessed 11-2-19 at https://headwaterseconomics.org/wp-content/uploads/Trail_Study_82-burke-gilman-trail-property-values.pdf.

Stark, L. 2014. Washington's Centennial Trail State Park – Trail of the Month: February 2014. Accessed 11-2-19 at https://www.railstotrails.org/trailblog/2014/february/01/washingtons-centennial-trail-state-park/.

Trask, B. 2015. New Economic Analysis: Bicycling Means Business in Washington. Accessed 11-2-19 at http://wabikes.org/2015/01/08/bicycling-means-business-in-wa/.

References: Chapter 52
– Yellowstone-Grand Teton Loop Bicycle Pathway, Wyoming-Idaho-Montana: Thinking Big Out West

Friends of Pathways. 2021. Friends of Pathways – Jackson Hole. Accessed on 10-14-21 at https://friendsofpathways.org/.

Idaho. 2021. Ashton – Tetonia Trail. Accessed on 10-15-21 at https://parksandrecreation.idaho.gov/parks/ashton-to-tetonia-trail/.

Jackson Hole Mountain Resort. 2021. Biking in Jackson Hole. Accessed 10-16-21 at https://www.jacksonhole.com/biking-in-jackson-hole.html.

Jensen, W. and K. Scoresby. 2015. Yellowstone-Grand Teton Loop Pathway Estimated Economic Impact. Rexburg, ID: Eastern Idaho Entrepreneurial Center. Accessed 10-14-21 at https://headwaterseconomics.org/wp-content/uploads/Trail_Study_97-Yellowstone-Grand-Teton-Cycling-Loop.pdf.

Wyoming Pathways. 2021. Greater Yellowstone Trail Plan Update 2021. Accessed 10-16-21 at https://www.wyopath.org/wp-content/uploads/2021/03/Greater-Yellowstone-Trail-Plan-Update-2021.pdf.

ABOUT THE AUTHOR

Rick Pruetz is a former city planner who writes about bicycling, ecocities, and the preservation of ecosystems, farmland, and historic landmarks. Most recently, he wrote *Smart Climate Action through Transfer of Development Rights* and *Ecocity Snapshots: Learning from Europe's Greenest Places*. He is a Fellow of the American Institute of Certified Planners and currently serves as Board Vice President of Ecocity Builders, a non-profit organization promoting the emerging of cities in balance with nature.

www.ingramcontent.com/pod-product-compliance
Lightning Source LLC
Chambersburg PA
CBHW051906160426
43198CB00012B/1765